Excellent casebook! The cases are contemporary and truly reflect the marketing challenges of SMEs in India. Great learning resource for business education in India.

Prof. Dinesh Sharma, Indian Institute of Technology, Bombay

Finally a casebook which is highly readable and focused on marketing issues faced by SMEs, particularly in the Indian context. This book is a 'must-have' for all those tasked with teaching marketing concepts to students, prospective entrepreneurs and owners, and executives of small and medium enterprises.

Prof. Somayajulu Garimella, Director, International Management Institute, Bhubaneswar

Not many Indian authors have been able to strike the right balance between the theories of marketing and the changing marketing practices in the Indian environment, especially in the SME sector. As a result, students often find a lot of what they read on the subject, redundant. I thank Dr Neeraj Pandey and Gaganpreet Singh for writing this book of cases covering the SME sector, which addresses the gap between theory and practice in marketing.

Prof. Debasis Mallik, S. P. Jain Institute of Management & Research, Mumbai

Excellent cases providing great insights into the inner workings of SMEs and their business challenges. The cases cover a wide range of industries and scenarios. It will provide an excellent tool for thought-provoking analysis and discussions.

Chandan Singh, Vice-President, Barclays, USA

The authors present a balanced view of the marketing and strategy issues confronted by SMEs in India. Despite the fact that SMEs generate very high level of employment in India, research and cases on SMEs are rather scarce as the focus is disproportionately high on larger organizations. This well-researched book offers powerful lessons for managers, academicians, entrepreneurs and students of business studies.

Prof. Manas Ranjan Tripathy, IBS Hyderabad

The book *Marketing Issues in SMEs: Cases from India* by Dr Neeraj Pandey and Gaganpreet Singh is an interesting study on dilemmas faced by SMEs in India. This book differentiates itself from other casebooks by doing a thorough primary investigation of diverse SMEs and their predicament in almost real time situations. It is a useful resource for practising managers, entrepreneurs, academicians and students. Congratulations to the authors for their thoughtful compilation!

Dilip Nandkeolyar, Managing Director, ET ElecTrans Limited, Pune

Marketing Issues in SMEs

Cases from India

Neeraj Pandey
Assistant Professor
National Institute of Industrial Engineering (NITIE), Mumbai

Gaganpreet Singh
Business Analyst
Viom Networks Limited, Mohali

Pearson

Assistant Editor–Acquisitions: Saumya Chawla
Associate Editor–Production: Amrita Naskar

ISBN 978-81-317-8505-8

First Impression, 2013

Published by Pearson India Education Services Pvt. Ltd, CIN: U72200TN2005PTC057128.

Head Office: 15th Floor, Tower-B, World Trade Tower, Plot No. 1, Block-C, Sector 16, Noida 201 301, Uttar Pradesh, India.

Registered Office: The HIVE, 3 rd Floor, Metro Zone, No 44, Pilliar Koil Street, Jawaharlal Nehru Road, Anna Nagar, Chennai,Tamil Nadu 600040, Phone: 044-66540100
Website: in.pearson.com; Email:companysecretary.india@pearson.com

Compositor: White Lotus Infotech Pvt. Ltd, Puducherry

Digitally printed in India by Trinity Academy For Corporate Training Limited, New Delhi in the year of 2020.

To my parents,
D. S. Pandey and Renuka Pandey, and
to my wife, Chitra Pandey.

—Neeraj Pandey

To my parents,
Pritam Singh and Kanwaljeet Kaur.

—Gaganpreet Singh

CONTENTS

FOREWORD

SMEs are one of the major pillars of the Indian economy. It is estimated that there are 29.8 million SME units in India, and they account for 95 per cent of the total number of industrial units in the country. What is even more impressive is that 45 per cent of India's industrial output, 40 per cent of India's exports and around 90 per cent of India's employment are accounted for by SMEs. SMEs create one million jobs annually. Despite SMEs accounting for 95 per cent of industrial units in India, they contribute to just 22 per cent of India's GDP and about the same percentage of India's total banking sector lending. They are small and vulnerable as can be gauged from the fact that 70 per cent are in the services businesses and over 75 per cent are single proprietor firms, lacking professional expertise for driving growth (Data Source: CRISIL).

CRISIL analysis points to the interesting fact that many of them are highly leveraged and even a 1 per cent increase in interest rates can reduce profit by 14 per cent on an average. This affects manufacturing units more severely than it does service units; and consequently, their ability to invest in technology upgrading or capital expenditure is impaired—in turn impairing their ability to attract and retain customers and grow the top line more aggressively. Therefore, a more sustainable revenue growth, year on year, is needed for the SMEs to have the safety cushion and to generate the growth capital that they need.

Intuit Inc., a leading provider of business and financial management solutions for small- and mid-sized businesses across the globe, believes that most of the challenges faced by small businesses in India are not unique and are shared by small businesses in developed economies as well. In a worldwide study (including in India) conducted with small businesses, Intuit found that the major pain points among small businesses consistently centre around getting and retaining customers and financial management. Customer facing issues, which is what this book is about, were also seen by most as being important in addition to being painful.

With this situation prevailing on the ground, a book like this is extremely valuable, relevant and timely. The authors Neeraj Pandey and Gaganpreet Singh must be congratulated for giving us such a book of real-life case studies of SMEs, drawn from diverse industries and addressing different marketing challenges. Since the case studies are based on actual field surveys, they provide a real-life flavour which the other SMEs can easily identify with. Marketing theory, tool and methods come alive and are easy to implement and gain from, if told through practical examples, and this is exactly what this book does. It covers various aspects of marketing challenges and dilemmas and it is told through the eyes of the entrepreneurs who faced it and dealt with it. It covers both 'routine' operational (how to do) and strategic (what to do) marketing issues as well as special problem situations.

I commend this book to all the SMEs and also businesses interested in SMEs, be they banks or technology companies or other service providers including educational institutions. This book will definitely inspire and coach several SMEs and help them grow stronger.

Rama Bijapurkar
Independent Market Strategy Consultant and Author

PREFACE

India has a unique business fabric. There is enormous diversity within the consumer base and across the domestic markets, and there are specific structural constraints. The industrial clusters in India not only fulfill the high domestic demand but also act as an outsourcing hub for many developed countries. The SMEs play a crucial role in matching this demand as a supplier, both directly and indirectly. In India, SMEs generate revenue equivalent to 17 per cent of the country's GDP, constitute 40 per cent of exports and contribute 45 per cent to overall manufacturing output. SMEs supply mainly to other businesses (B2B) and at times directly to the consumers (B2C) too. SMEs face a variety of marketing dilemmas during their decision-making processes. All such decisions have to be taken within the given budget, human resource and infrastructural constraints. The deregulation and globalization have further enhanced competition and brought forth new challenges for Indian SMEs.

This book captures actual marketing dilemmas faced by SMEs in India. It covers operational and strategic marketing scenarios/issues the SMEs face while they are expanding, diversifying, scaling up, promoting innovation, pricing products and services, undertaking new product development, handling sales problem or negotiating with bigger organizations to which they are marketing their products as vendors, apart from special marketing dilemmas. All the case studies in the book are based on primary research and field visits to the respective organizations. Each case study covers a different industry so as to provide readers insights into a variety of marketing issues across industries. It covers both manufacturing-focused and services-focused SMEs. Each case study tries to connect marketing theory with the documented business case dilemma. This book would not only make readers aware and learn about practical marketing issues but also invigorate thought-provoking classroom analysis and discussions to find sustainable solutions to SME marketing problems. Such discussions make the reader a better decision-maker in tackling marketing problems besides appreciating the context and constraints within which SMEs operate.

The book also caters to the international readers who, off late, have developed a keen interest in the emerging markets. The emerging markets, mainly comprising BRICS (Brazil, Russia, India, China and South Africa), have drawn the attention of the whole world due to their higher GDP and market growth rate. So, this book will be a useful resource for anyone who is interested in knowing about marketing canvas in such economies and particularly in India. It also gives a glimpse of the opportunities and constraints which an Indian SME faces on its journey to become an established and bigger enterprise.

Lastly, the book was written with a lot of passion, interest and academic rigor. However, there is still scope for further improvement. We will heartily appreciate any suggestions for further refinement of this book.

Neeraj Pandey
Gaganpreet Singh

ACKNOWLEDGEMENTS

This book is the culmination of support from many quarters. Firstly, we want to acknowledge the CEOs/owners of the SMEs, who granted permission to write cases for their respective organizations. Their cooperation and candidness in sharing their company data, besides timely response to various queries, helped us in drafting the actual marketing decision points with sufficient background information. The company officials were available for interactive sessions whenever required in spite of their busy schedules. We are truly indebted to all these organizations for their immense cooperation.

We are also thankful to Inderjit Singh Gill, Pawanpreet Singh, Jaskaran Singh Bains, Kulvinder Pal Singh, Amritpal Singh, G. S. Kahlon and Sukhwinder Singh for providing references and support during the data collection regarding case study. We are grateful to Dr Manas Ranjan Tripathy, Dilip Nandkeolyar, Teja Jayanthi, Lakshmikanth Hari and other academicians and practitioners who gave their valuable inputs to the initial draft of the chapters.

We thank the entire publication team at Pearson Education. Special thanks are due to Raza Khan, Amrita Naskar and Saumya Chawla for their support during the entire publication process.

Neeraj Pandey
Gaganpreet Singh

I want to thank the students and faculty peers at NITIE, IIT Bombay, Thapar University and Johns Hopkins University, who provided the motivation to write this marketing case book with an Indian perspective. I express sincere gratitude to my mentors, Prof. Dipankar Chakravarti, Johns Hopkins University, USA, and Prof. Geetika, MNNIT, Allahabad, for extending their continued support. I also express my gratitude to Prof. Amitabh De, Director, NITIE, for extending his full support whenever required.

I want to thank my family members who have been very supportive of my intense involvement with the book. I want to heartily thank my eldest brother, Anil Kumar Pandey, who has always helped me realize my potential. He is a great source of energy for me. Also, thanks are due to my brothers, Sunil Pandey and Sanjay Pandey and also to my sister, Prof. Anita Ojha, for their constant support and encouragement. I want to express heartfelt gratitude to my wife, Chitra Pandey, to my son, Atharvasheersh and daughter, Avantika, for their constant support and faith in me.

Neeraj Pandey

I want to thank my sister, Dr Ravneet Pal Kaur and brother-in-law, Dr Simarpreet Singh, for their constant encouragement and support and for keeping me inspired.

Gaganpreet Singh

ABOUT THE AUTHORS

Neeraj Pandey, MBA, Ph.D., PDF (Johns Hopkins University, USA), is Assistant Professor of Marketing at the National Institute of Industrial Engineering (NITIE), Mumbai. Dr Pandey has been actively involved in teaching, training, research and consultancy. He has more than ten years of academic and industrial experience. He has done consulting assignments for various organizations including MRF Limited, Bharat Petroleum Corporation Limited (BPCL), Gujarat State Fertilizers & Chemicals Limited (GSFCL), Owens Corning Limited, Marpol, EMCO Transformers and Oil and Natural Gas Corporation Limited (ONGC). His current teaching and research interests include B2B marketing, CRM, pricing and marketing research. He is also a visiting faculty at IIT Bombay. He was awarded the 'International Award for Excellence in the World Universities Field' by the *Journal of the World Universities Forum*. He has published several research papers in reputed international and national journals like *Journal of Medical Marketing*, *Journal of World Universities Forum*, *Journal of Services Research*, *International Journal of Indian Culture and Business Management*, etc.; and contributed chapters in several books. He has given invited talks and presented research papers in many international conferences, such as at NYIT, New York; University of Maryland; University of Cologne, Germany and Harvard University, USA. Dr Pandey lives in Mumbai with his wife Chitra, son Atharvasheersh and daughter Avatika. He can be reached at neerajpandey100@gmail.com.

Gaganpreet Singh, B.Tech., MBA (Thapar University), is currently working with Viom Networks Limited, a Tata enterprise as Business Analyst. He has more than two years of industrial experience. Prior to joining his first job, he used to own two dot com companies, which were later acquired after achieving significant milestones. He is an active researcher and writer in the area of social media marketing with expertise in green products and services. He has presented research papers in various national and international conferences. His research interests include marketing analytics, services marketing and pricing. He lives in Chandigarh and can be reached at gagan5787@yahoo.co.in.

1

NOVA BICYCLE INDUSTRIES: THE DIVERSIFICATION PUZZLE

It was during lunchtime on 20 June 2011 at NOVA Bicycles dining hall, when intense discussions on the company's expansion strategy for the next five years took place. Members on the dining table included Chairman Mr H. M. S. Pahwa (Exhibit 1.1), Director Mr Rohit Pahwa and GM (Marketing) Mr S. C. Chakraborty (Exhibit 1.1). During this unofficial and unplanned conversation, interesting and diverse viewpoints emerged. The chairman's viewpoint was that apart from stabilizing and expanding the existing business of bicycle manufacturing, there was a need to diversify by entering into e-bikes[1] division and health equipments. He strongly believed that bicycle industry had been shrinking in the past and will further contract at a faster rate in the coming years as threat from low cost China bicycles was increasing each year. However, Mr Chakraborty had a different viewpoint of the cycle industry, in general, and NOVA, in particular. He believed in focussing on the core competency of the company. He was of the view that any foray in new products may distract NOVA from its current market position. He cited some statistics highlighting the huge untapped potential in the existing cycle business. Difference in beliefs had put the Pahwas in serious dilemma on whether to invest in diversification of group business or to stick to their basics and core competence and capture more business within the bicycle industry. Since both the options seemed lucrative, it had become quite a tough decision for the top management.

NOVA GROUP OF COMPANIES

After family partition took place in 1999 at Avon group of companies, Avon Bicycle Components Pvt. Ltd. came in the share of Mr H. M. S. Pahwa under the settlement. Avon Bicycle components—a fifty year old company—manufactured bicycle components, namely, spoke, hubs, brakes and chains.

Exhibit 1.1 | *Profile of Management Team*

Mr H. M. S. Pahwa: Mr H. M. S. Pahwa was born in Sialkot, now in Pakistan in 1944. After completing his studies, he joined his family business under the name of M/S Avon Cycles Limited at an age of 17. He remained with the group for almost four decades until family partition took place and he took over the reins of Avon Bicycles Components Pvt. Ltd. During his association with the group, he had looked after all the functions of business; however, his main focus had been on 'marketing'. Under his leadership, the company had achieved many milestones. As a result of his strong dedication and passion towards the business, his new trademark, namely, NOVA had been a successful brand and was consistently achieving higher market share.

Mr Rohit Pahwa: Mr Rohit after doing his masters in engineering from Bangalore joined his father's business in 1995. He has always set high standards for himself and the company. He also conceptualized and founded V. S. Auto Industries which manufactured automotive parts. He looks after the marketing and engineering division at NOVA Bicycles Industries.

Mr S. C. Chakraborty: Mr Chakraborty, currently working as General Manager (Marketing), is an alumnus of Calcutta University. A mechanical engineer and PGDBM (Post Graduate Diploma in Business Management), he started his corporate life in 1974 with Raleigh (A joint venture between Government of India and Government of England) based in Calcutta. He worked with Raleigh for 12 years. Then he had a long stint with one of the leading export houses. He had warm personal relations with Pahwa family since early years and was acting as an unofficial consultant. Finally, when NOVA was founded in 2002, he was officially recruited and had been serving the company since then.

Source: Company records and interview with Mr Chakraborty

It was supplying its entire product mix to all across the nation along with catering to the needs of its group companies. Indirectly the company had also been exporting its products to Africa.

After a few years of its sole dedication towards manufacturing bicycle spare parts, Mr Pahwa started manufacturing complete bicycles under the brand name of NOVA. NOVA Bicycle Industries was started in 2002 with the initial production capacity of just 5,000 bicycles monthly. At that stage, the company had eight cycle variants in their portfolio. The top management had always been fascinated about new designs and variants, thus, moving towards more inNOVAtion. Launching of new models was quite motivating for NOVA's enthusiastic manufacturing team. As a result, presently, the company has a range of 56 bicycle variants in their basket, with the production capacity of more than 15,000 bicycles per month.

In 1995, when Mr Rohit Pahwa (Director), joined his father's business, he could realize the impact of low cost China's bicycle variants on NOVA and other domestic bicycle companies.

This was the time when Chinese products were starting to capture the Indian market at a rapid pace. Besides supporting his father's business, Mr Rohit also initiated investment in the automobile industry. He founded V. S. Auto Industries, an automotive parts manufacturing company. It was a quite successful venture and was a major profit earner for NOVA group of companies. Thus, NOVA group comprised three progressive organizations, viz., NOVA Bicycle Industries, V.S. Auto Industries and Avon Bicycle Components Private Limited.

GLOBAL BICYCLE INDUSTRY

The global market for bicycles is projected to be more than $77.7 billion by 2015[2]. Throughout the world, utility of bicycles varied from region to region depending upon whether it is a rural area, semi-urban or an urban area. In developed countries, bicycles were mostly used for sports activities. China, with a population of around 1.2 billion, had a domestic consumption of about 30 million bicycles per year. It also exports more than 15 million bicycles to different countries. If the comparison was done for developed countries like Japan and United States of America, interesting results were observed. The bicycle sales were fewer in developed countries like USA and Japan. For example, the United States and Japan with a population of 300 million and 125 million, respectively, had a consumption rate of just 20 million and 7 million each year[3].

Major bicycle manufacturing countries include China, India, Japan and Taiwan. In 2000, China held the first position by manufacturing 52% of the world's bicycle production, followed by India (11%), Taiwan (7%) and Japan (5%). Taiwan, with its maximum clientele in the United States had nearly 400 bicycle manufacturing units and has been facing setback from the time the United States's major manufacturers had started direct outsourcing from original OEMs (Original Equipment Manufacturers). China had flooded U.S. market through its manufactured bicycles especially due to its cost competitiveness. Out of 19 million bicycles sold in the United States in 2001, 90 per cent were imported from China and Taiwan. This was mainly due to availability of cheap labour, economies of scale and availability of cheap raw material in China.

INDIAN BICYCLE INDUSTRY

India is the second largest player in the global bicycle industry. The ₹17 billion Indian bicycle industry sells about 12 million bicycles a year, after China which manufactured every two out of three units made globally. Indian bicycle industry had been broadly classified into two segments, namely, standard bicycles and fancy bicycles.

In the recent past, sales of Indian bicycle industry had transitioned from standard bicycles towards fancy bicycles because of continuous changing consumer behaviour and higher disposable income levels of middle- and lower-middle classes in urban and semi-urban areas. Back in the 1990s, standard bicycles which almost captured almost 90 per cent of the total Indian market share had come down by almost 35 per cent. This was because of increasing inclination of urban and semi-urban community towards fancy bicycles. During the last decade, lifestyle or fancy bicycle segment had recorded CAGR (Compounded Annual Growth Rate) of over 30 per cent. (Exhibit 1.2). Irregular monsoon seasons had also negatively impacted the sales of standard bicycles as rural incomes were highly dependent on monsoons and standard bicycles have majority of potential customers located in semi-urban and rural areas. Approximately 90 per cent of Indian manufactured bicycles are domestically consumed and quite fewer are exported. Comparative cost disadvantage over Chinese manufactured bicycles, especially in the fancy bicycle segment, also detered manufacturers from exporting bicycles. The Indian bicycle industry had been dominated by three major players, namely, Hero Cycles Limited (Hero); Tube Investments of India Limited (TI) and Atlas Cycles Limited (Atlas) (Exhibit 1.3).

Exhibit 1.2 | *Indian Bicycle Industry at a Glance*

	Size of Market (Mn. Units)	% of Total	CAGR 1996–97 to 2001–02	CAGR 1999–2000 to 2001–02
Standards	8.0	66.4%	2.70%	–2.40%
Specials:				
SLRs	0.5	4.4%	2.0%	–2.3%
MTBs	1.6	13.3%	22.4%	26.9%
Juveniles	1.1	9.5%	12.6%	2.2%
Kids	0.8	6.4%	15.5%	9.9%
Total Specials	4.0	33.6%	14.0%	12.5%
Grand Total	12	100.0%	5.8%	1.9%

CAGR: Compound Annual Growth Rate, SLR: Sports Light Roadster MTB: Mountain Terrain Bikes
Source: http://www.crisil.com/Ratings/Commentary/CommentaryDocs/cycle-ind0103.pdf, accessed on 27 November 2011

Exhibit 1.3 | *Major Cycle Players/Competitors*

	Hero Cycles	TI Cycles	Avon Cycles	Atlas Cycles
Founded	1944	1949	1948	1951
Brand(s)	Hero	BSA, Hercules	Avon, Buke, Apsara	Atlas
Production (million units)	4.9	2.8	1.7	1.2

Source: http://dare.co.in/opportunities/manufacturing/the-business-of-bicycles.htm, accessed on 19 November 2011

NOVA'S JOURNEY OF 9 YEARS (2002–11)

In 2002, Mr Pahwa introduced a new brand in bicycle market by the name of NOVA. Within nine years of its operations, it got established as a strong brand in the Indian bicycle industry, which was earlier dominated by big names like Hero, Avon and Atlas. During this short journey, the company had crossed sales of 1 lakh (0.1 million) bicycles and thereby increasing its annual turnover each year by many folds. In January 2005, the company received ISO-2001 certification.

Due to its excellent quality and competitive prices, NOVA was many times awarded government tenders of providing bicycles to the 'below poverty line' (BPL) people. During participation in such welfare campaigns, NOVA had supplied more than 1 lakh bicycles to various state governments, namely, Punjab, Rajasthan, Chhattisgarh, Maharashtra and Gujarat. At the state level, the Punjab government had rated NOVA as the safest bicycle provider organization. Recently, the Gujarat government had recognized NOVA as amongst the select few SSI units that was at par with large scale manufacturers for applying state government contracts. During this tenure, NOVA had also become the first company to introduce improvised inNOVAtive packaging style of bicycles which had been highly accepted across the nation. These achievements had been accomplished due to the expertise, experience and vision of NOVA's chairman. The chairman was actively supported by his son who was busy in conceptualizing, designing and implementing new manufacturing and marketing strategies to expand the footprints of NOVA's operations.

PRODUCT PORTFOLIO AND THREAT FROM CHINA

NOVA Bicycle Industries had a large product range. NOVA group's various product lines included complete bicycles, ancillary bicycle components and auto parts. Complete bicycle range at NOVA had been further classified into Roadster (Standard Bicycles), Mountain Bikes, Lady Bikes, Kid Bikes and Racer Bikes (Exhibit 1.4). NOVA had eight different variants for Roadster. It was one of the bicycles that were categorized as heavy duty[4] in India. As per Mr Chakraborty, Roadster occupied almost 80 per cent share of total sales and had maximum demand in the domestic market as it has the capability to perform versatile purposes. As per the company officials, if the comparative analysis between price and utility for Roadster was measured, customers would see very high value as utility was quite high, given the domestic price[5]. In India, the target market of Roadster was rural and semi-urban population where it was being used for various purposes. Roadster was used by some segment of people for cycling exercise purposes, while others used it also as a mode of transportation and carrying light luggage. It was not only heavily used by rural background individuals but also by semi-urban individuals who used it to carry out their daily businesses; for instance, milk vendors used it to deliver milk within limited territories, the local cloth merchant, etc. used it for their daily door-to-door sales movement. NOVA's inhouse R&D team was able to develop unique designs which had also been trademarked in the company's name. Roadster was one of those uniquely designed successful product of NOVA.

The other segment which NOVA focussed on was Fancy bicycles. It included ladies bicycles, kids bicycles, racer bikes and mountain bikes. In all these variants, plastic was used as the core raw material. China had managed well to maintain competitive edge in this segment. It had been comfortably supplying such products at a price which was quite less in comparison to ones manufactured in India. For instance, the cost of production for children bicycles manufactured in India equals ₹850 per cycle. However, the Chinese manufactured bicycles cost around ₹650[6]. This is possible due to availability of cheap raw material, especially plastics, mass production (economies of scale) and cheap labour costs in China. Moreover, comparatively the usage of plastic content in Chinese bicycle was much higher than Indian bicycles. The quality and durability of Indian bicycles were better than Chinese manufactured bicycles. However, the Indian bicycle prices were higher than Chinese bicycles. This price gap proved favourable to Chinese bicycle manufacturers for price-conscious Indian customers.

China had also been supplying raw materials for kids bicycle segment frequently. The Ludhiana dry port alone had been receiving about 100 containers of Chinese cycle parts each month[7]. The Chinese bicycle industry, due to its unique price advantage, had already grabbed 25 per cent of the market share in the fancy bicycle segment in India.

Exhibit 1.4 | *Product Portfolio of NOVA Bicycles (Standard and Fancy)*

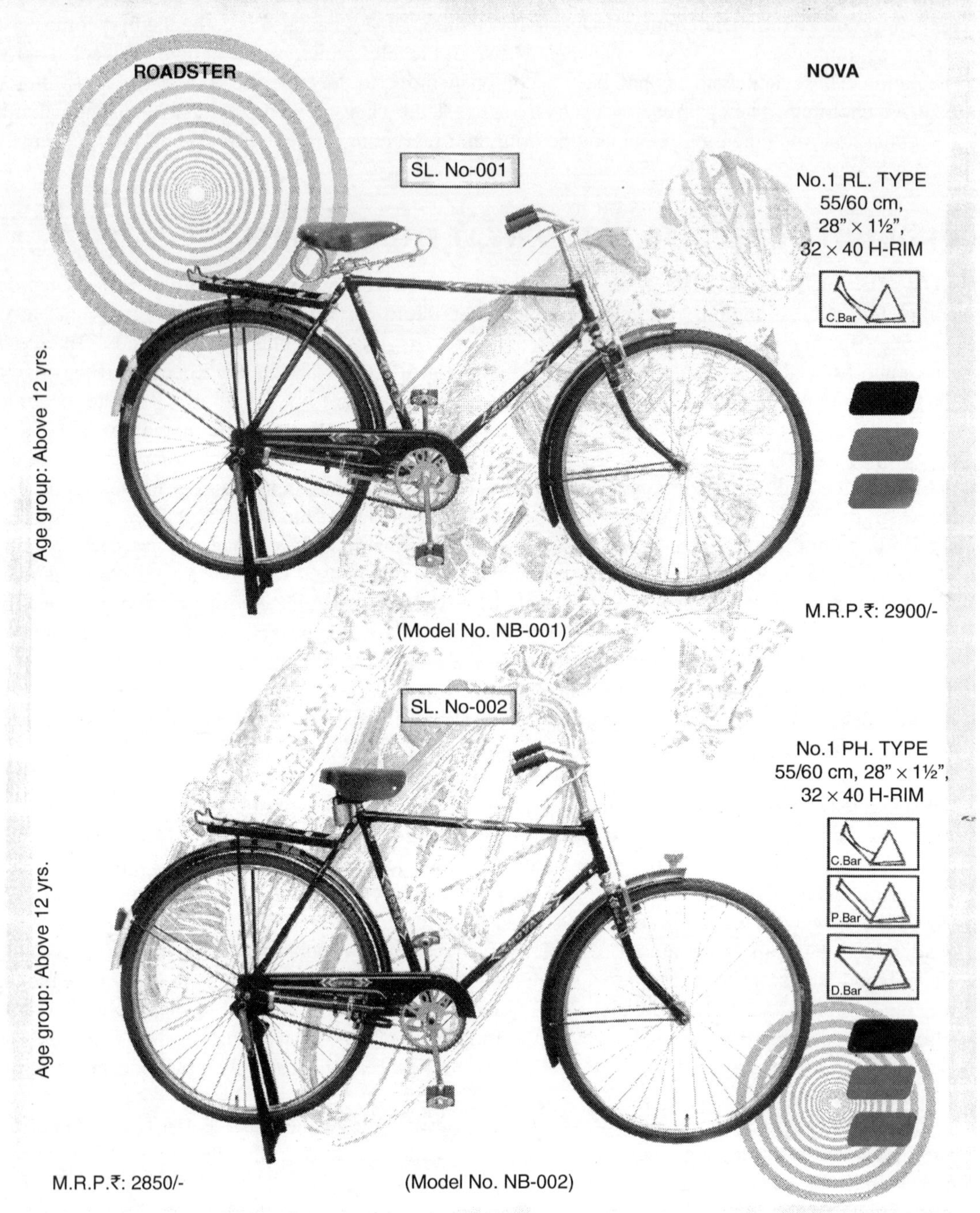

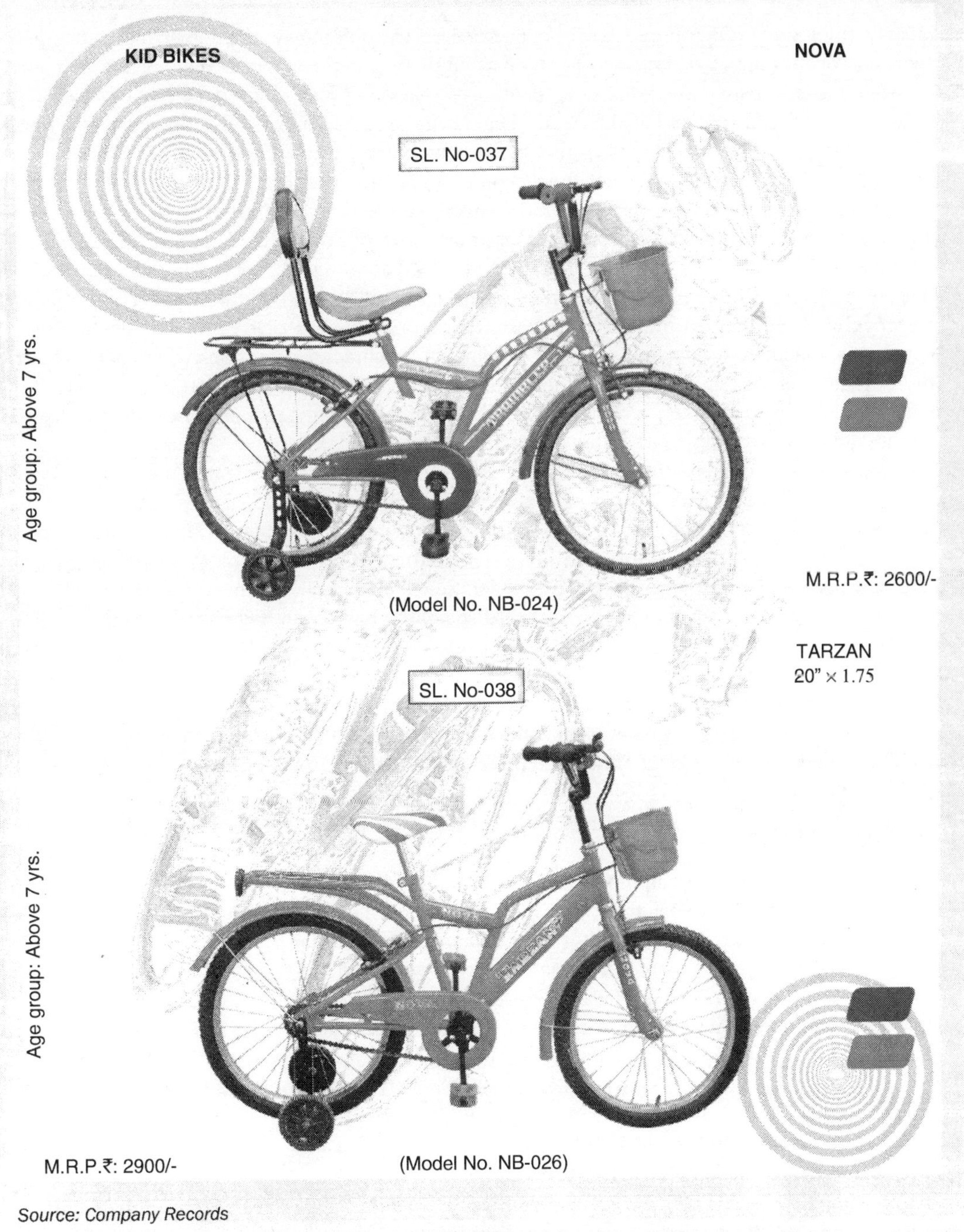

Source: Company Records

PRICING

As far as pricing of NOVA products was concerned, it was quite lower than other Indian competitor's products. This pricing advantage was possible as NOVA's group companies manufactured majority of individual bicycle spare parts. Inhouse production of spares not only reduced the cost of finished goods production to a greater extent but also gave advantage of assured timely supply of quality raw materials to NOVA. This core competence of quality product with competitive price gave NOVA a unique edge over other domestic competitors since the inception of the organization.

On comparing cost of raw materials of Indian manufactured bicycles and Chinese bicycles, India had a disadvantageous position. This was because in India, price of raw materials such as MS round, CRCA (Cold Rolled Close Annealed) Sheet and Tube was priced at around ₹29,000, ₹36,000 and ₹43,000 per tonne, respectively, while in China their prices stood at around ₹14,400, ₹21,000 and ₹25,000 per tonne[8], respectively[9]. According to the Ludhiana-based largest association of bicycle manufacturers, Indian Bicycle Manufacturer Association (IBMA), the Indian manufactured bicycles were about 30 per cent costlier than those manufactured by China. Though China was heavily exporting complete bicycles along with individual ancillary components across the globe at much reduced price, the quality parameters are quite inferior compared to Indian products.

According to Mr Pahwa, the present bicycle industry had to stay contented with thinner margins, however, the volume of sales would be a key criterion in deciding the success path for any bicycle manufacturing and marketing organization (Exhibit 1.5). Everyday fluctuations in iron, steel and rubber prices were an area of concern for Indian bicycle manufacturers. According to the company officials, there had been many instances in NOVA's operational history, when the variations in steel prices between the stage of order booking and actual dispatching had led to huge losses to the organization. In such situations, NOVA had no other option than to deliver the goods by incurring huge losses; else there was every chance of not just loosing the customer but also the organizational credibility. Since the cycle manufacturing companies have negligible control over fluctuating prices of raw materials, effective designing and execution of manufacturing processes, sound procurement policies and effective marketing allocation may play a critical role in reducing overall product cost.

DISTRIBUTION

NOVA had its manufacturing unit located in Ludhiana, Punjab, India (Exhibit 1.6). As per United Cycle Parts and Manufacturers Association (UCPMA), Asia's largest cycle manufacturer's body, Ludhiana had more than 1,800 registered members. Besides Ludhiana had more than 2,500 industrial units which were either manufacturing cycle parts or complete bicycles. More than 25,000 bicycles each day were being manufactured in the city[10]. Being located in Ludhiana, NOVA had another added advantage of abundant supply of desired raw material. Besides complete in-house state-of-the-art quality testing facilities, NOVA had built separate tool room, assembly units, packaging area and R&D department. Recently, the organization had modernized its enamelling and phosphate plant for better finish and quality of final product.

NOVA had a well-defined distribution strategy. It supplied and marketed its entire portfolio of bicycles throughout the country. The finished products were transported from the NOVA warehouse to the distributors across the country as per the orders collected by the marketing department. NOVA had appointed one distributor in each major city, who further had engaged dealers as part of the distribution network. The retailers were being supplied products by their respective local dealers in the region.

Exhibit 1.5 | *Year-on-Year Performance*

Performance at a Glance (2006–2011)

		2006–07	2007–08	2008–09	2009–10	2010–11
1	Number of bicycles sold	1,43,244	1,70,405	1,55,192	1,77,255	1,80,081
		11.40%	18.96%	(–)8.92%	(+) 14.22%	(+)1.59%
2	Turnover (In crores)	28.94	34.54	34.58	41.5	42.85
		35.86%	19.35%	0.90%	(+) 19.08%	(+) 3.27%
3	Production: Total number of pieces painted	5,76,614	6,95,774	6,46,240	8,25,149	8,65,180
		6.38%	20.66%	(–)7.12%	(+)27.68%	(+)4.85%
4	Rejection (Paint)	1.56%	0.93%	1.20%	2.03%	1.55%
5	Process Cost/Cycle Rs.	53.52	42.29	51.82	68.36	71.04
	(Base-black enamel)					
6	Number of orders received	1125	1457	1134	1464	1514
		6.53%	42%	(–)22.17%	(+)29.10%	(+)3.41%
7	Order execution	92.69%	95.55%	95.94%	95.50%	97.70%
8	Number of complaints	17	17	34	12	10
9	New model introduction	3	5	4	10	8
10	Customer feedback				2	7
11	**Addition in manufacturing plant**					
	Oven (Existing -2)	1			1	
	Spray booth (Existing-2)		1		1	
	Lift (Existing-1)		1			
	Electrostatic gun (Existing-3)		1	1	2	
	Phosphate VAT (Existing-7Tank)	1	1		1	
	New phosphate plant				1	
	Threading M/C					1

Source: Company Records

NOVA's marketing managers and sales team appointed distributors for each city. The entire network of distributors and dealers was being handled by the marketing department of NOVA Bicycle Industries (Exhibit 1.7).NOVA used road transportation for sending finished goods to distributors across India from its central warehouse in Ludhiana.

Exhibit 1.6 | *Ludhiana, Punjab, India*

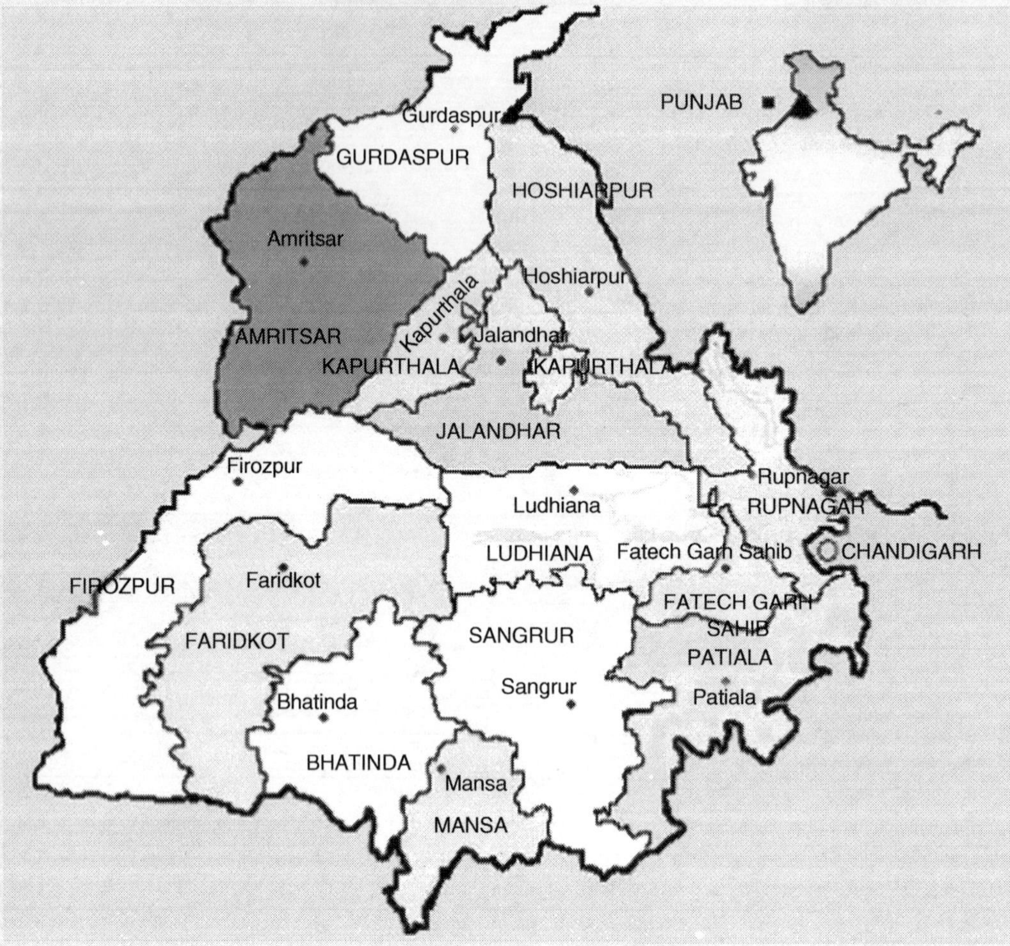

Source: www.travelmadeeasy.in
www.travelmadeeasy.in, accessed on 21 November 2011

PROMOTION

Owing to the ever-changing nature and demand of consumers, bringing new bicycle models with latest design, colours and other specifications have become essential for survival of any bicycle manufacturer. Besides manufacturing quality bicycles, promoting it through effective communication medium has also become the necessity because of the rising competition. NOVA had been actively involved in conceptualizing, designing and implementing new marketing approaches for its product promotion.

Exhibit 1.7 | *Distribution Network*

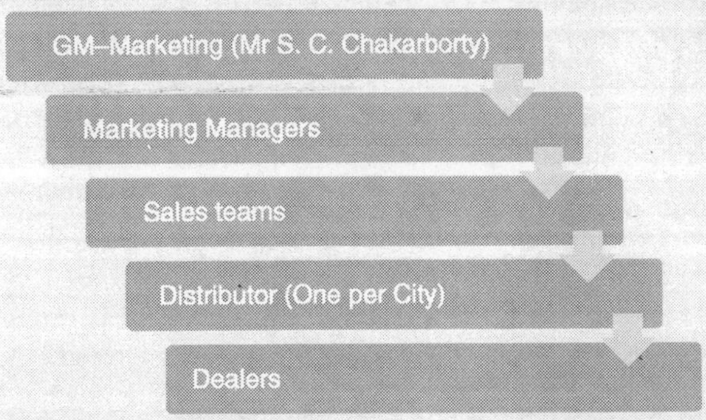

Source: Interview with Mr Chakraborty; dated 4 November 2011

NOVA primarily followed push marketing strategy. It believed that if the dealer and retailer margins were better they would be able to convince and sell the product to the customer. Besides the push marketing strategy, NOVA also issues advertisement for its products. During the product launch, NOVA undertook extensive mass media campaigns and introduction of promotional offers apart from banner advertisement, newspaper advertisements and circus meet promotions. The organization was an active participant at all bike-expo exhibitions. Company's top management had implemented incentive schemes for its entire sales team and marketing managers.

Although advertisement played a vital role in increasing the sales of the product, as per Mr Pahwa, strong interpersonal links were a must for survival in the present scenario of Indian bicycle market, which was already dominated by big players. Thus, for any organization like NOVA which had just nine years of operational existence, creating and maintaining high brand equity was always a challenge. But for NOVA, Mr Pahwa's 40 years of rich experience came as an asset. It was because of mutual respectable personal relations with dealers, retailers and customers that NOVA had been progressing at an impressive growth rate since its inception.

As per Mr Pahwa, in coming days, increasing market share will be crucial for any organization for its long-term survival. He envisioned that relationship management had played a very critical role in improving the company's sales revenue and NOVA will further progress by strengthening this relationship bond with the dealers, retailers and customers. Dealer meets were a key part of NOVA's marketing operations. Such meets not only gave dealers associated with NOVA a sense of recognition but also kept them motivated for further progress with regard to product promotion and sales. As per the GM (Marketing), such meetings acted as a single platform for feedback and grievance handling within NOVA. During these meets, dealers were also made aware of the organizational goals and strategies, besides the upcoming product by NOVA. As extensive cost cutting in bicycle industry had been a major requirement, the organization had come up with many inNOVAtive techniques for product promotion. Some of them included promotion through wall paintings and mobile vans.

MARKETING STRATEGY AT NOVA

NOVA bicycle industries had unique STP (segmentation, targeting and positioning) strategy. Depending upon the utility of the product, the company had been targeting different population segments for different products. For some of its product lines like Roadster, the company had been targeting the rural and semi-urban population. This was because Indian rural and semi-urban population still used bicycles for carrying out their daily personal and professional works; which was in complete contrast to the lifestyle of urban population. Also rural and people 'below poverty line' prioritized usage utility over the bicycle design. This was one of the reasons for Roadster's higher acceptance among rural and semi-urban population than amongst the urban population.

As far as the other segment, that is, fancy bicycles was concerned, companies had been targeting the urban population. This was because these bicycles were expensive in comparison to Roadster bicycles and targeted higher purchasing power customers. The acceptance of such fancy bicycles among urban population was high. For the last few years, the demand of fancy bicycles from this segment had been on the rise and the same trend was expected to be followed in the coming years[11]. Interestingly, the definition of high-end bicycles was also changing. Earlier the high-end bicycles were considered as those selling between ₹5,000 to 8,000. However, with the global brands coming into the country this definition had changed to price-points starting from ₹15,000 to 1 lakh (0.1 million).

PORTER'S DIAMOND MODEL

Mr Rohit Pahwa was reading Harvard Business's School professor Michael Porter's Diamond Model for competitive advantages of nations (Exhibit 1.8). The model talked about analysing the five factors, viz., factor conditions; demand conditions; firm strategy, structure and rivalry; related and supporting industries and government; in order to assess competitive position of a nation in global competition. Mr Rohit was trying to draw a parallel with the business model in the bicycle industry and NOVA and analysed NOVA's industrial location in Ludhiana with the five factors given in the Porter's Diamond model. Porter in this theory had also opined on 'clusters' or groups of interconnected firms, suppliers and related industries. Mr Rohit introspected about each of the five factors with respect to NOVA's competitive position regarding its location at Ludhiana.

Exhibit 1.8 | *Michael Porter's Diamond Model for Competitive Advantage of Nations*

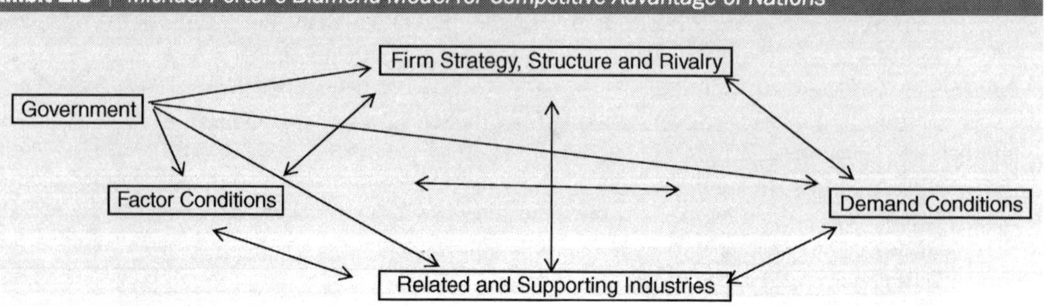

Source: www.valuebasedmanagement.in, accessed on 21 November 2011

Factor Conditions

It includes human resources, raw material resources, knowledge resources, capital resources and infrastructure. 'Ludhiana', the industrial city of Punjab, had ample supply of all these resources. Ludhiana had a huge skilled labour pool required by NOVA Bicycle Industries for attaining competitive advantage. The inhouse product development team of NOVA had designed machinery layout and developed machinery-related infrastructure thereby saving a lot of capital cost. The raw material like iron, steel, plastics, etc. a sub-part of factor conditions was also available in abundance in the vicinity of Ludhiana.

Demand Conditions

The customers of bicycle industry were quite demanding especially in the fancy bicycle segment. In bicycle industry, demand in terms of new designs, shapes, variants, colour had been periodically required by customers in the past, which was acting as a major driving force for NOVA to continuously come up with new variants. Also with the population becoming more health conscious and adopting green practices, the demand of bicycles is likely to increase.

Firm Strategy, Structure and Rivalry

Strong intra and intercity competition within Ludhiana created pressure to further inNOVAte in order to upgrade competitiveness. NOVA had to compete with small, medium and large scale bicycle manufacturers. Such competition directly impacted all bicycle manufacturers to improve their production capacities and marketing campaigns. Each firm endeavoured to reduce the price by refining across the value chain, that is, minimizing cost in procurement of raw materials, reducing cost in operations and warehousing, and optimizing the marketing and overhead expenditure.

Related and Supporting Industries

Supporting industries for bicycle manufacturing unit included production units or furnaces which moulded steel in desired shape, size and design by undergoing processes such as annealing. Such industries were present in large numbers in Ludhiana. NOVA had been getting the desired raw material in adequate quantity from within the city. It helped in reducing the manufacturing and procurement cost.

Government

The government had been strongly promoting the use of bicycles in view of increasing pollution and health hazards. The state government was aggressively promoting the use of bicycles, especially in crowded cities in order to decongest it and also reduce vehicular pollution. The Centre and various state governments in India had distributed free bicycles to poorer population during the various state-sponsored social campaigns. For instance, Assam and Uttar Pradesh government had separate budget allocation for providing bicycles to girl students from 'below poverty line' families. Punjab and Haryana government had been distributing free bicycles each year under various government social schemes.

THE ROAD AHEAD FOR NOVA

For NOVA Bicycle Industries, the business was running at its usual pace. However, the Chairman, Mr H. M. S. Pahwa, was worried on certain issues facing the company. He was convinced that some initiatives had to be taken as soon as possible for sustained profitability and better future of the organization. Mr H. M. S. Pahwa was introspecting over the following options:

Diversification into E-bikes and Health Equipments

Chairman, Mr H. M. S. Pahwa, mainly focussed on three objectives, viz., stabilizing the present business, expanding into new areas and exploring diversification, especially in related areas. He felt that stronger foothold in the fancy bicycle segment was required to sustain the existing business in the long-term, especially due to high margins in this segment. According to him, standard bicycle industry would shrink in the coming years and the margins will get further reduced. The economies of scale would be the key to survival in such a scenario. Therefore, he envisioned that in order to achieve NOVA's economies of scale and thereby get the most competitive manufacturing cost, it will have to invest in its production capacity.

Further Mr Pahwa was interested in diversification of NOVA product line. This was because of the following underlying factors:

Imposition of Excise Duties

During the initial phase of the business—that is, during 2002–03—the excise duties were 4 per cent and part of increase in total cost of production was added to sale price by each manufacturer. This provided lot of comfort and margin to the manufacturers. However, now the situation had altered with high percentage of excise duty and highly competitive pricing within the industry. According to Mr Pahwa, there was need to increase prices in the Roadster bicycle segment in the near future as prices of raw materials have increased by many folds since the price of Roadster bicycle segment was last fixed. Presently, India has maximum sales of standard (Roadster bicycles) and competition in same segment was anticipated to further surge as new excise duties would widen the price differential between the organized players and unorganized sector.

Changing Automotive Lifestyle

In India, the socio-economic patterns were altering rapidly. As a result of easy and extensive availability of credit facilities, the purchasing power of the lower middle class had improved drastically. Therefore, quite comfortably the middle class people were making a transition from bicycles to motorcycles. The usage of motorcycles among school and college students had been on rise for the past many years.

Poor Road Infrastructure of India

Overcrowded roads with heavy vehicles running at jet speeds make Indian roads quite risky and hard to ride bicycles. With no provision of separate bicycle lanes in present Indian infrastructure, bicycle riders face high risks while travelling, especially in urban localities. Also urban populations preferred motor bikes as they had to travel long distances, especially in the metro and large cities.

Out Migration to Cities from Rural Areas

Due to the increasing opportunities for both personal and professional growth, large number of rural population had migrated and settled in urban and semi-urban areas. This out migration of population from the rural areas had affected the sales of bicycles to this large target population, especially in Roadster segment bicycles.

Fluctuating Monsoons

More than two-thirds of the Indian population was dependent on agriculture for their livelihood. The income of the agriculture-dependent rural population had a high correlation with the monsoon. If the monsoon arrives timely and brings adequate rainfall, it leads to a bumper harvest and, thereby, brings more income to the rural population. The rural population income each year had an impact on their purchase and spending including the purchase of bicycles. However, fluctuation in monsoon was quite common in entire India and this also affected the sales of roadster bicycles. This frequency of fluctuation in the monsoon rainfall had increased with the aggravating global warming phenomenon. Chairman Mr Pahwa further added that the instability in steel and rubber prices had been bothering manufacturers a lot in the recent past and it was directly affecting their profit margins.

These were amongst the many reasons which were motivating Mr Pahwa to broaden his horizons by entering into new product lines. Mr Pahwa envisaged that if the plan to diversify was successfully rolled out, it may help in some international tie-ups.

Undoubtedly, Mr Pahwa also saw a lot of hurdles in e-bikes division. He was quite apprehensive that whether people would accept e-bikes as they would cost a lot more than traditional bicycles. He added that since India was already an electricity-deficient nation, so adding such a product in their portfolio which was completely dependent on electricity may be risky. Also he was aware that rural and semi-urban population used bicycles for multi-faced functions, on the contrast, e-bikes cannot be used to carry huge loads which might also act as a hurdle for its acceptance.

Strengthening the Existing Business

Mr Chakraborty had a different opinion regarding the future of NOVA product lines. He believed that instead of diversification, if NOVA focussed on its core competence which it had acquired over the last many years; the probability of success would be higher. He confidently stated that:

> If we are able to sell one bicycle per family, it will take us another 25 years to do the same provided population and production remains same. Indian population is also increasing at a comparatively faster rate in world. So, NOVA's mission should be to sell at least one bicycle in each and every house of this nation irrespective of the purpose for which it would be used.

Mr Chakraborty was completely convinced about growing challenges in the bicycle industry as stated by Mr Pahwa in the dining hall. However, he had a different viewpoint about how NOVA should undertake the future initiatives. Mr Chakraborty's advice was that NOVA should focus more on high margin fancy bicycle segment. He believed that with the increasing growth of fancy bicycle segment, demand of high end accessories such as gears would increase. He opined that pricing strategy of earning much higher margins on accessories than the main product would bring large revenue to NOVA. Mr Chakraborty also suggested that NOVA should increase the number of product lines of fancy bicycles. He stated that since NOVA enjoyed high brand equity, marketing strategy of product differentiation and consistent new launches would augur well for NOVA's future. Mr Chakraborty opined that promotion of NOVA's fancy bicycle product line should leverage its association with NOVA's successful and widely accepted Roadster bicycle segment.

Further, Mr Chakraborty suggested opening one of the NOVA Bicycle Industries' offices in China or hiring agents in China, which would facilitate the import of cheaper raw materials from China. This would enable NOVA to further lower its market price of fancy bicycle segment without compromising on the quality. He was confident that Chinese bicycles cannot enter into Roadster segment. He had reached this conclusion after doing complete cost-benefit analysis for the same. He stated that because of higher steel prices than plastic in China, the cost of production for such segment in China automatically got increased and further when freight cost (from China to India) and 30 per cent import duty gets added, the actual price becomes quite high in comparison to that available in India. He believed that even if tariff rates were lowered to 15–20 per cent as per WTO norms or even reduced to zero, Chinese manufacturers were unlikely to beat Indian manufacturers in Roadster segment since higher freight cost would act as an obstacle to achieve price advantage.

Hearing about the statistics of Roadster bicycle cost advantage over Chinese bicycle and logic of building upon NOVA's core competence as stated by Mr Chakraborty; infused lot of confidence in him for the moment. However, the shrinking profit margin, promising growth of green products like e-bikes, increasing Chinese low-cost product influx in high-margin fancy bicycle segment, changing automotive lifestyles and out migration to cities of the target population; made Chairman Mr H. M. S. Pahwa have a second thought on the suggestion given by Mr Chakraborty. He was in complete dilemma regarding what steps to undertake to ensure a successful and sustained profitable future for NOVA Bicycle Industries.

DISCUSSION QUESTIONS

1. On the basis of facts given in the case, what would be your advice to Chairman Mr H. M. S. Pahwa regarding future strategic initiatives at NOVA Bicycle Industries?
2. Discuss the implications on the organization in case NOVA Bicycle Industries decides to diversify into e-bikes and health equipments?
3. Suggest marketing strategies to the top management of NOVA Bicycles Industries to counter the low cost Chinese bicycle variants in the domestic market.
4. Do a SWOT analysis of NOVA Bicycles Industries. Also suggest strategies for NOVA Bicycles Industries on how to capitalize on their strengths in tapping the opportunities in the domestic market.
5. Discuss how the Porter's Diamond Model is relevant to NOVA Bicycle Industries location at Ludhiana. Also suggest additional initiatives to be taken by NOVA Bicycle Industries in order to further strengthen its competitive advantage.
6. Should NOVA Bicycles Industries engage market research agency to do an in-depth study about sales revenue potential and prospects of bicycles, e-bikes and health equipments in the domestic market; before making a major strategic decision?

ENDNOTES

1. An e-bike is an electric motor powered bicycle which may look like a bicycle, scooter or motorcycle depending on the product design. It does not require conventional petroleum product to run it and therefore is environment friendly.
2. http://www.prweb.com/releases/bicycles_adult/mountain_electric_bikes/prweb4515734.htm, accessed 22 November 2011.
3. http://www.crisil.com/Ratings/Commentary/CommentaryDocs/cycle-ind0103.pdf, accessed 22 November 2011.
4. Heavy duty bicycles are entirely made up of steel and iron.
5. Value = Price/Utility
6. http://www.business-standard.com/india/news/indian-bicycle-industry-to-lose-huge-market-shares-to-china/292669, accessed on 27 November 2011.
7. Ibid.
8. Tonee is a unit of measurement equaling 1,000 Kilograms.

9. http://www.business-standard.com/india/news/indian-bicycle-industry-to-lose-huge-market-shares-to-china/292669, accessed on 27 November 2011.
10. http://www.dare.co.in/opportunities/manufacturing/the-business-of-bicycles.htm, accessed on 27 November 2011.
11. http://indianindustrystatistics.blogspot.com/2010/01/bicycle-industry-in-india-pedal-for.html, accessed on 27 November 2011.

REFERENCE

http://www.valuebasedmanagement.in, accessed on 21 November 2011.

2

Rakesh Chemicals (P) Limited: The Pricing Muddle

Rakesh Chemicals (P) Limited (RCPL[1]) was about to undertake certain strategic initiatives that would impact its product pricing. The organization had a track record of accomplishing successful structural changes. The last few board meetings at RCPL were dominated by discussions and brainstorming sessions on plans and proposals to reduce RCPL's PCC pricing. As a result, when one of these board meetings started, the opening agenda was to discuss on various options that the committee constituted by the top management had recommended so as to achieve competitive product pricing.

THE BEGINNING

RCPL was started by Mr Khoob Chand in 1982 as a precipitated calcium carbonate (PCC) manufacturing unit. PCC is used as synthetic filler in various industries like rubber, plastic, cable and dentifrice (toothpaste). Mr Chand headed the organization for 15 years. However, due to heavy financial losses during the early 1990s, he sold out his venture, which was named after his son in 1997, to three renowned personalities of Saharanpur district of Uttar Pradesh (Exhibit 2.1). One of the new promoters who took over the reins of the debt-ridden RCPL was Mr Kanwar Pal Majra, a successful political leader and famous personality of the state. The other two new promoters were Mr Satwant Singh Batra and Mr Rajinder Chawla. Both of them had vast experience in the chemical industry. All of the three promoters chalked out a strategic plan to revive RCPL's old glory of a profit-making successful enterprise. Streamlining the operations along with reorganization required huge infusion of capital which was a real challenge for the new promoters.

BUSINESS HIERARCHY

RCPL, though an SME, had structured processes and was managed on lines of multinational corporations. The new top management was optimistic and market savvy. They believed in strategic planning

Exhibit 2.1 | *Saharanpur, Uttar Pradesh, India*

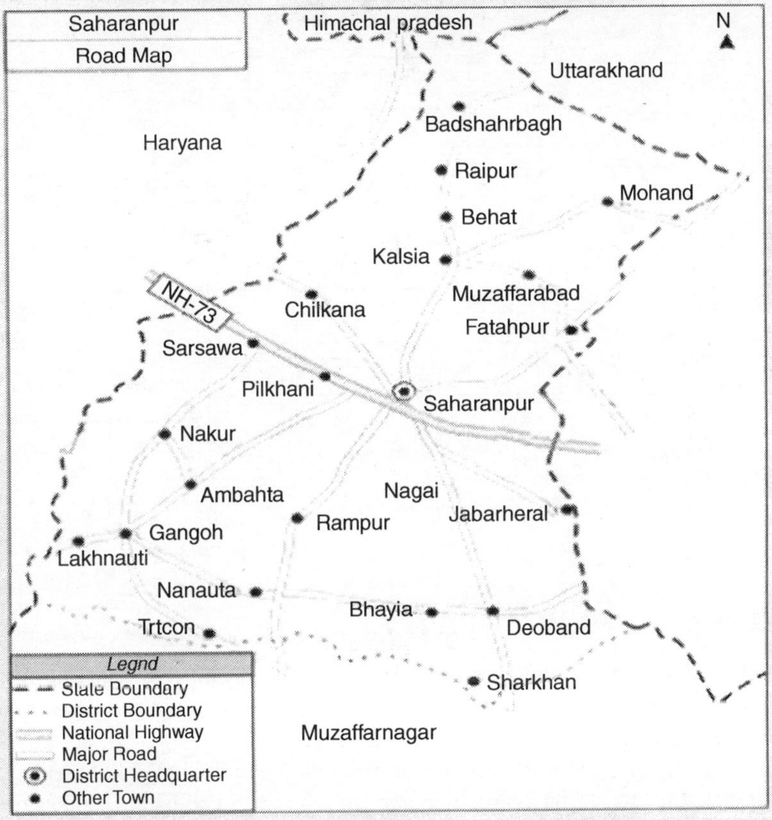

Source: www.mapsofindia.com/maps/uttarpradesh/districts/saharanpur.htm, accessed on 15 December 2011

and its meticulous execution. The new management added talented and experienced manpower to the existing human resource pool. RCPL was reorganized along functional departments. Each department was led by its respective functional head. Each functional head reported directly to the directors (Exhibit 2.2). The director was the highest hierarchy at RCPL. One of the co-owners and director Mr Satwant Singh Batra looked after production and warehousing division. The other co-owner and director, Mr Rajinder Chawla looked after rest of divisions including marketing and finance.

RCPL had recently recruited Mr Rajesh Goswami to head its marketing and sales function. His mandate was to explore new potential markets and suggest strategic market penetration strategies for these new markets. Mr Viresh Kumar, Head (Production), a mechanical engineer by training, had served in various chemical manufacturing organizations since 1990. He had joined RCPL in 1998. Other verticals reporting directly to top management included finance and purchase. According to the company officials, monthly reviews of financial targets, production targets and profitability were undertaken by all functional heads with the directors.

Exhibit 2.2 | *Organization Structure at RCPL*

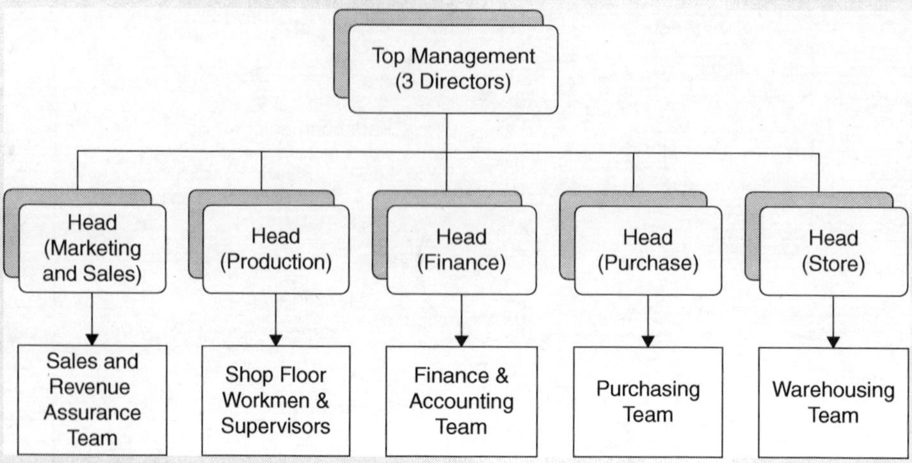

Source: Company Records

1997 RESTRUCTURING ACTIVITY

During the late 1990s, RCPL faced serious cash flow crunch and news spread among the business community regarding its negative profitability. Its vendors like charcoal and limestone merchants were reluctant to provide raw materials on credit. RCPL started to lose its permanent customers because of their inability to promptly cater to the demands of its clients. Owing to the negative word of mouth, the credibility of RCPL was seriously affected and Mr Khoob Chand had no other option but to sell the company. As soon as new management took over, priority was given to clearance of vendor invoices, restructuring of business processes and streamlining of warehouse procedures. Responding positively to needs and desires of the workforce at RCPL, the new management generated trust, motivation, job security and positive attitude amongst the employees. Consistent adherence to such employee and vendor practices and making it a part of organizational culture helped in revitalization of RCPL.

Since then, RCPL has never looked back and has been achieving new milestones each year. The organization had planned to expand its production capacity in order to meet the growing market demand. RCPL has sales revenue of more than ₹3 crores (30 million) in the financial year 2010–11 (Exhibit 2.3).

CALCIUM CARBONATE

Calcium is the fifth most abundant element on earth. Because of its ability to form compounds on reaction with oxygen and water, it is not available freely in the environment. It was discovered by Sir Humphry Davy, in 1808, through the electrolysis of lime (CaO) and mercuric oxide (HgO)[2]. Commercially for the first time it was manufactured by the English company John E Sturge Ltd. in 1941.About 4.2 per cent of the earth's crust is composed of calcium. Chalk, marble and limestone are various other forms of calcium carbonate. Other common compounds of calcium are calcium sulfate ($CaSO_4$), also known as

Exhibit 2.3 | *Balance Sheet of RCPL as on 31 March 2011*

S.No	Particulars	31/03/2011	31/03/2010
	Source of funds		
	Shareholders fund		
A	Share Capital	4,990,000	4,990,000
	Reserve and Surplus	220,740	220,740
	Total (A)	5,210,740	5,210,740
	Loan Fund		
	Secured Loans	1,255,397	2,556,950
B	Unsecured Loan	11,098,004	11,798,004
	Total (B)	12,353,401	14,354,954
	Grand Total (A+B)	17,564,141	19,565,694
	Application Fund		
	Fixed Assets		
C	Gross Block	4,832,984	5,318,366
	Less: Depreciation	563,272	628,062
		4,269,712	4,690,304
	Current Assets and Advances and Loans		
	Inventories	7,678,801	5,219,218
	Sundry Debtors	8,160,264	8,302,385
	Cash & Bank Balance	196,125	205,571
D	Other Current Assets	1,441,823	1,404,125
	Loans and Advances	110,000	111,484
	Deferred Tax Assets	14,853	1,943
	Total Current Assets	17,601,768	15,244,727
	Less: Current Liabilities & Provisions	13,061,278	9,693,491
		-	-
E		4,540,490	5,551,236
	Profit and Loss APP A/C	8,753,940	9,324,154
		17,564,141	19,565,694

Profit and Loss Account of RCPL as on 31 March 2011

S.No	Particulars	31/03/2011	31/03/2010
	Sales	32,748,030	29,314,845
A	Interest on Power Security	21,273	21,273
	Increase/Decrease in Stoke	2,261,250	(1,181,250)
		35,030,553	28,154,868
	Expenditure		
	Cost of Raw materials consumed	24,260,609	13,727,793
	Manufacturing Exp	6,394,511	10,010,985
B	Admn. Expenses	1,916,375	1,853,951
	Employees welfares exp	606,383	571,699
	Depreciation	563,272	628,062
	Financial Charges	287,279	160,723
		34,028,430	26,953,214

C	Profit and Loss before tax(A-B)	1,002,122	1,207,653
D	Deffered tax assets	12,910	10,415
E	Profit and Loss after tax(C+D)	1,015,032	1,218,069
F	Retained Earning	1,015,032	1,218,069

Source: Company Records

gypsum, which is main constituent in Plaster of Paris; calcium nitrate (Ca $(NO_3)_2$), a naturally occurring fertilizer; and calcium phosphate (Ca_3 $(PO_4)_2$), the main material found in bones and teeth.

Some of the properties of calcium are[3]:

- Atomic number: 20
- Atomic weight: 40.078
- Melting point: 1115 K (842°C or 1548°F)
- Boiling point: 1757 K (1484°C or 2703°F)
- Density: 1.54 grams per cubic centimetre
- Phase at room temperature: Solid
- Period number: 4 group number: 2 group name: Alkaline Earth Metal
- Estimated crustal abundance: 4.15×10^4 milligrams per kilogram
- Estimated oceanic abundance: 4.12×10^2 milligrams per litre
- Number of stable isotopes: 4
- Ionization energy: 6.113 eV

PRECIPITATED CALCIUM CARBONATE (PCC)

RCPL is the leading manufacturer of precipitated calcium carbonate (PCC), which acts as a synthetic filler in various industries such as rubber, plastic, cable and dentifrice. Iron, magnesium, copper, arsenic, chloride, fluoride, phosphate, sulphate, silica and magnesia are main components of PCC (Exhibit 2.4). The other form of calcium carbonate is ground calcium carbonate (GCC). RCPL had not entered in GCC production business. RCPL manufactured PCC of international quality standards in two distinct types of structures, namely, *Rakcal Aragonite series* and *Rakcal Calcite Series.*

Though, chemically, both the series are same, they have different crystal lattice and thus have different appearances and classifications.

1. **Rakcal aragonite series:** Various grades manufactured by RCPL in aragonite series were RAKCAL, RAKCAL-999, RAKCAL-D, RAKCAL-11 and RAKCAL 44 (refer to Exhibit 2.5). These grades of PCC were fine white powders of aragonite structures with different particle size, distribution and apparent density. These were widely used as fillers in rubber, paint, PVC, pharmaceuticals and food industry.
2. **Rakcal calcite series:** Various grades manufactured by RCPL in calcite series were RAKCAL-F, RAKCAL-212 and RAKCAL-313 (refer to Exhibit 2.5). These grades of PCC were ultra fine white powder with smoother texture having calcite structure. Due to its high opacity, it was widely used as filler for surface coating of paper, printing inks, PVC leather cloths, foam leather and compounding of cables and shoes.

Both PCC and GCC have similar chemical compositions, however, they occur in different shapes and sizes. Under microscopic view, GCC is rhombohedral in shape. Particle sizes in GCC are larger than PCC of the same size (Exhibit 2.6).

Exhibit 2.4 | *Chemical Analysis of PCC*

Colour	Bright White
Specific Gravity	2.65
Solution in Hydrochloric Acid 5 N	Clear
Soluble Alkali (as NaO)	Less than 0.15%
pH	9.5 to 9.8
Loss On Drying at 1050 C + 50 C	0.5 Max
Iron as Fe	Less than 0.01%
Manganese as Mn	Less than 0.003%
Copper as Cu	Negligible
Arsenic as As	Nil
Chloride as Cl	Traces
Fluoride as F	0.05% Max
Phosphate as P04	0.05% Max
Sulphate as S04	0.2% Max
Silica as Si02	Less than 0.5%
Aluminium, Iron, Phosphorus and matter insoluble in Hydrochloric Acid	Less than 0.5%
Magnesia as Mgo	Less than 0.5%
Calcium Carbonate (Test method as is IS-918-1968)	98.5% Minimum

Source: Company Records

Exhibit 2.5 | *Properties of Aragonite and Calcite Series*

Aragonite Series

Grade	RAKCAL-EVA SPL	RAKCAL-999 (Fine)	RAKCAL-D	RAKCAL-11	RAKCAL-44
Description	Extra Light	Superior Quality	Light	Dense	Extra Dense
Apparent Density (gm/ml)	.30–.33	.34–.35	.36–.37	.50–.58	.68–.82
Particle weight median diameter (micron)	3.8	4.0	4.0	8.4	10.2
Surface area by nitrogen (Absorption m2g)	6.8	6.4	6.5	4.9	2.02
Specific Surface diameter from surface area (micron)	0.33	0.34	0.34	0.47	1.10
Flow Point (ml/15gm)	32	26	27.5	25.5	12
Settled Bulk (ml/gm)	3.2	2.8	3.0	2.6	1.4
Fineness Residue on 75- Micron IS Seive % by weight (IS-918-1968) (200 Mesh)	0.1	0.1	0.1	0.1	0.1

Calcite Series

Grade	RAKCAL-F	RAKCAL-212	RAKCAL-333
Description	Fine	Ultra Fine	Ultra Fine
Apparent Density (gm/ml)	.36–.40	.44–.45	.44–.50
Surface area by nitrogen (Absorption m2g)	6.5	12	18-22
Specific Surface diameter from surface area (micron)	0.34	0.10	0.10
Oil Absorption (gm/100gm)	32	34	38
Fineness Residue on 75- Micron IS Seive % by weight (IS-918-1968) (200 Mesh)	0.1	0.1	0.1

Source: Company Records

Exhibit 2.6 | *Pictorial View of PCC and GCC*

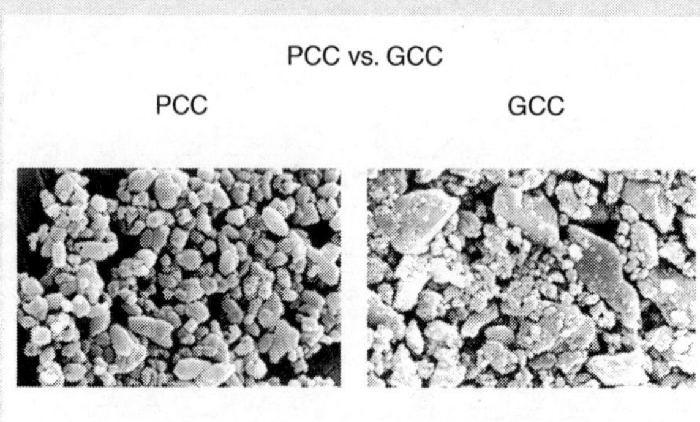

Source: http://www.specialtyminerals.com/our-minerals/what-is-pcc/ accessed on 15 December 2011

APPLICATIONS OF PCC IN DIFFERENT INDUSTRIES

Various grades of PCC manufactured by RCPL had distinct applications in varied industries. In these industries, PCC acted as an ingredient to the main product and was used for altering and improving the physical properties besides overall processing of the finished product. The purpose of PCC's specific grade for respective industries is mentioned in Table 2.1.

Table 2.1 *PCC Grade and Their Applications in Industry*

Industry	Typical Application	Suitable Grade
Plastics	As a filler in rigid and plasticized PVC to improve impact strength	RAKCAL-11, RAKCAL-F,RAKCAL-212,RAKCAL-333
	As a filler in PVC footwear and cable compound / cables to improve surface gloss and other physical properties	
Rubber and Paints	As a reinforcing filler in natural and synthetic rubber for tyre & tube application	RAKCAL-D,RAKCAL-999,RAKCAL-EVA SPL
	As a filler for Hawaii chappals soles/straps to improve the strength as well as whiteness	
	As an anti-settling agent in paints and in emulsion	
	As a white opacifying agent	
Pharmaceuticals	As a calcium source	RAKCAL-999
	As an anti-acid	
	For neutralization and filtration aid in antibiotic products	
	As a buffering and dissolution aid in soluble tablets	
	As a bulking agent in tableting	
	For strengthening bones	
Dentifrice	In powder and tooth paste, as cleaning and polishing agent	RAKCAL-44
Food & Beverages	In chcwing gums	RAKCAL-999
	As a calcium supplement	
	In effervescent powder drinks	
	To neutralize excess acid in food and wine manufacturer	
	As a filtration aid	
Cosmetics	In talcum powder, to increase fluffiness and control absorption characteristics	RAKCAL-999
	In face powders, as a perfume carrier and in sunscreen preparations	
Paper	In paper, coating for brightness, smoothness, opacity and ink receptivity	RAKCAL-D
	In cigarette paper, for control of opacity and burning rate	
	As a cost effective filler in alkaline-sized paper giving high brightness and opacity	

RCPL MANUFACTURING PLANT

RCPL manufacturing plant had large warehouses to store bulky raw materials at its premises. RCPL had its own mechanical workshop to maintain and repair machine tools. It had heavy equipments like boilers, dryers and kiln which were prone to disruptions. RCPL also had an in-house laboratory within its production facility to monitor various quality parameters like bulk density, moisture, purity, alkanity, etc. The organization had recently installed boiler cum turbine unit to ensure uninterrupted electricity supply to the entire manufacturing plant. The plant layout was done in a scientific manner so as to ensure smooth manufacturing operations. The RCPL's boilers had existing capacity of 5tph (tons per hour) besides having 8 running dryers and 4 dryers in standby mode to provide replacements in case of any breakdown. In addition to the existing infrastructure, 2 kilns and 2 settling tanks were also installed within RCPL premises.

PCC PRODUCT DEVELOPMENT

PCC was manufactured through a series of continuous processes at RCPL. The basic raw materials required for manufacturing PCC were limestone and charcoal. RCPL's charcoal vendors were located in Gujarat, Rajasthan and Assam. Initially, carbon monoxide was produced separately in gas producer by burning charcoal in the presence of air. The gas was then mixed with limestone (small stones or powder) along with presence of air inside kiln to initiate the process of calcination at temperature range varying from 800° C to 1200° C. In order to ensure high level of purity, calcination process was carried out using natural gas at RCPL. The resultant material developed was calcium oxide or lime (CaO) and carbon dioxide (CO_2) gas Further CO_2 was made cold and stored in scrubbler. Simultaneously, calcium oxide was amalgamated with water (H_2O) in a hydrolyser to form calcium hydroxide Ca $(OH)_2$. Calcium hydroxide also known as hydrated lime or slake was further mixed with individually stored carbon dioxide inside the carbonator to form liquid calcium carbonate. Liquid calcium carbonate was then further screened using a vibratory screen to allow its solid particles to settle inside settling tanks while keeping the liquid afloat. These screens had configurations of approximately 300 mesh.

Subsequently, settled particles were hardened by allowing its passage through rotary vacuum filter (RVF). Calcium carbonate particles were further dried using steam generated by huge boilers (Exhibit 2.7). Though the manufacturing process as shown below seemed simple, its industrial production requires strong adherence to various quality parameters and related processes to ensure uniformity in particle size and shape, surface area and its chemistry.

Burning of limestone -------- $CaCO_3$ $CaO + CO_2$

Slacking of quicklime ------- $CaO + H_2O$ $Ca(OH)_2$

Precipitation ----------------- $Ca(OH)_2 + CO_2$ $CaCO_3 + H_2O$(PCC)

Locational Advantage

RCPL was located in the heart of Saharanpur city (Exhibit 2.1). Situated in Uttar Pradesh, RCPL had another added advantage of its close proximity to Shivalik hills. Located to the north of the Saharanpur city, Shivalik hills have an abundance of natural limestone. Limestone available from hills of Shivalik had appropriate combination of various chemical elements which ensured RCPL availability of best quality raw material in the close vicinity. Saharanpur and Yamuna Nagar (Located west of Saharanpur city and is part of Haryana state) are known for thriving wood carving industries. This ensured sufficient saw dust of wood for all RCPL's boilers. Also RCPL had abundant supply of bagasse due to Saharanpur's proximity with Uttar Pradesh's sugarcane belt.

The strategic location of production plant gave RCPL competitive cost advantage besides quality production output. The quality raw material was available in abundant quantity within close proximity which reduced freight charges and reduced uncertainty regarding timely availability of raw material.

Exhibit 2.7 | *Production Phases of PCC*

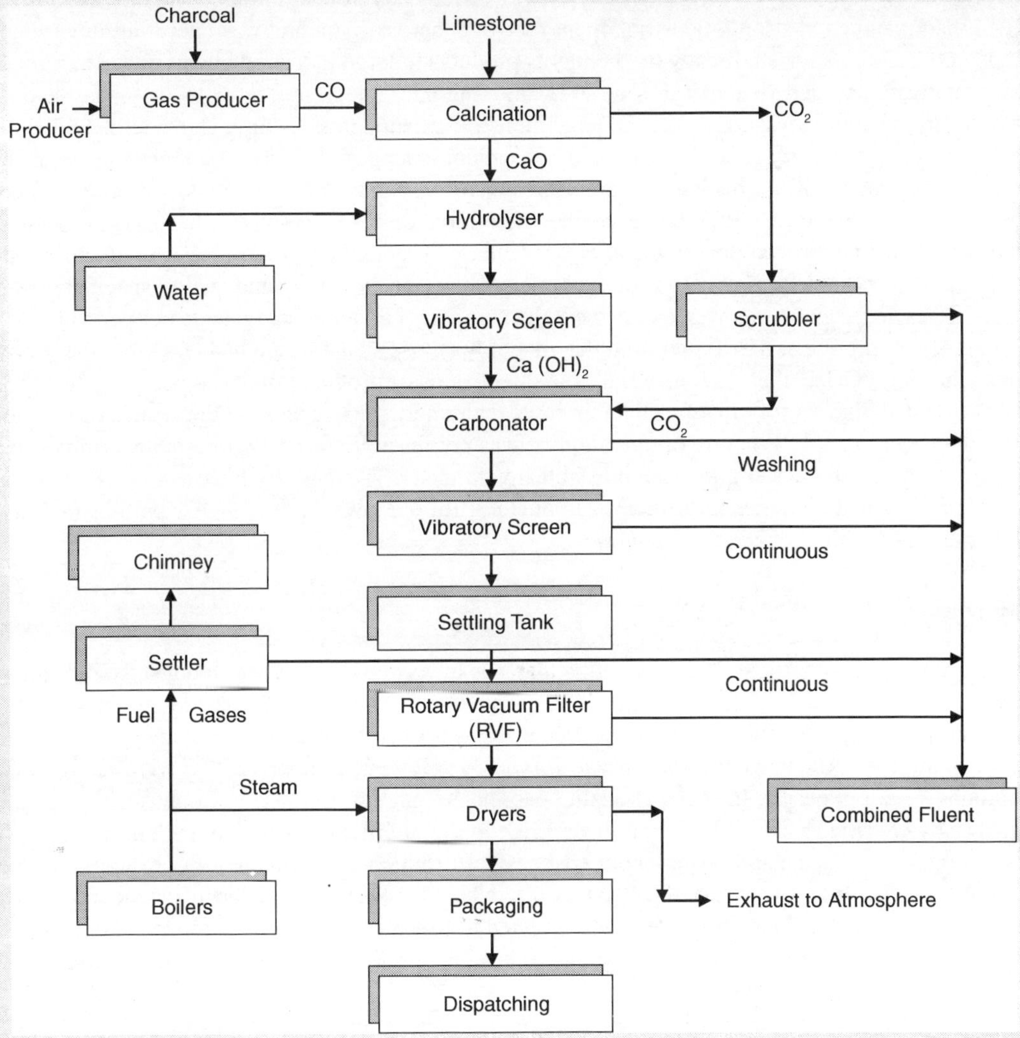

Source: Company Records

However, industrial cities like Saharanpur were facing labour shortage problems. Being a mostly manually operated plant, RCPL was heavily dependent on labour to run its activities. The main reason for severe shortage was increasing number of industrial units in Bihar state during the last few years. Bihar had an enormous pool of labour class but higher daily wages, and that to close to their hometown, besides Central government's sponsored MGNREGA (Mahatma Gandhi National Rural Employment Guarantee Act) had drastically reduced out-migration of labourers from Bihar to other states of the country. According to the company officials, there had been reduction of about 30 per cent of labourers from Bihar at RCPL in the financial year 2010–11. RCPL used road transport for delivering its products from its warehouses throughout the country and even for its exports to Nepal.

PROMOTION

RCPL had been aggressively targeting industries of varied background through its marketing initiatives. RCPL had maintained strong industrial client networks across India and was exporting its products to Nepal too. RCPL had been directly marketing its products to large industrial clients and also through its dealer network. As per Mr Goswami, Head (Marketing and Sales), presently, the company had 40:60 ratio regarding company's direct sales to large industrial client and sales through dealer networks. In its direct marketing process, RCPL's business development managers (BDM) set up meetings with supply chain management (SCM) manager or purchase department manager of various concerned industries. The BDM submitted the RCPL product sample, after initial discussions and clarifications. As soon as the (industrial) client approved the sample after their internal product approval process, number of negotiation meetings was held to finalize various parameters like price, quantity and quality specifications.

As far as dealer networks were concerned, the company had appointed one dealer per state to stock and market its products. RCPL preferred this model for those states which had lesser number of industries requiring PCC as their raw material. The direct sales of products from the company to industrial clients yielded higher profit margins than through dealer networks because of elimination of intermediaries. However, given the nature of operations it was not feasible for RCPL to establish offices in each major city due to higher employee and establishment costs. Till date, RCPL was not using any mass media promotional activities to market its product portfolio. However, it regularly participated in trade shows and PCC-related trade conferences.

PRICING

Pricing was the most critical 'P' of marketing that was in current discussions amongst RCPL's top management. Intense competition from China, Malaysia and other South East Asian countries were making survival quite tough for RCPL and its local competitors. According to the company officials, the cost of production for PCC in RCPL was close to ₹10 per kg. However, imported PCC were easily available at around ₹8.5 to 9 per kg. In terms of quality parameters, they were inferior. Countries like China and Malaysia were able to export PCC at a lower price in the international market, including India, due to their economies of scale and lower labour cost besides production automation. For example, in India it took about seven steps to produce finished PCC product, whereas in China, due to advanced automation, the entire product development cycle was completed in four steps. The production cycle time reduction helped Chinese PCC producing organizations to enhance production volumes and thus also helped in achieving economies of scale.

The other reasons for high price of RCPL's product line were its non-presence in GCC production and high energy cost. The GCC price was about ₹4 per kg and majority of the PCC producing organizations, including exporters, were partially mixing GCC with PCC in their finished products and, thus, reducing their production cost. Also the state of Uttar Pradesh where RCPL was situated was highly deficient in electricity. Uninterrupted power supply was the essential requirement for RCPL's manufacturing plants. In the past, the organization relied on state electricity supply and the diesel electricity generators for its power supply. However, due to rising diesel prices and other overheads of maintaining this uninterrupted electricity supply system, the top management decided to undergo one-time capital investment of installing boiler-cum-turbine unit at RCPL's premises to generate steam that would be used to run the dryers and dehydrate PCC. Besides electricity generated in this process would be used to run the manufacturing plant. Though the installation of boiler-cum-turbine unit had removed the problem of electricity interruption, the running expenditure of such unit was significantly higher and was increasing the cost of production of finished goods for RCPL.

PCC was used as raw material in various industries like plastic, rubber, cable and dentifrice industry. Besides PCC, another product called 'resin' was also used to develop final products such as PVC pipes. High fluctuations of resin prices had seriously affected the production of ultimate products, viz., PVC pipes, shoe soles, etc. which in turn impacted the usage of PCC. Strong resistance to high prices of plastic, rubber and paint goods forced its manufacturers to use GCC or mixture of GCC and PCC as ingredient raw material. These developments, at times, interrupted the production schedule of RCPL due to demand fluctuations.

Charcoal was one of the main raw materials used for producing PCC. It was available in requisite quantity and quality in Assam, Gujarat and Rajasthan. However, imposition of comparatively higher excise duties on incoming raw materials from other states by Uttar Pradesh government increased the cost of PCC production by the organization. The increased diesel prices were also making it hard for RCPL to compete with the imported PCC products.

These issues were taken into consideration by RCPL's top management when they were considering restructuring of entire pricing strategy.

GLOBAL PCC INDUSTRY

As per Global Industry Analysts Inc., international calcium carbonate market was estimated to touch 108.5 million tonnes by 2015. One of the key drivers supporting this exponential growth included increased use of PCC in paper industry[4]. Most of the paper manufacturing organizations were getting their processes automated and were transforming from acid-based process technology to alkaline-based process technology, thus, increasing the usage of PCC by manifolds. Asia was at the top in terms of PCC consumption in the world, followed by Europe and North America. Within Asia, 70 per cent of the total production capacity was in China[5]. Asia had also the largest PCC consumption due to significant growth in plastic and paper industry in the last few decades. The European PCC market had quite low growth rate due to economic recession and intense international competition. As far as calcium carbonate was concerned, Asia-Pacific represented the largest regional market as per new market research report on calcium carbonate. Apart from Asia-Pacific, Latin America and Middle East were upcoming potential markets for PCC in the coming years. Solely, Latin America was expected to post a CAGR of 3.6 per cent in PCC consumption[6].

Though GCC represented principal type of calcium carbonate, PCC was anticipated to have higher demand growth rates till 2015. Growth in Europe was expected to be higher than North America. Also the consumption of calcium carbonate was expected to be higher in plastic industry globally. In other parts of the world, particularly Asia, the global recession had lesser impacts since major demand was driven by domestic consumption. The Asian market was expected to continue to grow in the forecasted period (Exhibit 2.8)[7].

OPTIONS AVAILABLE

The top management had constituted a cross functional committee of senior members to give proposals and recommendations on steps to be taken to overcome the present PCC pricing problem; after taking into account the prevailing industry and organizational conditions. The team had proposed the following options in its report to the top management:

Product diversification: Since inception RCPL had completely focused on production of quality PCC product. There had been no initiative by RCPL for starting GCC production. However, lately the utility of GCC as fillers among various industries such as paper, plastic and paints had risen, both

Exhibit 2.8 | *Consumption Trend of PCC (2010)*

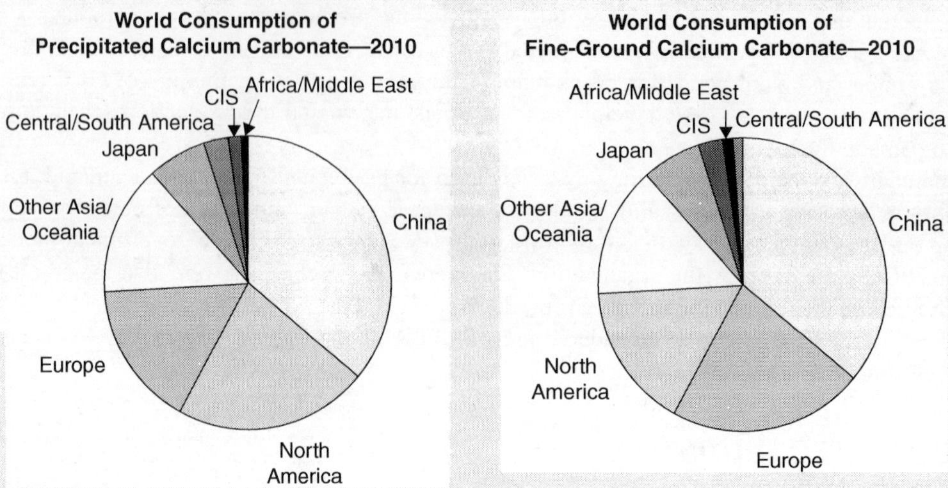

Source: http://chemical.ihs.com/CEH/Public/Reports/724.6000/, accessed on 18 December 2011

domestically and internationally. The main reason for GCC's higher acceptance was much lesser price than PCC. The cost of production for GCC per kg was about ₹6 lower in comparison to that of PCC.

Calcium carbonate, whether GCC or PCC, was used for altering the properties of the final product. Since it was an ingredient and did not contribute to the outward appearance, GCC became a preferred option over PCC due to its cost advantage. Because of increasing fluctuations in prices of rest of raw materials for finished products (resin in case of plastic pipes), manufacturers started exploring alternative raw material. GCC was found to be the best alternative because of its lower price and already proven utility.

The committee recommended that one of the options for tackling Chinese PCC lower prices and also enhancing revenue and profitability of RCPL was to diversify into production of GCC. It elaborated that since GCC had high approval amongst the target market, initiating GCC's production and promoting it through existing marketing channels would be a good alternative. This product mix in RCPL calcium carbonate product line would also help in reducing PCC cost and thereby take care of imported PCC onslaught, especially the Chinese PCC prices.

Enhancing Production Capacity

The committee recommended that in order to further reduce the RCPL's PCC prices, it should enhance its economies of scale. The committee proposed to the top management to augment the production capacity from 16 tonnes per day to 25 tonnes per day. Increasing production capacity would require installation of new infrastructure. As per the new proposal, active boilers will have to be upgraded from 5 tph to 8 tph. RCPL will also have to add at least 2 to 4 boilers and 2 settling tanks to support new production capacity plan. RCPL already possessed core competency in PCC manufacturing, so increasing PCC's production capacity with some initial capital investment seemed one of the viable options. The committee further suggested that since demand of PCC was expected to increase, increased sales due to the competitive prices would result in ultimately higher revenue and profitability. The lower prices achieved through economies of scale would also result in increased RCPL's market share in PCC market.

Increase Direct Organizational Sales to Clients than Through Dealer Networks

Presently, RCPL's marketing operation had 40:60 proportions for its direct sales to industrial clients and sales through dealer networks. The committee suggested reversing this percentage so as to increase the organizational revenue by eliminating intermediaries. The committee cautioned that the direct organizational sales should be only to bulk buyers from large industrial corporations else it may affect the expected profit margins. This will help in reducing logistics cost and enhance profits thereby enabling competitive pricing by RCPL.

Global Product Rollout

The committee suggested that owing to huge international demand of calcium carbonate, product rollout by RCPL to international markets had high chances of success. RCPL already had its export license sanctioned by the Government of India. The global product rollout would give RCPL an opportunity for achieving economies of scale and, thereby, decreasing cost. The competitive product pricing in the international market by RCPL would also help the organization hedge its risk against cheap and low quality Chinese calcium carbonate products in the domestic market. The committee also cautioned about the risk of currency fluctuation dynamics in the international market.

The RCPL board was discussing these four options for taking the next strategic initiative which would have a direct impact on RCPL's product pricing.

DISCUSSION QUESTIONS

1. Give your suggestions on the option that the top management should choose in order to respond to Chinese cheaper PCC product offer.
2. Discuss the role of cost, competition and marketing channels in pricing of a product.
3. Should RCPL invest in product diversification to GCC? Justify your answers by quoting facts from the case.
4. What do you mean by marketing mix? Discuss the marketing mix of RCPL.
5. Comment on the committee's recommendation for enhancing the percentage share of direct organizational sales to clients as compared to sales through dealers. What would be the impact on RCPL operating cost in case it enhances share of direct organization sales to clients? Support your answer with examples.
6. Suggest innovative pricing strategy for RCPL's calcium carbonate product line, not suggested by the committee, so as to successfully compete in the international market.
7. Given the fact that the PCC market is set to grow, could there be any non-pricing strategies adopted by RCPL to support its current pricing? If so, what could be done and how?

ENDNOTES

1. Rakesh Chemicals (P) Limited is often referred to as RCPL in the case study.
2. http://education.jlab.org/itselemental/ele020.html, accessed on 15 December 2011.

3. Ibid.
4. http://www.prweb.com/releases/calcium_carbonate/ground_precipitated/prweb8064439.htm, accessed on 15 December 2011.
5. Ibid.
6. Ibid.
7. Ibid.

REFERENCES

http://www.mapsofindia.com/maps/uttarpradesh/districts/saharanpur.htm, accessed on 15 December 2011.

http://www.specialtyminerals.com/our-minerals/what-is-pcc/, accessed on 15 December 2011.

http://chemical.ihs.com/CEH/Public/Reports/724.6000/, accessed on 18 December 2011.

3

Cheers Food & Beverages

Mr H. P. S. Lamba, CEO, Cheers Food & Beverages, was going through the profile of *Business World's* top 100 Indian companies. After he completed reading the entire article, he started introspecting why his company Cheers Food & Beverages was not amongst those top 100 companies. He thought about reasons from capital infusion, innovation, new product development, branding to issues like scaling up to enhance production volumes in order to achieve substantial jump in revenue and profit. The vision of Mr H. P. S. Lamba was to make Cheers Food & Beverages amongst the top 10 leading Indian players in food and beverages industry.

THE BEGINNING

Mr H. P. S. Lamba, an engineer with an MBA (Exhibit 3.1), started off his career with Crompton Greaves, Mumbai, and worked there for 3 years before joining Mukut Pipes at Patiala, Punjab. He initiated his entrepreneurial career along with his partner Mr Sukhpinder Singh in December 1999 by starting a company named Cheers Food & Beverages. In 2000, the promoters formed another new company named Beverly Beverages which launched sparkling fruit-flavoured drinks after tying up with an European company for supply of flavours and know how. After initial acceptance, the idea faced a stumbling block with return of material from the market as the product was ahead of its times and more so as it was launched in small cities. The company launched many other innovative drinks like Crush concentrates, energy drinks and re-launched sparkling drinks as exotic drinks. The need for introducing new products were two pronged—firstly, Yupp soda business was going down due to many players entering the field due to low entry barriers; and secondly, to keep the profitability of business intact. After nearly 10 years, Mr Lamba, with the support of his wife Mrs Deepika Lamba, launched another product line, by the name of Tanmeh Foods. Tanmeh Foods is a part of Cheers Food & Beverages. Tanmeh Foods included wheat-free and gluten-free products for celiac patients (Exhibit 3.2). This idea struck them after their own daughter was found to be allergic to wheat. Lambas had a lot of trouble in procuring wheat-free and gluten-free products for their daughter[1]. Unfortunately, the products from Western countries were not suited to Indian taste.

Exhibit 3.1 | *Profile of Mr H. P. S. Lamba*

H. P. S. Lamba, an alumnus of Punjab School of Management Studies, Punjabi University, Patiala, and graduate in mechanical engineering, started his professional career with Crompton Greaves after his MBA. He served there for 3 years. Thereafter, he joined Mukut Pipes at the middle management level. Due to his versatile capabilities and his hard work, within two years, he became Senior Manager (Projects and Marketing). Being an entrepreneur by heart, a desire to do something of his own was always there. Sukhpinder Singh, another entrepreneur to the core, was working as an engineer in PSEB (Punjab State Electricity Board) but was also pursuing private business of assembling and supplying computers to corporate clients. As a vendor for supplies of computers to Mukut Pipes, he got acquainted with H. P. S. Lamba. A strong desire to become an entrepreneur made H. P. S. Lamba quit his job in 1997. Sukhpinder, being a friend, offered him to open up a hi-tech franchise computer centre of Tata InfoTech Ltd., namely TULEC, to impart quality computer education to students and professionals. Soon after that a private limited company named Trias InfoTech Ltd. was formed by them with total investment of 15 lakhs (1.5 million) with half of the money coming from loans. The TULEC centre opened in early 1997 at Leela Bhavan, Patiala. Though computer education at that time was in growing stage of its life cycle but market was mature with leaders such as NIIT and Aptech. Further the smaller players like SSI, STG, CAL-C made competition and sustainability much tougher. TULEC, Patiala, with its quality education and state-of-the-art infrastructure clocked a turnover of ₹20 lakhs (2 million), thus crossing the breakeven in its first year of operations. Over the next 3 years, it gained reputation as quality institute with a growth rate of 10 per cent and with student strength of more than 200. Tata InfoTech Ltd. in the mean time got contract of imparting computer education in government colleges of Punjab that catapulted TULEC as a major league player in computer education. In the meantime in November 1998, due to interesting turn of events, the whole scenario of the company and its directors changed (Exhibit 3.3).

Source: Interview with H. P. S. Lamba dated 20 August 2011

Exhibit 3.2 | *Celiac Disease*

Celiac disease is caused by reaction to gliadin, a prolamin (gluten protein) found in wheat and similar proteins found in the crops like barley and rye. Upon exposure to gliadin, and certain other prolamins, the enzyme tissue transglutaminase modifies the protein, and the immune system cross-reacts with the small-bowel tissue, causing an inflammatory reaction. That leads to a truncating of the villi lining the small intestine (called villous atrophy). This interferes with the absorption of nutrients, because the intestinal villi are responsible for absorption. The only known effective treatment is a lifelong gluten-free diet.

Source: www.wikipedia.com accessed on 20 August 2011

Wheafree is the brand name of Tanmeh Foods. India lacked both in testing facilities and awareness, so no manufacturer in the past ever took interest in producing or trading in wheat-free and gluten-free products. But due to increase in the number of celiac cases, there was a growing demand for a complete range of wheat-free and gluten-free products.

Initially Mrs Deepika Lamba with lot of maternal care and culinary skills developed tasty gluten-free products for her daughter. Later Mr & Mrs Lamba thought of sharing it with others as there were a sizable number of celiac patients. This was how commercial production of Wheafree products started. To make it hygienic, Wheafree products were specially produced in most sanitized and wheat-free and gluten-free environment besides keeping strict check on ingredients which were sourced from the certified gluten-free suppliers. Moreover, these products were also checked clinically for presence of gluten through kits imported from the United Kingdom.

CHEERS FOOD & BEVERAGES

Yupp soda (Exhibit 3.3) is the flagship brand of Cheers Food & Beverages. Cheers Food & Beverages had 80 employees. Initially, Cheers Food & Beverages started production of carbonated water (soda). However, later on, the CEO Mr Lamba decided to add flavoured drinks and wheat-free products into its product portfolio. Yupp was introduced in market at the time when all major players in the market were using glass bottle for packaging of soda. Yupp was bottled in unique packaging of PET (Poly Ethylene Tetraphlate). It was a challenge for the marketing team to persuade people about the utility of PET bottle. The concept was very well received by the retailers as glass bottles were bulky, broken in transport and more over securities for glass bottles was not highly appreciated by the retailers.

Exhibit 3.3 | *Inception of YUPP as a Brand*

Yupp, which means YES, got its foundation in a unique way. *The Hindu* was promoting their new business newspaper called *Business Line*. During their campaigning, they offered H. P. S. Lamba at TULEC one month complimentary copy. Coincidentally on the first day of the delivery of the newspaper, the newspaper had a photo caption of a company showing bottles being filled. The heading read that one company in Hyderabad is doing roaring business of packing soda in PET bottles under the brand name of SRICO and is likely to touch ₹8 crores (80 millions) of business in the first year. The article fascinated H. P. S. Lamba who always admired and got encouraged from such innovative business ideas. Incidentally, Sukhpinder Singh's father-in-law who was a superintendent at the Railways at AP Express brought some PET bottles of SRICO soda for his son-in-law. The unique packaging concept of SRICO soda also attracted the attention of Sukhpinder. Sukhpinder brought same PET bottles to his friend H. P. S. Lamba and shared his viewpoint of initiating a new venture of soda with unique packaging style. Immediately, H. P. S. Lamba showed him the newspaper cutting of the same company and expressed his interest in the same business. This coincidence brought two persons who were full of entrepreneurial passion, together on a single platform. Both started exploring the new opportunity with full determination. A letter seeking appointment was prepared and faxed to the company in Hyderabad showing interest in their venture. On 1 November 1998, both went to Hyderabad to meet the owners of SRICO. The company was working in totally traditional manner and wanted to give out franchisees. But they asked exorbitant know-how fee. Being a mechanical engineer, the seed of project was sown, and on the return journey a detailed layout of the plant was drawn by H. P. S. Lamba but the only problem was to arrange the funds. The initial contribution was given by Sukhpinder Singh who contributed ₹10 lakhs (1 million); and ₹2 lakhs (0.2 million) were taken out of Trias InfoTech Ltd. The amount quoted by the Hyderabad-based company was ₹50 lakhs (5 million) which was negotiated and brought down to ₹20 lakhs (2 million). With lot of exercise, the right kinds of parties were developed as idea was new and as such no standard manufacturers were available. The project started commercial production with effect from 13 April 1999.

Source: Interview with H. P. S. Lamba, dated 20 August 2011

The thought behind soda in PET was to enhance consumer's comfort by providing portable bottles. Because of the convenience involved, retail shopkeepers accepted the novel idea. With use and throw nature of Yupp PET bottles, it was easier to control the impurities issue as was in case of glass bottles. However, there were many hurdles that came during execution of operations for Yupp, for example, inadequate availability of quality caps and pre-forms. Moreover, none of the partners had any prior experience in beverages industry except Mr Lamba, who did his summer internship in Campa Cola way back in 1988. So, along with the management issues, technical complications also came in the way of the growth path of Cheers Food & Beverages. For instance, company officials were unaware of bottling temperatures and pressures. Due to this, bottles started becoming swollen and started bursting. Also due to excessive pressure inside the bottle, many of the bottles started opening on their own. This led to customer dissatisfaction and negative word of mouth spread widely. This resulted in lots of stock being returned to the warehouse. The problems were mounting for H. P. S. Lamba and Sukhpinder. By this time, the initial capital was exhausted. Also because of rented factory place and non-standardized machines, none of the banks were ready to give any loan to Cheers Food & Beverages. But both the partners never let their entrepreneurial passion diminish. They maintained their calm and started working again in a more methodical way to understand the technical problem they were facing. Because of past relationship and trust developed with the suppliers, they came up with bottles which were of better design and were able to handle high day temperatures of North India. Only obstacle left was working capital. Ultimately after rigorous follow-ups, one bank came up with a loan of ₹2 Lakhs (0.2 million) and therefore after 4 months of disappointment, the product was re-launched in September 1999 with the hope of better results. The new variant was highly accepted in market with company working for 24 hours to meet its orders and reaching production capacity of 3,00,000 bottles (0.3 million) per month. Subsequently new sizes of 1.5 litres as party soda and 2 litres as jumbo Yupp were introduced (Exhibit 3.4 and 3.5).

Exhibit 3.4 | *Yupp Product Line*

Yupp Family

- Party Yupp 1.5 litres
- Jumbo Yupp 2 litres
- Mini Yupp 400 ml
- Regular Yupp 600 ml
- Yupp Orange
- Yupp Lemon

Source: www.cheersfood.net, accessed on 20 August 2011

Exhibit 3.5 | *Financial Results of Cheers Food & Beverages*

Balance Sheet as on 31-03-2011

Liabilities	Amount (₹)	Assets	Amount (₹)
Partners Capital (as per Capital Account)	6,43,414	Fixed Assets (as per Depreciation Chart)	33,50,944
Secured Loans		Securities	81,399
O.B.C Bank O/D	16,48,007	Current Assets, Loan and Advances	
O.B.C Loan	11,96,447	Closing Stock	16,42,979
Cholamandalam Investments	2,44,015	Sundry Debtors	3,83,077
Unsecured Loans		Cash and Bank Balances	
Deepika Rajpal	1,00,000	Cash in Hand	48,912
Mohan Hot Billion (P) Ltd	1,00,000	Others	
Trade Securities	50,000	Pre Paid Insurance	9,938
Current Liabilities and Provisions		Advance Tax	35,000
Sundry Creditors	9,55,872		
Sundry Payable	3,95,993		
Cheques Issued But Not Yet Presented	2,18,501		
	55,52,249		55,52,249

Manufacturing and Trading Account (Wheafree & Corrugated)
For the Year Ended 31.3.2011

Particulars	Amount (₹)	Particulars	Amount (₹)
To Opening Stock	5,27,501	By Sales	
To Purchases		Wheafree (5.5%)	12,75,836
Wheafree 1,434,926		Wheafree (13.75%)	6,15,025
Corrugation 7,095,570		Wheafree (Tax Free)	1,10,796
	85,30,496	Wheafree (Int.2%)	2,74,487
To Freight Inward Expenses	1,17,876	Wheafree (Int. T/Free)	72,041
To Printing Expenses (Job Work)	2,34,287	Wheafree (Int.5%)	3,39,979
To Wages Expenses	3,92,755	Wheafree (Int.13.75%)	3,00,728
To Electricity Expenses	3,92,750	Corrugated Box (5.5%)	40,25,912
To Generator Expenses	65,897	Sale Interstate 2%	37,49,836
To Vat input on tax free sale	410	Sale Interstate 5%	14,575
To Vat Tax W/O (Tax free Sale)	4,155		
To Gross Profit	21,56,070	By Closing Stock	16,42,979
	1,24,22,198		1,24,22,198

(Continued)

Exhibit 3.5 | *Financial Results of Cheers Food & Beverages (Continued)*

Trading Account (Yupp Soda) For the Year Ended 31.3.2011

Particulars	Amount (₹)	Particulars	Amount (₹)
To Opening Stock	1,89,299	By Sales	
To Gross Profit	–98,461	Goods sent on consignment	81,320
		Scrap Sale 5%	9,518
			90,838
	90,838	By Closing Stock	90,838

TWO COMPANIES AND ONE CEO

Instead of forming a single entity comprising all the companies, Mr Lamba and his partner preferred forming separate companies, viz. Cheers Food & Beverages and Beverly Beverages. The main reason behind this was to avail tax savings and exemption schemes offered by the Government of India for the small and medium enterprises (SMEs). As per the Government of India, each SME having turnover of less than 5 crores (50 million) availed certain excise duty exemptions. The other reason behind forming of separate company was to hedge the risks associated with each business. However, as per the latest statement of the CEO Mr Lamba, after the effective implementation of GST (Goods and Service Tax) policy by Government of India, all the companies would be merged within one group, thus, making it a single entity.

The reason behind two companies being looked by a single CEO was due to the social and personal life of one of the partners. Though initially the entire business was established in partnership with each division being managed separately by the two young entrepreneurs, later Sukhpinder, because of some personal reasons, immigrated to Canada in 2002 and thereafter Mr Lamba was looking after the entire business for some time. Because of the decreasing soda business, Cheers Food & Beverages demanded serious attention in order to revive it. Individually, Mr Lamba found it really hard to manage the entire operations of the group and ultimately the day came when HPS Lamba had no other choice than to ask Sukhpinder to either share the responsibility of the business or sell off his share. On 13 July 2004, they formally parted with the terms and conditions of diluting the share in next 18 months and Mr Lamba becoming the CEO for both the companies, that is, Cheers Food & Beverages and Beverly Beverages.

Beverly Beverages

In 2000, promoters thought of renouncing their IT business as it was hampering the desired resource commitment to beverages business which had a lot of potential. IT business demanded much attention and energy to sustain it further. So, ultimately they decided to close their first venture and focus completely on the newly formed company named Beverly Beverages. Beverly Beverages was started with the aim to launch an indigenous brand with international quality standards. The company became operational in the year 2000. Thereafter, it had no looking back. It launched many sparkling flavoured fruit drinks and other products. Beverly Beverages had HACCP (Hazard Analysis and Critical Control Points) certified production units. It followed international standards on food safety. Moreover, Beverly Beverages was a member of GS1 to adopt barcodes for its complete range of products. This was the first step towards adopting global supply chain business standards. Beverley Beverages was also the official bottler of Cadila Healthcare Limited for their sugar-free energy drinks under the brand name of D'Lite.

Beverly Beverages came up with 'Beverly Hills' (Exhibit 3.6) as their initial product in the market. Beverly Hills were sparkling aerated drinks. Beverly Hills drinks were available in four different

Exhibit 3.6 | *Product Line of Beverly Beverages*

Fun Drinks

Flavours available: Orange, Cola and Lime

Beverly Hills

- Flavours available: Litchi, Peach, Ginger Lemon and Strawberry

Tom & Jelly

Source: www.beverlybeverages.net accessed on 20 August 2011

flavours, viz., peach, ginger, lemon and strawberry, with bottles available in two sizes, that is, 330 ml and 1.5 litres. It was followed by Fun drinks and Crush drinks. Crush drinks were concentrated flavoured syrups. Also 'Mast' energy drinks for children were added to the product portfolio. Fun drinks were available in three popular flavours ,viz., cola, lime and orange. They were packed aesthetically in PET bottles of various sizes such as 330 ml and 2 litres. Other popular products of Beverly Beverages included crush concentrates which were available in three different flavours such as cola, lemon and orange. These concentrated drinks were available in aesthetically designed bottles with a jug-like handle making it convenient to use.

Beverly Beverages had launched a product called Tom & Jelly. The target segment was kids. A mouth watering semi-solid jelly was available in three different flavours, viz., orange, mango and litchi (strawberry). It was packed in pouches, which made it easy to use and carry. An attractive 200 ml bottle was very popular among children because of its mouth watering taste and economical price. It had become the largest selling drink of the company with sales touching 0.6 million bottles per month (Exhibit 3.7).

The traditional taste of Indian people was always a top priority for the company and as a result company revived drink named Yummy Jeera. A drink justifying its name—Yummy was a cocktail snack made from pure herbal and natural oils of zeera (cummins), kali mirch (black pepper), pudina (mint) and nimbu (lemon).

Tanmeh Foods

Tanmeh foods—part of Cheers Food & Beverages Company, grabbed the first mover's advantage by entering into wheat-free and gluten-free segment. Keeping in mind the regular eating interests of people from northern India, Tanmeh foods developed dishes that were meant to be readily consumed. The range of Wheafree products included inter alia gluten-free flour, gluten-free bhatura mix, gluten-free puri mix, gluten-free besan (gram flour), gluten-free noodles, gluten-free chocolate biscuits, gluten-free sweet and salty biscuits and gluten-free khatai biscuits (Exhibit 3.8). Tanmeh Food also planned to launch Western products such as macaroni, spaghetti, pasta and ice cream cones in order to cover more market segments. The company had also provided an option of placing orders directly through their e-interface on www.wheafree.com, thereby saving the distribution cost. In compliance with the food laws of Government of India, the company got its products tested from MARKFED.

MARKETING INITIATIVES

Yupp, a familiar brand among wine lovers and headquartered at Royal city of Punjab-Patiala, had a strong marketing footholds in its nearby areas. The organization was managing its entire marketing operations through 160 distributors and seven Clearing and Forwarding (C & F) agents spread over eight states and one union territory, viz., Punjab, Haryana, Himachal Pradesh, Jammu & Kashmir, Rajasthan, Uttar Pradesh, Uttaranchal, National Capital territory of Delhi, and Union Territory of Chandigarh, respectively. The unique selling proposition (USP) of Yupp was as follows:

- No deposit from retailer to ensure safe return of bottle as was the case for the glass bottles.
- Disposable packaging nature of product.
- Use of PP caps instead of crown caps so that consumers may recap and reuse the bottle.

Exhibit 3.7 | *Financial Results of Beverly Beverages*

Balance Sheet as on 31-03-2011

Liabilities	Amount (₹)	Assets	Amount (₹)
Owner Capital	15,93,270	Fixed Assets	48,27,859
Secured Loans	22,30,222	Securities	
Unsecured Loan	14,85,000	Electricity Security	55,400
Trade Securities	1,92,500	Sponsor Retail	1,500
Current Liabilities and Provisions		Current Assets, Loan and Advances	
Sundry Creditors	12,50,456	Closing Stock	21,62,580
Sundry Payables	3,99,191	Cash and Bank Balances	87,802
Cheques Issued But Not Yet Presented	9,02,581	Sundry Debtors	7,95,470
		Others	
		Pre Paid Insurance	36,548
		Advance Tax	75,000
		Deferred Expenses	9,632
		Amount recoverable	1,429
	80,53,220		80,53,220

Trading Account for the Year Ended 31-03-2011 (Beverly Beverages)

Particulars	Amount (₹)	Particulars	Amount (₹)
To Opening Stock	21,34,925	By Sales	
To Purchases		Consignement Sale	32,54,221
Purchase Interstate	1,01,40,559	Sale Agt Form C	1,57,27,885
Purchase Tax free	6,14,055	Sales Interstate Form C	5,52,280
VAT Purchase 12.5%	4,220	Sale Within State 12.5%	3,65,150
VAT Purchase 5%	39,58,487	Sale (Excisable)	350
	1,47,17,321		1,98,89,886
To Direct Expenses		By Closing Stock	21,62,580
Blowing of PET Bottles	40,000		
Diesel for Boiler/Generator	2,36,133		
Wages	3,13,673		
Electricity Expenses	10,56,260		
Cartrage and Octroi	1,09,104		
Testing Fee	8,151		
VAT ITC w/o for Consignment	31,389		
To Gross Profit	34,15,510		
	2,20,62,466		2,20,62,466

- Corrugated trays along with shrink pouch replaced the wooden or plastic crates and were also disposable in nature.
- Every bottle was fresh and pure due to its disposable nature.

Yupp was considered to be the largest selling mineral soda in north India. Because of the ever-increasing demand of mineral soda, and to reduce the dependency on local suppliers, Cheers Food & Beverages was forced to maintain in-house warehouse for its raw material such as PET performs which were used for bottles and CSD closures (Exhibit 3.9). Cheers Food & Beverages while extending its reach for suppliers had tied up with Zamil Plastic Industries Limited, Saudi Arabia; Hon Chuan Enterprise Co. Limited, Taiwan; Hercules, Malaysia; Indo Rama, Thailand and Kien-Joo, Malaysia.

Exhibit 3.8 | *Product Mix of Tanmeh Foods*

Gluten-free Flour, Gluten-free Bhatura Mix, Gluten-free Puri Mix, Gluten-free Besan (Gram Flour), Gluten-free Noodles, Gluten-free Chocolate Biscuits, Gluten-free Sweet & Salty Biscuits, Gluten-free Khatai Biscuits , Gluten-free Comb Biscuits, Gluten-free Pappars (Daal & Rice), Gluten-free Cake Mix, Gluten-free Panjeeri Mix, Gluten-free Dalia, Gluten-free Namkeens (Bhujia), Gluten-free Readymade Panjeeri, Gluten-free Rice Pappar Rolls, Gluten-free Dosa Mix, Gluten-free Chocolates, Gluten-free Namkeen Matthi, Gluten-free Sweet Shakarpara, Gluten-free Boondi Laddu, Gluten-free Bread.

Source: www.wheafree.com, accessed on 21 August 2011

Exhibit 3.9 | *Operational Management of Yupp Soda*

Cheers Food & Beverages manufactured soda. Soda is nothing but passing CO_2 through water with no addition of any kind of flavour or sugar. The water used is exceptionally pure both from chemical and bacteriological perspective. Generally, soda is made from ordinary or filtered water but Yupp soda was made from the water that was treated to make it low TDS (total dissolved solids) by removal of undesired hard minerals. As soon as Yupp was formed by passing CO_2 through water, it was then blended and chilled for effective carbonation. The carbonated water was then filled into bottles. The supervisor had the responsibility of checking the quality of soda by maintaining the pressure of CO_2 and also by tasting the soda. Bottles were then inspected through illuminated light to check any kind of impurity that might have moved into the liquid. Bottles after inspection were capped. Then the bottles were tested for leakage and were sent for soaking bay where these bottles were kept for at least 72 hours for any kind of deformity, leakage, ballooning or bursting. Thereafter, the bottles were labelled. The labelled bottles were kept in trays for shrink wrap packaging. After packaging, finished products were transported to the warehouse.

Source: www.cheersfood.net accessed on 21 August 2011

VISION OF THE CEO

Like any other CEO, Mr Lamba had separate vision statements for beverages and functional foods. As far as beverages were concerned, apart from bringing improvements in quality and taste, Mr Lamba was quite eager to achieve economies of scale with bigger production plants. Presently, being the official bottler for Cadilla Healthcare Limited for their new sugar-free drink D'lite, Mr Lamba also wanted to cater to 2–3 more big retail chains by becoming their official bottler. Being a strong preacher of innovation, Mr Lamba hoped to set up its exclusive Research and Development (R & D) centre which would give birth to more innovative products for the organization. In coming years, he planned to hire large number of marketing executives from various reputed B-schools who would undergo an exclusive training programme thus catapulting Yupp as a national brand from its present status of regional brand. However, as far as functional foods were concerned, Mr Lamba was confident that by 2017, its food division would be amongst the best in the country. He hoped to add various other dishes and variants of wheat-free and gluten-free products as per the market potential thus enhancing its product portfolio and ultimately meeting the demands of the rising customers. By 2013, Mr Lamba envisioned to bring food for diabetic patients also.

ISSUES AT HAND

Broadly things looked positive and encouraging for Mr Lamba. However, he was concerned about some pertinent issues in the organization:

Product Issues

Quality and taste had always remained the core of Cheers Food & Beverages. Some of its products such as Peach and Litchi (Strawberry) drink were at par with Coke on these two parameters. However, being a SME some of the product issues still prevailed at Cheers Food & Beverages. The lack of infrastructure was restricting the organization to achieve economies of scale for its products. Company's functional food portfolio included products that were heavily dependent on taste, and taste varied drastically from person to person and region to region. Some people demanded various other variants of biscuits and some wanted gluten- and wheat-free sweets. Inability to cater to the needs of various customer segments was disturbing Mr Lamba.

Pricing Issues

Cheers Food & Beverages was facing pricing issue as compared to its competitors. Although equipped with the best technology available and quality wise at par with brands like Coke and Pepsi, Cheers Food & Beverages was not able to generate same money as compared to these bigger brands. Cheers Food & Beverages product lied in between the unorganized sector of beverages industry and organized beverages market. Quality and taste wise they were being compared with Coke, Pepsi and other big brands but when it came to pricing they were being compared to unorganized market. Hence, Cheers Food & Beverages was forced to put their prices low as compared to its competitors. For the same reason, the company had curtailed its product portfolio from 18 items to just 9 items. For instance, the company was forced to shut down the production of one of the highly demanded pure products named Jal Jeera because of the price issue. Despite the product being extracted from fresh seeds without adulterating with artificial colours, the company failed to sell the product because of availability of similar products at a lower price by one of the close competitors. As of now, the company only manufactured limited quantity of Jal Jeera without any label for relatives/friends who preferred quality and taste over price. The company recently came up with a new packing and labelling of Yupp soda. According to the company officials, the company had invested lakhs of rupees while bringing this new variant into the market, and was facing pricing issue due to the rise of 2 rupees per bottle. Similar situation existed in the case of functional foods also. Tanmeh Foods, a division of Cheers Food & Beverages, was the first one to manufacture wheat-free and gluten-free products. The entire ranges of product were in high demand due to surge in celiac diseases. The cost of manufacturing gluten-free and wheat-free products was high as compared to wheat products, but customers found it difficult to understand this fact and were reluctant to pay higher price of wheat-free and gluten-free products as compared to conventional products.

Distribution Issue

Like other SMEs, Cheers Food & Beverages also had distribution issues. Distributing its products to distant areas had always remained an issue with Cheers Food & Beverages because of lesser margins and lower priced products. Due to low entry barriers prevalent in the beverages industry many new manufacturers of soda had came in existence in various parts of the country. The stockists/distributors preferred buying products from nearby industries rather than purchasing products from distant areas as it added to their transportation costs. Setting up of more industrial units in other parts of country was not feasible for Cheers Food & Beverages because of seed capital and plant management issues.

Promotional Issue

Promotion had always remained a big question mark for Cheers Food & Beverages. Big brands such as Coke and Pepsi intensively advertised their products. Their product promotions were quite popular in metro cities. Hence, SMEs such as Cheers Food & Beverages, with low budget for advertisements, focussed more on rural and semi-urban markets. According to the company officials, whenever the company allocated a specific budget for media advertisement, the company experienced huge losses. Probably the reason behind this was that consumers required continuous advertisement throughout the year to keep reminding them about the product and deliverables. But media being expensive it was not possible for any SME to sustain and bear the high cost of advertisement for longer duration. On the contrary, big brands promoted their brand throughout the year. Hence, for Cheers Food & Beverages it was becoming imperative to find out innovative and inexpensive ways of advertisement and promotion of their products.

Push or Pull Strategy

The organization always followed a push strategy instead of pull strategy due to inadequate budget for expensive advertisements. The company preferred to maintain warm relations with its distributors and believed in giving higher margins to distributors and retailers instead of investing on promotional activities. Mr Lamba was wondering whether it was the right marketing strategy or he may switch to the pull strategy and focus more on the brand awareness and customer loyalty.

DISCUSSION QUESTIONS

1. Among 'issues at hand' discussed in the case study, which issue is the most important for Cheers Food & Beverages? Enumerate facts from the case to justify your answer.
2. Was it a good management decision to have two separate companies, viz., Cheers Food & Beverages and Beverly Beverages? How was it beneficial to the owners? What would be the financial and operational impact of proposed merger of these two organizations into a single entity?

3. Given the facts from the case, envisage the future of Tanmeh Foods. Also suggest new product lines for Tanmeh Foods so that it may become a major revenue earner for Cheers Food & Beverages.
4. What should be the future marketing strategy of Cheers Food & Beverages given the prevailing organizational conditions?
5. Should Mr H. P. S. Lamba consider a detailed marketing research study before making any significant changes in the marketing mix? Should he hire a marketing research agency or rely on his internal team for the same?
6. 'Cheers Food & Beverages should adopt a pull sales strategy for its products'. Do you agree with the statement? Give examples in support of your answer.

ENDNOTE

1. www.cheersfood.net, accessed on 21 August 2011.

REFERENCES

www.beverlybeverages.net, accessed on 20 August 2011.
www.wheafree.com, accessed on 20 August 2011.
www.wikipedia.com, accessed on 20 August 2011.

4

BOOKSHELLS.COM: ISSUES IN PRODUCT MANAGEMENT

As soon as Shrey Kaushik wound up his discussions with his close friends at NITIE (National Institute of Industrial Engineering) regarding his venture, bookshells.com, he was feeling quite confident about its launch and acceptance of bookshells.com among its target customers. The entrepreneurial journey of Shrey Kaushik began as he joined his first year at Vellore Institute of Technology (VIT) for his engineering studies. His inherent passion to be independent and the desire to fulfil his monetary necessities without any parental help, motivated him to initiate entrepreneurial career early in his life. In the first year of his college, he joined a MLM (multi-level marketing) online education marketing organization for promoting its product line (Exhibit 4.1).

The Web site bookshells.com went live in March 2011 with the vision: *To strengthen the triple bottom line approach*[1] *by streamlining the used book supply chain for Indian student community.* Bookshells.com aimed at bridging the gap between unorganized sector and organized sector of used books industry. After about one year of its operations, CEO Shrey Kaushik was confident of achieving a targeted revenue of ₹10 lakhs (1 million) by 2012 (Exhibit 4.7). The organization in its first phase of implementation leveraged social networking site Facebook to promote its innovative idea of selling and buying second hand/used books. Though bookshells.com received an enthusiastic response during initial phase, CEO Shrey Kaushik still had concerns about rolling-out of the marketing mix in its second and third phase of business expansion. Also the low entry barriers to business model adopted by bookshells.com were worrying him.

THE BUSINESS IDEA

Shrey Kaushik had completed his graduation and was waiting to join TCS (Tata Consultancy Services). While he was in his home town Jaipur, Rajasthan, in May 2009, he came to know through his friends and website blogs that TCS had delayed its recruitment for a while, due to global economic downturn in 2009. As a stopgap solution and to keep himself positively engaged, he joined a local engineering college to teach physics. Simultaneously, he was also preparing for his CAT (Common Admission Test) entrance exam for MBA admissions.

Exhibit 4.1 | *Profile of the Founder CEO*

Shrey Kaushik, an electronics and communication engineer from Vellore Institute of Technology (VIT), Vellore, Tamil Nadu, was pursuing his MBA degree from NITIE, Mumbai. Since Shrey wanted to be financially independent, he joined a MLM (multi-level marketing) online education marketing organization while he was in his first year of engineering studies. An extrovert by personality, he used to travel to different parts of the country related to his studies. The marketing of product line of MLM firm also gave him this travelling opportunity. As part of MLM, he promoted a consolidated teaching module CD having all software languages which was quite useful for a prospective software engineer. He also used to appoint associates who further promoted the software CDs; thus further adding to his incentives as per the existing MLM incentive plan model. Shrey through his rigorous efforts and natural marketing talent was able to appoint 1,858 associates in just 2 years. Thereafter, as soon as his above network got drifted to another company named Club Freedom Travels Limited; Shrey also got associated with the same. It was an Australian firm headquartered in Bangalore for its India operations. It had a product portfolio related to world travel packages. There also he had made 100 associates in just 3 months. Thus, marketing became an inherent trait of Shrey Kaushik, which he cherishes till date.

Shrey, during his engineering studies was a frequent visitor to various technical fests being organized across the nation. During one of such visits at IIT-Bombay fest he thought to develop and promote a web portal which would aggregate all information of events happening across various colleges and universities in India. He shared this idea with one of his friends whom he knew through the network of the MLM firm. They together implemented the idea and it was Shrey's first entrepreneurial foray. After about 6 months the portal was sold by Shrey Kaushik to his business partner. Thus, his first entrepreneurial journey was a short one. But the passion to do something of his own and being financially independent always motivated him to think about new ventures. Bookshells was one such innovative entrepreneurial ideas that Shrey Kaushik wanted to implement professionally.

Source: As per interview with Mr Shrey Kaushik, dated 20 December 2011

On one rainy evening in August 2009, Shrey Kaushik, along with a colleague, was stranded in a second hand/used books market in his home town in Jaipur. Shrey was unable to locate some second hand physics books due to its limited availability with the local vendors. Suddenly amidst the heavy downpour and disappointment of not being able to find the desired book from the existing second hand book sellers; the idea of starting a used books portal crossed Shrey Kaushik's mind. However, due to his December 2009 CAT exam preparations, his teaching job and other mundane engagements; he could not devote any further thought towards his 'used book portal' idea.

Shrey performed quite well in CAT exams, which finally helped him to get admission in a prestigious B-School of India. In June 2010, he shifted to NITIE (National Institute of Industrial Engineering), Mumbai, for his management education after resigning his academic job at Jaipur. With his admission in NITIE, he felt secure regarding his future placement. His passion to do something of his own and being independent made the entrepreneurial mind think again of his 'used book portal' idea. Incidentally, it was again pouring heavily in Mumbai for the entire month of September 2010, and Shrey Kaushik could transcendentally see the connection between his 'used book portal' idea and heavy downpour. However, he did not discuss anything about this rainfall connection with his business idea with any of his friends.

He discussed the entire business plan with his close friends at NITIE, who already had many years of corporate experience, both in India and abroad. Many issues about business model, challenges and opportunities related to the 'used book portal' were discussed and debated. Various inputs were added to his raw idea of 'used book portal' during these marathon meetings. After winding up one of such long discussions in September 2010, he was quite confident about the proposed launch and acceptance of used books portals among its target customers.

BOOKSHELLS.COM LAUNCH

The 'used book portal' with the domain and company name bookshells.com was launched on 10 March 2011. CEO Shrey Kaushik had planned and documented the entire business model with three successive stages of growth. He was convinced about the immense potential of online platform which would have the entire gamut of used books. According to him, it would not only remove the intermediary between buyers and sellers of used books but would also eliminate an individual's predicament of what to do with the used books after completion of their course, that is, how to gain value from already used books. This business model would also fulfil the desire of majority of students of buying books at minimum prices in good condition. His own research had shown that good quality used books were always the preferred choice over new books among majority of school and college students. To fulfil their used book requirements, the students were dependent on book vendors located in the college vicinity or 'weekend used book fair' stalls. However, Shrey identified that the poor condition of the used books, outdated edition and inadequate supply of requisite books were common problems with these vendors.

According to Shrey Kaushik, in Indian education scenario, out of 1.21 billion people, 40 million were students and, unfortunately, nearly one-sixth of the students were deprived of books. The reduced cost of the second-hand books provided through bookshells.com would enhance access to almost all 40 million students. Bookshells also intended to provide free books to the select schools across India in its third phase of growth, thus also fulfilling its corporate social responsibility. Shrey elaborated his business model as:

> Every college had its own book shops in the vicinity. These booksellers were selling fresh books at around 80–90 per cent of the MRP (Maximum Retail Price) mentioned in the book. Customers had the flexibility to return particular set of books which have further market of selling again as second hand or used books. These books are bought from customers by bookshells at 40–50 per cent of MRP and sold back again to the customers from the same area, at around 60–70 per cent of the MRP. This cycle continues "n" number of times until the book's condition is fit physically as per quality standards set by bookshells, thereby providing bookshells a healthy margin of 20–30 per cent of the MRP in each transaction.

Shrey envisaged that in the coming decade, Bookshells would be a leading player in Indian education industry. Bookshells endeavoured to provide the best platform to the Indian student community for not only selling their used books at the best prices but also buying best quality used books at the most competitive prices.

INDIAN EDUCATION INDUSTRY

Recently, Indian government enacted 'Right to Education', thereby, providing free and compulsory education to every child between the age of 6 and 14 years. The Indian education in terms of literacy rate, female literacy rate, number of schools, number of degree colleges and professional colleges, number of universities, gross enrollment ratio in elementary education and gender parity index at elementary level, had remarkable growth since the independence (Exhibit 4.2). The approved outlay for secondary education and higher (including vocational training) in the 10th Five Year Plan was ₹138.25 billion. Despite the huge investments by the government, the private sector spending in education in India had higher growth rate in terms of spending on education. For example, in the year 2009, about $10,000 million were invested by the private sector on education in India, out of which about $7,000 million were invested in professional courses. The market size for books for all grades starting from Grade 1–4 to professional courses had also witnessed an exponential growth thus infusing an investment of almost $1,732 million in 2009[2]. The numbers of students registered with various private colleges of varied disciplines in 2009 were close to 0.16 crores (Exhibit 4.3).

Exhibit 4.2 | *Growth of Indian Education Since 1950*

Item	Figures in 1950–51	Figures in 2005–06 (Unless Otherwise Stated)
Literacy rate	18.3%	64.8% (2001)
Female literacy rate	8.9%	53.7%
Schools	0.23 million	1.28 million
General colleges	370	11,698
Professional colleges	208	7,797
Universities	27	350
Gross enrolment ratio in elementary education	32.1%	94.85%
Gender parity index at elementary level	0.38	0.92
Public expenditure on education as % of GDP	1.5%	3.46%

Source: http://www.education.nic.in/sector.asp#size

Exhibit 4.3 | *Indian Education Industry*

Private Spending on Education in India (2009)	US $m/year
Schooling	***1,879***
Textbooks	1,732
Educational CD-ROMs	117
Multimedia in schools	30
Professional Courses	***7,054***
Engineering	5,850
Medical	473
MBA	731
Test Prep (Total)	***1,664***
Engineering test prep	1,000
UPSC (Indian Civil Services) Test preparation	120
MBA test preparation	104
Medical test preparation	420
GRE/GMAT/SAT test preparation	20
Skill Development	**54**
e-learning	27
IT/BPO finishing school	27
Estimated Total Market Size	***10,651***

Estimate of Market Size (Private) 2009	Size
Medical	
Private Colleges	140
Per College Per Batch	100
Total Students	70,000
Engineering	
Private Colleges	120
Per College Per Batch	300
Total Students	14,40,000
MBA	
Private Colleges	300
Per College Per Batch	150
Total Students	90,000

Market Size for Books (2009), US$ m

	Necessary Books	Augment Learning Books	Urban Market	Rural Market	Total Market
Grades 1-4	4	9	210	16	226
Grades 5-8	11	22	469	61	530
Grades 9-12	33	67	648	84	732
Professional courses	78	DNA	245		245
Total					***1733***

Source: CLSA Asia Pacific Markets, AICTE, Medical Council of India and 2002–07 Five Year Plan

The McKinsey–NASSCOM report forecasted that online sales will be more than $168.7 billion in 2011, and market share of B2C e-commerce would grow more than threefold from 4.1 per cent in 2006 to 14.3 per cent by 2011. Many e-commerce sites have registered a growth of 35–50 per cent registered users in the last couple of years. Flipkart had entered the online book selling industry in 2007. It recorded ₹20 crores (200 million) revenues in 2009, ₹100 crores (1 billion) in 2010 and had targeted ₹4,500 crores (45 billion) revenue generation by 2015. It had raised a capital of $31 million in two rounds of funding from venture capital funds Accel India (2009) and Tiger Global Management (2010)[3].

IMPLEMENTATION PHASES

Shrey Kaushik, in its execution strategy, had planned bookshells.com's business plan implementation in three distinct phases. The first phase was already operational. It served as a pilot project for the organization. The second phase focused on streamlining the supply chain which was under development and the third stage would be the full-fledged operational model of bookshells.com. Bookshells.com is presently being incubated by venture capitalist firm named The Hatch.

Phase 1 (Operational)

Phase 1, which was already operational, was floated with the objective to provide a platform where both buyer and seller can connect with each other. It would reduce their reliance on a single vendor/bookshop. Initially it was just an online platform where every student had been given the flexibility to share the information regarding the books they wanted to sell. The aim of the first phase was to attract the student community to an open platform where they can sell their books to the peers while developing customer loyalty towards bookshells.com. The buyer, upon logging on was navigated through various search stages and if he was successful in locating the desired book, he was given an option to close the deal directly. As soon as the seller uploaded the book information he intended to sell, notification appeared on his Facebook account, thereby intimating his friends regarding the book (Exhibit 4.4).

Exhibit 4.4 | *Unique Features of bookshells.com*

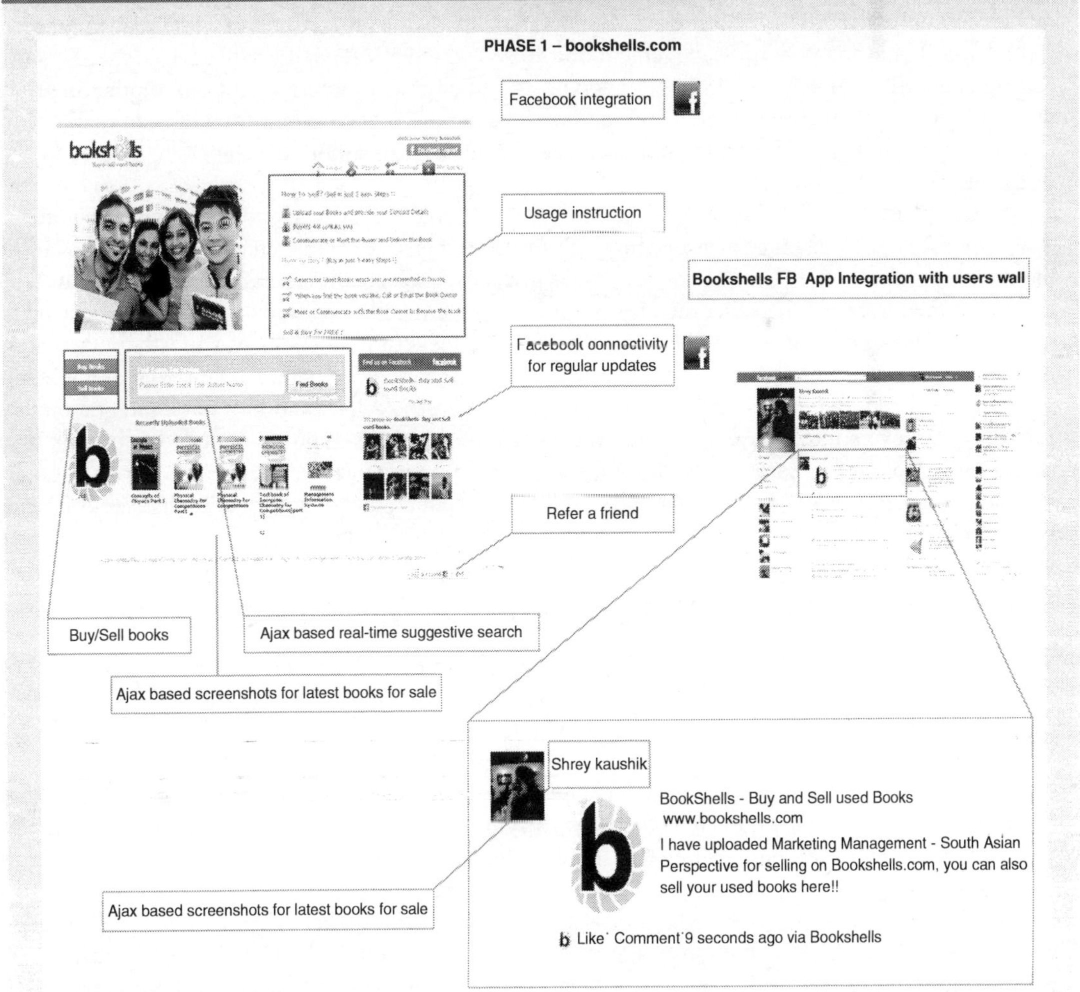

Source: Company Records

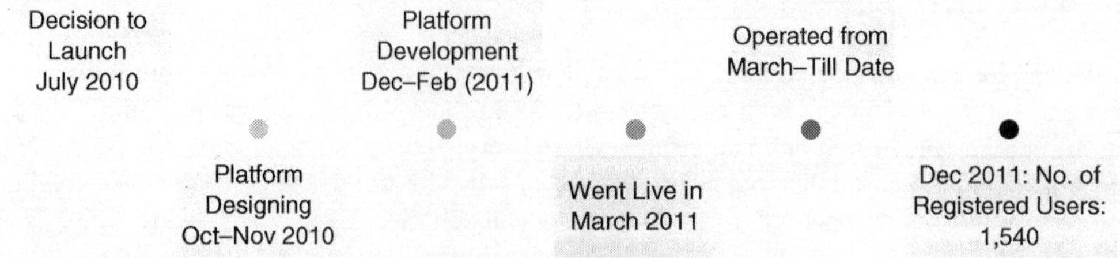

Figure 4.1 *Phase 1 Milestones*
Source: Company Records

During its first phase of launch, Bookshells did not intend to generate any revenue from its business. This phase mainly focused to garner acceptability of the online second hand/used book sales concept by the targeted customers, besides generating customer loyalty for bookshells.com. The first phase ran successfully in 3 MBA institutes of Mumbai, namely, National Institute of Industrial Engineering (NITIE), S.P. Jain Institute of Management and Research (SPJIMR) and Shailesh J. Mehta School of Management, IIT Bombay (SJMSOM). It served as a pilot project before its rollout to other metro cities and finally to the entire student community of the nation. It focused on the both intra-college and inter-college transactions during the pilot project. The phase-1 had more than 1,500 registered users as of December 2011(Figure 4.1).

The first phase also gave feedback to the Bookshells' team for improving their operations (Figure 4.2). The response of the first phase was encouraging for Bookshells. As predicted earlier by Shrey Kaushik, the students preferred used books over new books given the book condition was good. Importantly, it also connected the buyer and the seller directly, without any intermediary between them. It was realized that there was a latent need for such a platform. Currently business of used books was mostly in the unorganized sector and so the opportunity for Bookshells to attract the customers into organized sector was high.

Bookshells had used latest software tools like PHP/MYSQL/AJAX and Facebook integration using FB Apps for developing their web portal. Various features in its web portal included Facebook/bookshells login; Option for searching books at institute/city and region level; Facebook page connectivity–Book upload message gets updated on users wall; User account, that is, information hide/visible access rights and books account.

EXPERIENCES FROM IMPLEMENTATION OF THE FIRST PHASE

Shrey Kaushik had received a positive feedback from his peers and team on implementation of the first phase. One of the encouraging recommendations received was that the idea would work much better on expanding the horizon, that is, when a platform would be used for buying and selling of used books by a large student mass across the country, the business idea had higher chance of success. It was found that students were more interested in doorstep service, instead of putting an extra effort to go and meet people at other location (even if in the same town/city) for carrying out the transaction of buying/selling used book.

After receiving the feedback, Shrey Kaushik had instantly outsourced functions such as quality assurance to third party vendors and delivery at on site location through dedicated courier services. It was also realized that Bookshells needed a central warehousing facility where it may stock used books procured from different professional institutions. This way Bookshells would be able to adequately cater to requisite needs of specific books in case there was excess demand on the portal. It was realized that there was often mismatch in supply and demand for selected course books. The storage of used books with its live database with the organization would help in adequately matching the demand and supply situation. This will enhance buyer satisfaction in his/her each visit, thereby, enhancing customer loyalty.

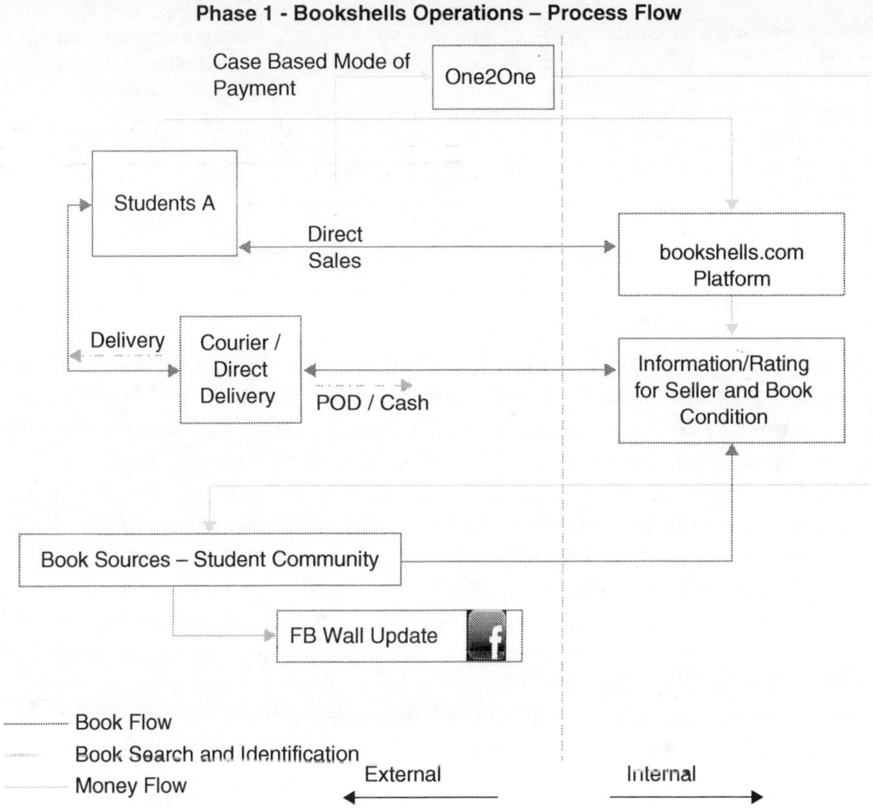

Figure 4.2 *Phase 1 Operations Process Flow Chart*
Source: Company Records

It was found that positive 'word of mouth' (WOM) promotion was quite important in this 'used book' business model. The students undertaking professional courses were well connected through various blogs and forums and any feedback about the organization was instantaneous and it spread like wild fire. It was found that Bookshells found positive mention in many of local student's blogs. The CEO Shrey Kaushik and his team wanted to sustain this positive WOM for Bookshells by consistently providing superior customer service to the targeted student population.

Phase 2 (Under Development)

Since Shrey Kaushik's innovative idea had received an overwhelming response in the first phase, he was all set to expand the footprints of Bookshells by streamlining various functional processes. In his second phase, the focus was to streamline the used book supply chain so that the target customer got what they required at their door step through back-end integration through courier services and payment gateways. The second phase was under development and the team was mulling over various entry barriers that could be embedded in the product development so as to minimize the risk of duplication by any prospective competitor. The team underwent intense brainstorming sessions on various critical parameters in order to streamline the businesses processes and build core competencies in select specific functional areas (Figure 4.3).

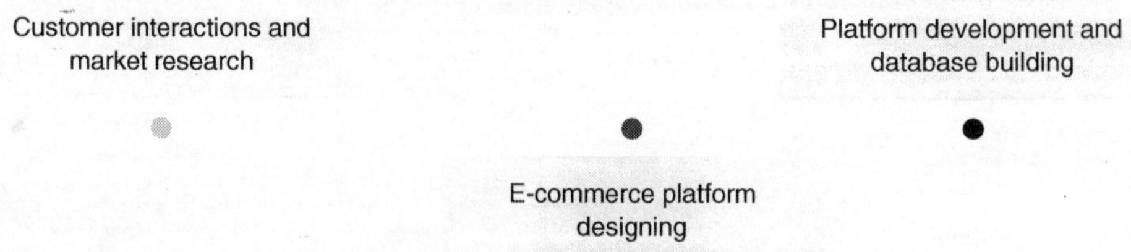

Figure 4.3 *Focus Areas in Phase 2*
Source: Company Records

Bookshells promoters had other plans too while they were getting ready for execution of its next operational phase. Apart from core business model of buying and selling used books to the targeted customers through online e-commerce portal; Shrey Kaushik was also planning to sell new books through the same portal to generate complimentary business. Also due to negative perceptions in India about bogus online transactions, Bookshells team was intensively involved in upgrading portal security to give users a positive e-transaction experience. The team had also worked on logistics by involving dedicated outsourced courier services for timely delivery to its customers.

The management had plans to charge minimal margins on each transaction in the near future. For streamlining its supply chain, Bookshells had planned its branch offices in three metro cities across India. These branch offices would serve the basic purpose of sourcing of used books to meet regular supply. It would also help in timely delivery of books to customers region-wise, which would help in reducing inventory and delivery costs. Bookshells had already started negotiation meetings with procurement vendors located across metro cities of India, viz., New Delhi, Mumbai and Bangalore. In New Delhi, Bookshells had reached preliminary agreement with many vendors. However, in Delhi, sourcing of used books was bit more expensive as compared to direct procurement but there was scope for further negotiation with the vendors. Mumbai could be managed more efficiently by sourcing books directly from college students, which would in turn also reduce procurement costs to a larger extent. The pilot study experience in Mumbai had given quite good insights about Mumbai market to the Bookshells team. In Bangalore, Bookshells had signed agreements with many vendors for supply of used books and with few vendors for fresh books (which provided good discounts). In Bangalore, the price of used books was almost stable. However, the Bangalore market was mature enough for operations and it would be easy to make foothold for Bookshells in Bangalore market.

Bookshells as part of its sourcing strategy had chosen two modes of operations, viz., sales driven (direct sourcing) and commission driven (indirect sourcing) for procurement of inventory (Figure 4.4). In the sales-driven model, direct sourcing in colleges was done for used books, and also through publishers to acquire some selective books whose used book copies were not available in colleges. In the colleges, used books were acquired through campus drive programmes directly just after college session got over.

In the commission-driven model, the sales of used books were done using vendors and customers. Bookshells would provide platform for vendors across India through its portal to upload their products (used books). This information would be accessible to the buyers. The buyers would buy the books based on its price and rating of vendors; and shipping happens directly from the seller to the buyer while the payment mechanism would be operated through bookshells e-commerce portal. The entire vendor based model would be similar to the US-based e-commerce portal eBay and Amazon. In case of procurement through customers, individuals who wished to sell the used books at the price they demand may sell them through the Bookshells portal in a similar manner as for the vendor-based model. The products

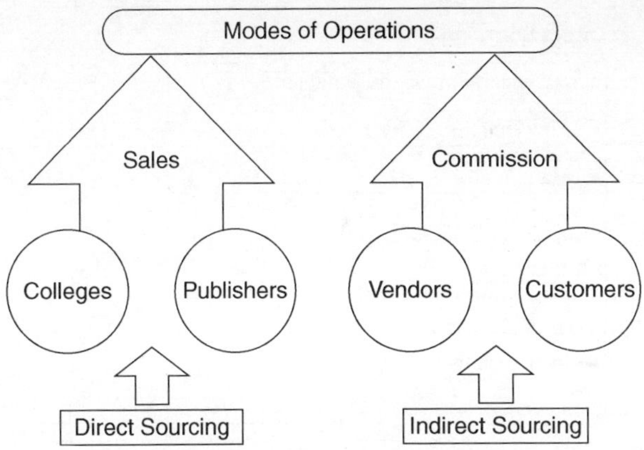

Figure 4.4 ***Sourcing of Inventory***
Source: Company Records

included education material as well as competitive exam materials which became useless once the exams were over. Bookshells planned to charge a minimal commission per sales in the near future.

Shrey Kaushik also disclosed that the company had long-term planning to switch completely from direct sourcing to indirect sourcing mode of operations. This would entail assured high scale of business with zero inventory, thereby, reducing the costs and enhancing profitabilty for Bookshells (Figure 4.5).

To design an efficient and reliable e-commerce platform, Bookshells team had researched on various technologies and was on the verge of finalizing it. Two popular open source platforms for designing online book store were Magneto and Zen-cart. Bookshells planned to use them in its second phase of operations (Figure 4.6). Magento was an open source which was new and dynamic but was less secure in comparison to Zen-cart. However, it provided excellent GUI (Graphical User interface) feature. Zen-cart was quite old and stable open source having features to support requirements, but was having issues with direct uploading of data (Figure 4.7).

Phase 3 (The Future)

In the coming 10 years, the company had two main plans for its business model. One was to diversify its existing product line of used books into other product lines such as computers, mobiles, cameras and music on the lines of eBay and Amazon. The second initiative planned for phase 3 was to leverage the Bookshells market foothold to become pioneer in Indian education industry by providing knowledge content on cloud-based platform. Since the coming era is of knowledge and it had potential of immense business opportunity due to its projected demand; the first mover advantage based on the cloud platform would enable it to provide quality knowledge content at the lowest price.

One of the reasons to diversify to other product lines in phase 3, according to Shrey Kaushik, was due to increased usage of e-books among students. Extensive use of new devices such as ipads, laptops, Kindle and Nook has further facilitated student's preference of online e-books over printed books. In the near future, with new technology further penetrating and getting popular amongst the students in India, there was mostly likely a scenario where students would be almost completely switching over to such technology-driven gadgets for their reading purposes and usage of printed books would be nearly minimal.

	Direct Sourcing	Indirect Sourcing
Cities covered	New Delhi, Mumbai and Bangalore	Available all across the nation
Deals done	• New Delhi-3 • Mumbai-3 • Bangalore-7	Any vendor can use integrated platform for his business
Shortage dealt with	• Region wise segmentation of delivery • Inter regions	Enhanced supply
Payment gateway costs	Yes	Yes
Procurement and delivery cost	Yes	Directly done by vendors
Margins/transactions	Old books–15% New books–7%	Old books 5% (volume based)
	Vendor Association Completed	Under Progress

Figure 4.5 ***Direct Sourcing Versus Indirect Sourcing***
Source: Company Records

According to Shrey Kaushik, the other futuristic trend in Indian education would be towards cloud computing. Bookshells' endeavour was to be ahead in this initiative. He envisaged that Bookshells mission would be *To provide a cloud for centralized content access*. It would not only provide platform to foster communication between students and faculty through private communities but would also reduce operational cost by moving management software to cloud. He further added that cloud computing would be the most demanding zone in the coming years with lucrative market opportunities. Moreover, it will also reduce high investments by higher education institutes on individual libraries and other hosting servers. Till now there has been no inter-institute online platform for student-faculty interaction, Bookshells cloud computing facilities also planned to incorporate such unique features (Figure 4.8).

The private cloud would be a dedicated cloud, especially for the university which would subscribe with Bookshells. Some of the other features for bookshells private cloud would be academic content access, student performance tracking and other administration focussed activities, and virtual community of student–faculty for better student–faculty interaction even after college study hours. The public cloud would be open to all with limited free access with focus on selling online content and training material.

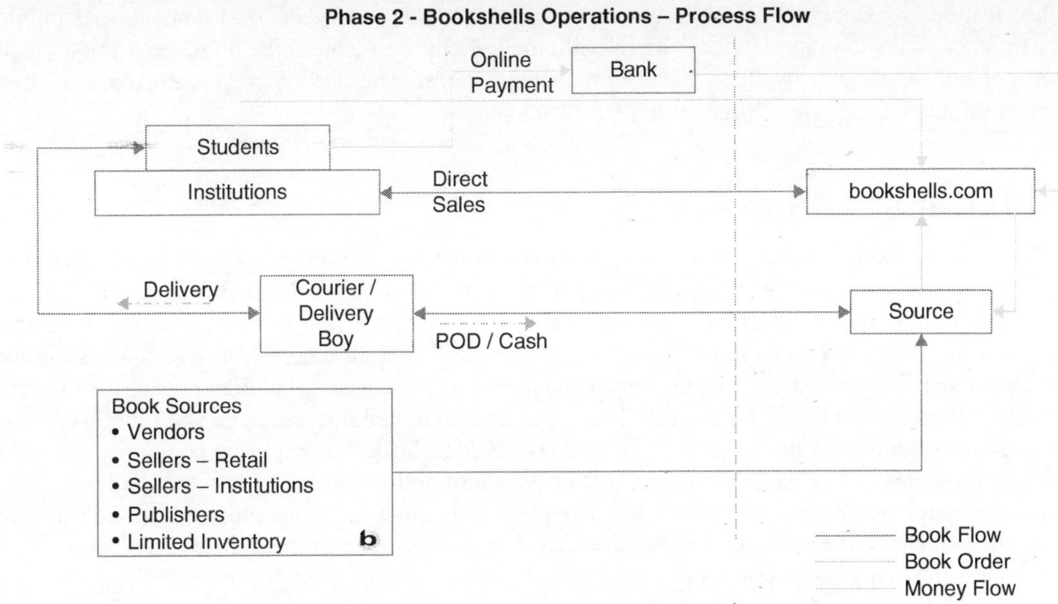

Figure 4.6 *Phase 2: Operations Process Flowchart*

Figure 4.7 *Popular Platforms for e-commerce Sites*
Source: Company Records

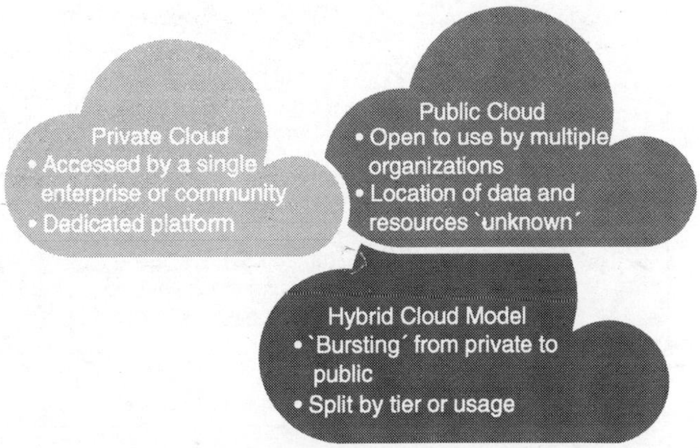

Figure 4.8 *Cloud Computing Platforms*
Source: Company Records

Other features of Bookshells' public cloud would be generic and specialized content, and public student–faculty community service. The hybrid cloud would be a consolidation of both private and public clouds. Its features would include common integrated student–faculty community and academic content for inter-stream knowledge for holistic development.

MARKETING PLAN

Bookshells was using online promotion as their main integrated marketing communication medium. Due to high penetration and immense popularity of social networking sites such as Facebook, LinkedIn, Twitter and Orkut in India, the visibility of bookshells had been widespread in very short span of time. The bookshells team had also gone for SEO (search engine optimization) to further enhance it visibility in online search for second hand books. They were promoting bookshells through Google AdSense, which cost it relatively lesser and had high visibility on blogs and other websites. Bookshells had attracted large fan base on Facebook which further added to its popularity amongst the college students. The bookshells team was also promoting its venture at various hotspots such as mobile recharge platforms, bookselling points and other popular locations (both online and offline) which had potential of gathering increased footfall at bookshells.com. Bookshells was also promoting green marketing in association with various NGO's in the Mumbai and Jaipur region (Figure 4.9). Bookshells had been also using physical banner advertisement across various cities for its promotion (Exhibit 4.5).

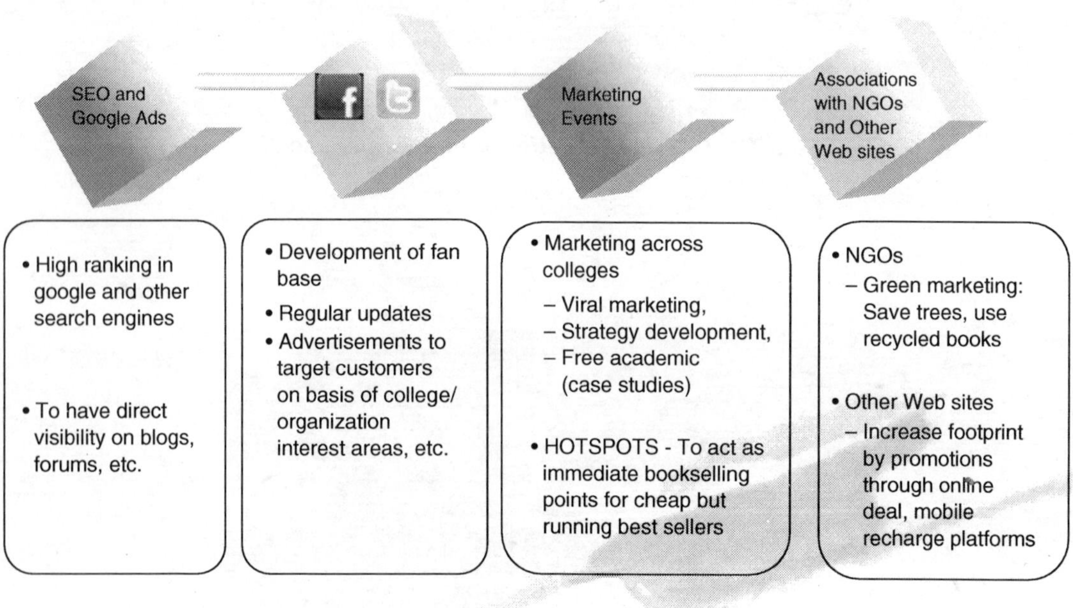

Figure 4.9 *Integrated Marketing Communication*
Source: Company Records

Exhibit 4.5 | *Product Promotion Through Banner Ads*

Source: Company Records

CORPORATE SOCIAL RESPONSIBILITY

Bookshells started with the vision *To strengthen the triple bottom line approach by streamlining the used book supply chain for Indian student community*. Shrey Kaushik stated that 'profit' was not the only way to measure business success. 'People' also mattered and so does the 'planet' on which we all live. Bookshells had also associated itself with various NGO's like REDSS in Rajasthan and NGO SIDART and contributed towards their vocational training programmes and scholarships to childerns.

Bookshells endeavoured to sustain people, planet and profit all together in its business operations. It believed that it was contributing to the planet as 25 reused books saved 1 tree cut and 'order 5 books and get a tree planted on individual's name' scheme also contributed positively to the planet.[4] Regarding profits, Bookshells through its business model contributed to monetary savings for society, carbon trading benefits and provided revenue earned via transactions. For people, it provided source of revenue generation for small vendors and every time one individual buys a book, others get some benefits too.

FINANCIAL PROJECTIONS

Shrey Kaushik did breakeven analysis (Exhibit 4.6) on the basis of financial projections (Exhibit 4.7 and Exhibit 4.8). Bookshells was able to achieve breakeven in third year of operations with consistent incremental growth in business except for one drop in the year, that is, 2014 because of expansion in new cities. Bookshells cost structure was divided among different heads such as initial office setup cost, web site cost, salaries and other overheads. Bookshells had started with two branch offices in Mumbai and Bangalore and was targeting other metros of India, namely, Delhi, Kolkata, Chennai and Hyderabad as next destinations in coming years. Each office would have a branch head for business development/vendor association along with a distribution head thus taking care of all sourcing and deliveries. Web-portal was initially developed by the in-house team so as to reduce the cost. However, the organization planned to upgrade its web interface and security aspects for a better online customer experience. Also, currently Bookshells had not kept any subscription/licensing fees for vendor association, this may become another stream of revenue depending on the market response.

Exhibit 4.6 | *Breakeven Analysis*

Breakeven Analysis	2012	2013	2014	2015	2016
Total revenue	1,000,250	2,995,250	7,221,150	10,715,914	14,282,226
Total cost	1,113,000	1,813,155	3,297,462	3,503,520	3,780,901
Income	(112,750)	1,182,095	3,923,688	7,212,394	10,501,325

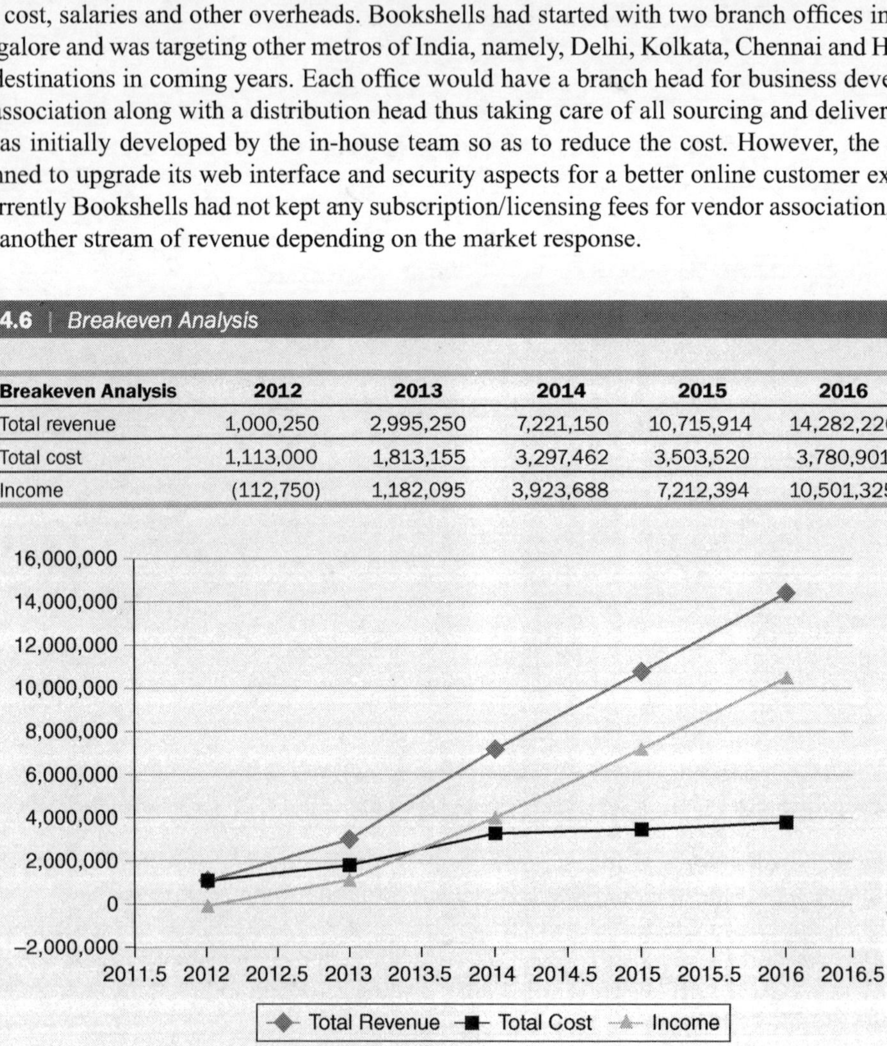

Source: Company Records

Exhibit 4.7 | *Financial Projections (In INR)*

Cost Projections

Cost Projections	**2012**	**2013**	**2014**	**2015**	**2016**
		Initial Outlay			
Printer	3,000	-	-	-	-
Packaging equipment	2,000	2,000	2,000	2,000	2,000
Stationery	6,000	6,000	6,000	6,000	6,000
		Website			
Website cost	40,000	-	-	-	-
Website AMC	-	10,000	10,000	10,000	10,000
Search engine optimization	50,000	45,455	41,322	37,566	34,151
Payment gateway	50,000	50,000	50,000	50,000	50,000
		Salaries and Wages			
Salaries	168,000	184,800	1,108,800	1,219,680	1,341,648
Website maintenance	5,000	5,500	16,500	18,150	19,965
Business registration fees	20,000	-	-	-	-
		Starting Inventory			
Old books	100,000	110,000	121,000	133,100	146,410
Fresh books	100,000	110,000	121,000	133,100	146,410
Security deposit	4,000	4,400	4,840	5,324	5,857
Office/Warehouse rent	200,000	220,000	726,000	798,600	878,460
Marketing budget	50,000	750,00	100,000	100,000	150,000
Logistics	315,000	990,000	990,000	990,000	990,000
Total Cost	1,113,000	1,813,155	3,297,462	3,503,520	3,780,901

Revenue Projections

Revenue/Margin Projections	**2012**	**2013**	**2014**	**2015**	**2016**
		Direct Model			
Margin from MBA	117,000	468,000	702,000	936,000	11,70,000
Margin from BE	702,000	2,106,000	5,616,000	8,424,000	11,232,000
		Commission from Vendor Model			
Margin from old books	93,750	146,250	228,150	355,914	555,226
		Commission from Student Model			
Margin from old books	87,500	275,000	675,000	1,000,000	1,325,000
Total revenue	1,000,250	2,995,250	7,221,150	10,715,914	14,282,226
Total cost	1,113,000	1,813,155	3,297,462	3,503,520	3,780,901
Income	(112,750)	1,182,095	3,923,688	7,212,394	10,501,325

Source: Company Records

Exhibit 4.8 | *Financial Figures and Assumptions*

Description	Instance/Percentage
Increment rates in salaries	10%
Number of new website maintenance heads	3
Increment in security deposit	10%
New branch offices in 2014 (additional)	3
Website AMC cost	25%
Rate of decrement in optimization	10%

Heads	Amount in INR/Percentage
Average SP of new book	400
Average SP of old book	250
Direct Model (Margins)	
Fresh books	7%
Margin in used books	20%
Number of vendors	30
Number of books/vendor	250
Total books	7,500
Books increment	20%
Indirect Model (Vendor)	
Vendor commission	5%
Vendor increment	30%
Logistics cost (per unit)	15

Year	Colleges Targeted	Frequency	Students	Market Share	No of Customers
2011	50	2	300	10%	3,000
	50	4	600	15%	18,000
2012	100	4	300	10%	12,000
	100	6	600	15%	54,000
2013	150	4	300	10%	18,000
	200	8	600	15%	144,000
2014	200	4	300	10%	24,000
	300	8	600	15%	216,000
2015	250	4	300	10%	30,000
	400	8	600	15%	288,000

Source: Company Records

PRODUCT MANAGEMENT ISSUES

The future looked promising for Bookshells, however, there were certain challenges that it had to navigate through with an adept marketing strategy. The phase 1 of launch had given them a good feel about the future opportunities and challenges of being in the Indian education industry and working on an e-commerce domain in India. Shrey Kaushik and his core team were concerned regarding certain product management issues.

Shrey Kaushik candidly admitted that the following product management issues would be crucial for Bookshells' next phase of growth:

- **Inadequate Social Marketing Tools:** Though Bookshells relied heavily on freely available SNS (social networking sites) like Facebook, Twitter, LinkedIn, blogs, forums and other social media for product promotion and as an integral part of product requisition operations; however, for the next growth phases, that is, second and third phase, it has to look for more innovative tools for its product promotion and product requisition operations. According to Shrey, these SNS may compliment an organization's operations but there can be many limitations of free sites in terms of bandwidth, server space, speed and security. However, going for a dedicated server and own high end web site would require time and money, which Bookshells lacked.
- **Lack of Technical Knowledge:** Since Bookshells was a start-up, so due to budgetary constraints it had to rely on smaller companies for its outsourced work. However, smaller companies in India mostly lacked in technical competence and the outsourced work was not delivered up to the expectation. For example, the Web site design was outsourced and it was getting delayed and still it was not shaping up properly. This forced the core team to learn and develop the web site themselves. Such constraints and involvement of core team in the mundane operational issues distracted them from getting involved in business development planning and deciding about other strategic initiatives for long-term growth of the company.
- **Lack of Resources (time and money):** Shrey Kaushik described his constraints in a very articulate way. He expressed his inability to appoint professionals like MBAs and engineering graduates, especially for marketing and other domains at initial stages due to lack of adequate resources. Hence handling all activities with limited resources and a small core team, along with his MBA studies, was the acting as obstacle in smooth execution of Bookshells. Shrey was looking for large venture capital infusion for the company to operate at much larger scale. The capital infusion will enable him to hire professionals so that he may devote his quality time for strategic business planning and implementation.
- **Continuously Engaging Customers:** In e-commerce business model like Bookshells, customers would visit and transact once or twice, but conceptualizing, designing and implementing marketing strategy to engage customers consistently for repeat visits was an important requirement and main goal of the company for sustained business growth. Bookshells was yet to finalize this marketing strategy for continuous engagement of customers. With similar competing e-commerce sites like secondhandbooksindia.com, buyselloldbooks.com, indianusedbooks.com and talash.com; devising innovative marketing strategy was essential for sustainable growth before implementation of the second and third phase of growth.
- **Consistency in Pricing:** Pricing of books varied from one educational domain to another. Bookshells maintained transparent and consistent pricing for its own book procurement and sales. However, in C2C procurement and sales model, it was tough and unfriendly to dictate pricing rules to seller and buyer. Also, maintaining same selling price of the same product becomes necessary

for brand building, on the other hand, leveraging different selling prices for different domains was also required for profitability. Bookshells has to come up with certain allowable pricing range for the same products. Hence, the product pricing needed to be revisited before the implementation of the second and third phase of Bookshells.

- **Addition of New Product Lines:** According to Shrey Kaushik, the culture of e-books was also catching up in India and gradually sales of printed books would see a decline. Hence, as envisaged by Shrey, Bookshells needed to diversify into different product lines such as computers, mobiles, cameras and music on the lines of Flipkart, eBay and Amazon for a sustainable future. This scaled up operations with multiple product lines would also act as entry barriers for other new firms planning to enter this segment. However, this will require huge capital investment to build the entire vendor and logistics network besides budget for integrated marketing communication. Funding from venture capitalists was one of the most viable options to implement this change at Bookshells. However, the demand of venture capitalist in terms of equity in the company (at times up to 80 per cent) and their intrusion in organizational affairs; made Shrey Kaushik uncomfortable with this idea. For Shrey Kaushik, bookshells.com was more than just a business idea; it was a passion and dream he had lived with for the last 2 years.

Shrey Kaushik planned to discuss the above product management issues with his core team. He was also thinking of taking the help of some marketing consultants to advise him on the above issues. He was keen to get clarity on these issues before the implementation of the second phase of bookshells.com.

DISCUSSION QUESTIONS

1. Among the 'product management issues' discussed in the case study, which issue was the most important for bookshells.com? Enumerate facts from the case to justify your answer.
2. Was it a good management decision by CEO Shrey Kaushik to have three distinct phases of business plan roll-out? How was it beneficial to bookshells.com? What could have been the alternate best launch strategy for bookshells.com?
3. Discuss the business model of bookshells.com. Also suggest marketing initiatives for bookshells.com so as create USP (Unique Selling Proposition) for its used book product line.
4. Given the facts from the case, envisage the future of bookshells.com. Also suggest new product lines for bookshells.com so that it may become a major online e-commerce web site like flipkart and amazon.com? Give examples to support your answer.
5. What should be the marketing strategy during second phase and third phase of business plan implementation given the prevailing organizational conditions at bookshells.com? Also suggest how bookshells.com may enhance the entry barrier to compete better with organizations planning to enter this online used book business.
6. Should CEO Shrey Kaushik consider a detailed marketing research programme before undertaking Phase 3 of his business plan? Should he hire a marketing research agency for this or rely on his internal team for the same?

ENDNOTES

1. The Triple Bottom Line approach focuses on planet, profit and people for business growth as part of sustainable growth.
2. http://education.nic.in, accessed on 21 December 2011.
3. Company records.
4. http://Conservatree.org/learn/EnviroIssues/Treestats.html, accessed on 23 December 2011.

REFERENCE

http://www.education.nic.in/sector.asp#size, accessed on 21 December 2011.

5

BHARAT INTERNATIONAL

It was 14 July 2011 and Mr G.S. Kahlon, Chairman, Bharat International (BI) was introspecting on the marketing strategy to increase BI's market share in the domestic market. BI[1] is an ISO 9001:2000 company having state-of-art production plant facilities at Ludhiana (Exhibit 5.1). It has 130 employees with an annual revenue of approximately 20 crores (200 million) rupees. This year (2010–2011), BI exported about 80 per cent of its production to heavy vehicles automotive parts distributors located across the globe. Growing fluctuations in the international market in terms of dollar value, high steel prices and other developments in the international market such as political disturbances in Egypt, Libya and Yemen made Mr Kahlon think of enhancing its domestic sales basket to 30 per cent by the next financial year. The top management of BI was of the view that a larger domestic market share will hedge BI's risk of over reliance on the international market. With established brand names like *Lit-lite* and the newly launched brand GPK, BI's top management saw this target as achievable.

INDIAN AUTO-ANCILLARY COMPONENT INDUSTRY

The Indian automotive industry comprises automobile and autocomponent sectors. The automotive ancillary component industry, a critical subsegment of the automotive sector, had about 500 firms in the organized sector and more than 10,000 firms in the small and unorganized sector. The Indian auto-ancillary industry had global recognition mainly due to its cost competitiveness. The low cost of steel besides lesser manpower cost helped in sustaining this cost advantage.

India, the fifth largest manufacturer of commercial vehicles, had witnessed consistent growth in automobile production (Exhibit 5.2) and has also emerged as a key auto component centre in Asia. The Government of India was actively promoting foreign direct investments (FDI) in the ancillary component industry. The Ministry of Heavy Industries and Public Enterprises had designed an automotive mission plan 2006–2016 to further accelerate the growth in this sector.[2] It included the following:

- Increase in total turnover to US$122–159 billion by 2016 from US$34 billion in 2006
- Increase in export revenue to US$35 billion by 2016

Exhibit 5.1 | *Ludhiana, Punjab (India)*

Source: www.travelmadeeasy.in[3]

- Providing employment to additional 25 million people by 2016
- Contributing 10 per cent of country GDP by 2016[4]

THE BEGINNING

Mr G.S. Kahlon, a mechanical engineer by training, started off his entrepreneurial career in 1971 (Exhibit 5.3). His initial business was the manufacturing of ancillary tractor parts. Being from an agricultural family, the utility of tractors was well known to him. Prior to his entrepreneurial career,

Exhibit 5.2 | *Indian Ancillary Component Industry*

Segment-wise Market share

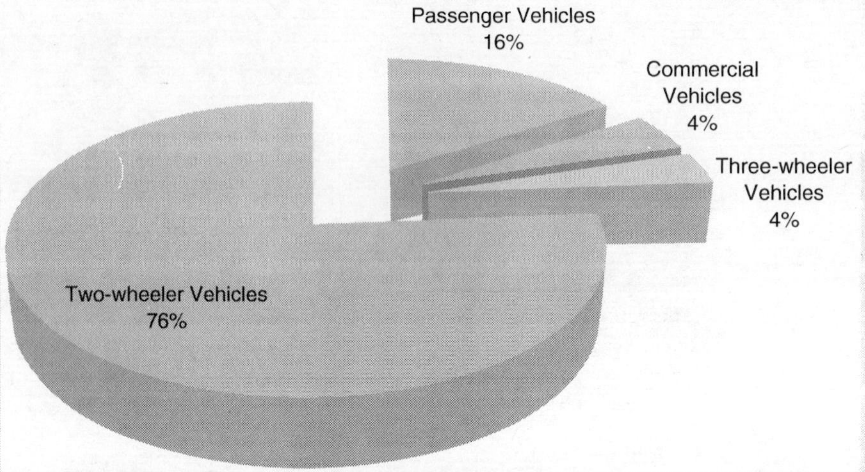

Production Trends

Automobile Production Trends (in lakhs)							Number of Vehicles
Category	**2003–04**	**2004–05**	**2005–06**	**2006–07**	**2007–08**	**2008–09**	**2009–10**
Passenger Vehicles	9.90	12.10	13.09	15.45	17.78	18.39	23.51
Commercial Vehicles	2.75	3.54	3.91	5.20	5.49	4.17	5.67
Three-wheelers	3.56	3.74	4.34	5.56	5.01	4.97	6.19
Two-wheelers	56.23	65.30	76.09	84.67	80.27	84.20	105.13
Grand Total	72.44	84.68	97.44	110.88	108.54	111.72	140.50

Source: Society of Indian Automobile Manufacturers

Mr Kahlon had served at Guru Nanak Dev Engineering College, Ludhiana, as Faculty of Mechanical Engineering.

The ancillary tractor parts manufactured by BI were serving the replacement spare parts market in the nearby automotive market. However, with the increased automation and the entry of large companies in tractor manufacturing, the market of tractor spare parts for BI shrunk. The customers preferred OEM (original equipment manufacturer) spare parts over the replacement tractor spare parts of local companies.

As a result, after few years, Mr Kahlon included ancillary auto parts of heavy vehicles to his product portfolio. The brand *Lit-lite* was born in the year 1978. Since then, Mr Kahlon never looked back. After a few years of business in the domestic market, one of his close friends encouraged him to start exports. Although there were a lot of initial constraints in terms of working capital and infrastructure,

Exhibit 5.3 | *Top Management at BI*

Mr G.S. Kahlon

Mr G.S. Kahlon, a mechanical engineer from Guru Nanak Dev Engineering College, Ludhiana, is the chairman of BI and its sister companies, namely, Kahlon International Private Limited and Gagan Tracto Industries Private Limited. He is also the president of Auto Parts Manufacturers Association of India and Patron of Chamber of Industrial and Commercial Undertakings. He holds key positions in Punjab Labor Welfare Board (Government of Punjab), RAC Central Excise (Government of India), Single Window Clearance Committee (Government of Punjab), Regional Committee NR Engineering Export Promotion Council (EEPC) and Member, Governing Council, Institute for Auto Parts and Hand Tools Technology. His holistic and structured approach in conceptualization, planning and implementation is something that needs to be learnt by today's entrepreneurs. .

Mr Gurpreet Kahlon

Gurpreet Kahlon, a Bachelor of Commerce, is the managing director of the company. He possessed a good knack of problem solving and is known for his leadership qualities at BI. His working style of 'management by heart' approach keeps the entire BI family motivated and loyal.

Mr Jashan Kahlon

Jashan Kahlon, a Bachelor in Arts, is head of operations at BI. He was actively involved in expanding the footprints of the company besides focusing on cost cutting initiatives at BI. He used innovative approaches in problem solving and delivery execution.

Source: Interview with Mr Kahlon, dated 12 July 2011

Mr Kahlon's strong determination enabled him to overcome such hurdles. Today, BI—with its headquarters at Ludhiana, the industrial hub of Punjab, India—is a major heavy vehicles automotive spare part exporter to many countries.

INITIAL OBSTACLES

India's image as a manufacturer and supplier of quality products was not quite positive in the international market. Being a developing country, India's infrastructure and technology in the early 1990s was poor and, therefore, a majority of the international buyers never preferred products that were manufactured in India. As per Mr Kahlon, the international customers possessed an image of inferior quality about Indian products.

It was a challenge for BI to develop higher quality products at par to Germany and Japan and that too at a lower price. This was essential for BI if it had to start exports. During his return from foreign countries, Mr Kahlon brought back benchmark samples and designed and manufactured similar or higher quality products. During the initial years, the company even sold its goods at razor thin margins in order to establish their brand name in the market. As the quality of the products was comparable to ones manufactured by German and Japanese companies, therefore, within a short span of time *Lit-lite* brand got well accepted in the major automobile hubs of the world. Since then, BI had never compromised on quality and it was the main reason besides cost competitiveness that currently the organization was exporting the ancillary auto parts of heavy vehicles all across the world (Exhibit 5.4).

Exhibit 5.4 | *International Network*

BI exported to the following countries and many others:

- Afghanistan
- Algeria
- Australia
- Canada
- Dubai
- Egypt
- Ethiopia
- Germany
- Iran
- Iraq
- Japan
- Libya
- Morocco
- South Africa
- Spain
- Sri Lanka
- Sudan
- Turkey
- United States of America

Source: Interview with Mr Kahlon, dated 12 July 2011

PRODUCT MIX AT BI

BI promoted all its product range mainly in the replacement market. Replacement market is a marketplace where the replica of original spare parts performing similar functions is available but under varied brand names and different price tags. The potential customer of replacement spare parts including users of a particular equipment or automobile generally preferred to buy the comparable quality replacement product but at a lesser price. Many of the small and medium enterprise (SME) manufacturers like BI, who had their core competency in manufacturing spare parts for the replacement market, preferred such target markets in comparison to supplying directly to OEMs because of their promotional budget restrictions, inability to meet standards in terms of production infrastructure and other budgetary constraints. As far as visibility was concerned, these markets had high customer footfalls because of better price deals. The end customers were generally more satisfied with the replacement spare parts market as they got comparable quality spare parts and at a much lower price.

BI, which had more than 1,000 ancillary components in their product range, included best quality auto fasteners, hub bolts, U-bolts, centre bolts, spring pins and other ancillary components of heavy vehicles (Exhibits 5.5, 5.6 and 5.7) under the brand name *Lit-lite*. These products were being used as replacement spare part of various heavy vehicles being manufactured by companies such as Mercedes Benz, MAN, Volvo, etc.

Apart from individual hub/wheel bolts, BI also manufactured complete hub-bolt assemblies for heavy and light vehicles of major OEMs such as Toyota, Dyna, Mitsubishi, Fuso, Isuzu, Nissan, Hyundai, KIA, etc. The most successful product from BI's product portfolio was wheel nuts with thrust washers. It was basically an alloy steel hardened washer which gave thrust to the spring section. It also protected bolts from breakage and gave better shock absorption, besides increasing life of the hub. Such products were highly suitable in heavy vehicles manufactured by MAN, DAF, SCANIA, UNIVERSAL (DIN) and others. As per the design specifications of various heavy vehicles, BI manufactured all shapes of nuts and bolts (Exhibit 5.6) along with complete adherence to other internationally accepted manufacturing specifications in terms of grade levels, hardness and tensile strength (Exhibits 5.7 and 5.8).

Besides standard fasteners, BI also manufactured fasteners used in railways, petrochemicals, power utilities, fertilizers and steel industries. Recently, BI had come up with wind turbine fasteners and fasteners for rotor blades. The organization had their mining and earthmoving equipment fastener patented in Australia and also had initiated the patenting process for the same in India (Exhibit 5.9). The patented fastener was highly useful for organizations like Caterpillar, Komatsu, Hitachi and JCB, as these organizations were involved in making mining and earthmoving equipments. BI's product collection also

Exhibit 5.5 | *Product Line of BI*

Hub/wheel bolts (heavy vehicles)
Hub/wheel bolts and nuts (light vehicles)
Spherical washer/ring
T-Bolt for trilex wheels
Pinion nut
Axle nut
Propeller shaft bolt with nylock nut
T-bolts and wheel clamp for Fiat
Spring centre bolts
Spring U-bolts
Axle stud with nuts
Spring pin/shackle pins
Shackle bolts for Fiat
Universal joint cross (UJ cross)
Wheel spanners
King pin kit
Brake cam shaft
Suspension parts for trailers
Automotive casting/chassis component
Banjo bolts/banjo/grease nipple
Union nut/drain plug
Adopter/double connectors
Accelerator end/tie rod end
Clutch release lever repair kit/over flow valve
Hand primer/con rod bolts/cylinder head bolts
Bushes (steel, brass/gunmetal, rubber mounting, nylon/PVC)
Mining and earthmoving equipment fasteners
Standard fasteners/fasteners for special application

Source: Company records

Exhibit 5.6 | *Shapes and Specifications of Nuts/Bolts*

Shapes

Bolts: Hex, square, round, plow bolts, track bolts, bent bolts, or in any shape

Nuts: Hex, square, collar, conical, tapper, or in any shape

Types of Nut: Plain, slotted, nylock and lock nuts

Metric Standards

Bolts: Property classes: 4.6, 6.6, 8.8, 10.9 and 12.9

Nuts:

Property Class of Nut	Use with Bolts of Property Class
4	4.6,4.8
6	6.6
8	8.8
12	10.9, 12.9

Specifications for Unified Precision Bolt, Screws and Nuts

As Per B.S. 1768: 1963

Bolts and studs: Grade A&B, P, S, T, V and X

Nuts:

Grade 0 Nuts	For Use With Bolts of Grade 'A', 'B' and 'P'
Grade 1 Nuts	For Use With Bolts of Grade 'S'
Grade 3 Nuts	For Use With Bolts of Grade 'T'
Grade 5 Nuts	For Use With Bolts of Grade 'V' and 'X'

Source: Company records

Exhibit 5.7 | *Lit-Lite Product Profile of Bolt, Screw and Studs*

Identification	Hardness (HRC)	Tensile Strength Rm (N/mm2)	Percentage of Elongation After Fracture (Minimum, %)
Lit-lite 4.6	18/20	400/500	22
Lit-lite 8.8	22/34	800/900	12
Lit-lite 9.8	28/37	900/1000	10
Lit-lite 10.9	32/39	1000/1200	9
Lit-lite 12.9	39/44	1200/1400	8

Source: Company records

included components such as U.J. cross, pinion nuts, axle nuts, chassis components and banjo bolts. Brake-cum-shaft kits, King pin kits and suspension kits were also in high demand amongst BI's product portfolio.

All the products were manufactured either through the hot forging process or cold forging process. The sequence of steps involved in both processes was almost the same (Exhibit 5.10). The cold forging process was automated at BI. The basic steps involved in both manufacturing processes included pickling, drawing, cutting, facing, forging, trimming, turning, grinding, threading, heat treatment, colouring and packaging. The hot forging process was manual. BI planned to automate it in the near future.

PRICING STRATEGY

As per Managing Director, Gurpreet Kahlon, BI followed a penetrative pricing strategy in the international market at the initial stage. The products were shipped to the clients at a highly competitive price. The margins were kept quite low and at times at par with the product manufacturing cost. As the product

Exhibit 5.8 | *Fasteners Specification*

Specification	Fastener Description	Material	Nominal Size Range	Proof Load (PSI)	Yield Strength (Minimum) (PSI)	Tensile Strength (Minimum) (PSI)
SAEJ429 Grade 5 ASTM A449	Bolts, Screws, Studs	Medium Carbon Steel Quenched and Tempered	¼" thru 1" Over 1' to 1 ½" ¼" thru 1" Over 1' thru 1 ½" Over 1 ½" thru 3"	85000 74000 85000 74000 55000	92000 81000 92000 81000 58000	120000 105000 120000 105000 90000
SAEJ429 Grade 7 Bolts and screws Roll threaded after heat treatment	Bolts, Screws, Studs	Medium Carbon Steel Quenched and Tempered	¼" thru 1 ½"	105000	115000	133000
SAEJ429 Grade 8 ASTM A354 Grade BD	Bolts, Screws, Studs	Medium Carbon Steel Quenched and Tempered	¼" thru 1 ½"	120000	130000	150000

Source: Company records

Exhibit 5.9 | *High Tensile Earth Moving Fasteners*

Standard System Fasteners	*Lit-lite* Special Fasteners	Identification/Grade Mark
Bolt: Tensile Strength = 170000PSI (min.)	**Bolt:** Tensile Strength = 185000PSI (min.)	*Lit-lite* 185.9
Hardness = 37 to 42 HRC	**Hardness** = 40 to 45 HRC	*Lit-lite* 185.9
Nut: System Designed Compatible	**Nut:** System Designed Compatible	*Lit-lite* 185.9

Source: Company records

Exhibit 5.10 | *Production Phases*

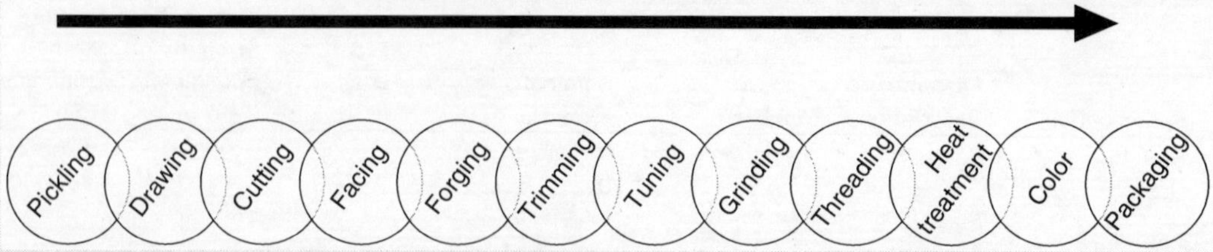

Source: Interview with Mr Kahlon, dated 12 July 2011

got accepted in the international market, which BI measured by the quantum of order enquiries it got from abroad, it charged premium prices on its subsequent export order bookings.

BI had better visibility in the heavy vehicle automotive replacement market of the world because of its ability to provide worth to customers in terms of quality and prices. However, automotive spare parts being derived demand, BI had often encountered difficulty in predicting demand and as a result there were problems in finalizing the manufacturing schedule. There was also always a risk that any time an OEM may stop manufacturing a particular model and it may lead to loss of BI's finished products inventory.

DISTRIBUTION AND PROMOTION

The distribution of BI products in the international spare parts market was through local established dealers. BI also maintained a relationship with other large dealers in the importing country, who could be leveraged during any issues with the regular dealer. BI could have booked higher profitability by selling its products directly to the end user by opening its own stores in the international market, but the top management had not explored that model. In the domestic market, the company followed a sales strategy of one dealer per city. With rising competition, the company was looking for more marketing executives who could generate leads in an efficient way and promote the *Lit-lite* brand. BI also wanted to promote *GPK*, which had lesser market visibility, thus leveraging the brand equity of *Lit-lite*.

BI followed both push and pull strategy while promoting its products. At initial stages, while promoting a product in the global market, it pushed its product in a limited quantity at the most competitive price. As soon as it got well established in the new marketplace, the industrial customers started looking for the same product. The unique selling proposition (USP) of BI products in the international market was that it had high-quality products and at a lower price than other international manufacturers. The lower price in the international market by BI was possible due to low labour cost, lesser overhead cost, less investment on R&D and excise exemption as BI had a 'Star Export House' status approved by the Government of India. The R&D cost in BI's balance sheet was minimal as they mostly adapted the design used by OEMs in their product design. Since Mr G.S. Kahlon is President of the Auto Parts Manufacturing Association of India, and a renowned personality in the industry, his personal image also facilitated the promotion of BI products in the industrial market. The company actively participated in many auto parts exhibitions and fairs both in the country and abroad.

EXPANSION STRATEGY AT BI

Initially, BI had no planned or structured expansion strategy. It started its exports to small countries like Egypt, Libya, Sudan, Ethiopia and Morocco, where technology and infrastructure were poor. Once BI's brand *Lit-lite* became popular and got established in these countries, it extended its presence to other continents such as Europe, America and Australia. This was how BI evolved from an Indian SME to an exporting enterprise.

Positive word of mouth acted as catalyst in the entire BI's expansion journey. For instance, after initial hiccups, BI had established itself as a quality vendor for replacement spare parts in Egypt. Some of the exporters from Libya visited Egypt's market, looking for some product alternatives. They heard about BI's *Lit-lite* brand and how it had created an excellent impact in Egypt's spare parts replacement market. It impressed Libyan importers and motivated them to take samples of *Lit-lite* manufactured components back home. As the samples met the requirements of Libyan automotive companies in terms of quality and price, the importers contacted BI directly. This was how BI's exports track path extended. The entry of BI in the international market had never been an issue except in few developed countries who had developed wrong perceptions about India's manufacturing infrastructure.

EXPLORING BRANDING

According to Managing Director, Mr Gurpreet Kahlon, brand plays a very important role in the industrial market even though the product was not visible after the final product was manufactured. The buyers correlated quality with the brand name. BI targeted the users who had automobile service stations catering to a large number of heavy vehicles. Such users always bought the branded product in bulk quantity, which met the same quality standards as used by OEMs. These organizations expected lower prices than the OEM prices. Even though the product was not visible while in use, its real utility was reflected in its quality during on-field usage. Therefore, the brand name was equally important in the automotive spare parts replacement market as in the consumer market.

BI AT CROSSROADS

Transition from an Unorganized Sector to an Organized Sector

BI started as an Indian SME[5] and initially its entire business was operated in an unorganized way. BI started when the Indian automotive spare parts industry had only a few manufacturing units. Not much importance was given to inventory management, plant layout, marketing and automation. As a result, BI produced desired quality products but the cost of production was high; however, now circumstances were completely different. Today's survival required a holistic control over operations, marketing, human resources and other overhead costs. Also, for international market BI required to come up with a much more competitive price so as to get more export orders.

In the following years, Mr Kahlon envisioned that his organization should have more automation, adopt modern management practices and build up state-of-art infrastructure. The company was highly dependent on labour for its daily operations as the level of automation was low at BI. Punjab (Exhibit 5.1) being highly deficient in manual labour had affected the entire industry. BI was planning for large-scale automation so that the dependency on manual labour was reduced.

However, BI was in a dilemma that whether such a huge investment in large-scale automation and infrastructure would commensurate with substantial increase in the market shares in the export and domestic market.

Expansion

The company planned to increase the production capacity through large-scale automation. It would decrease manufacturing cost in long term, besides decreasing dependency on manual labour. Also, it wanted to expand its product line. BI aimed to increase its customer base in the domestic as well as the international market through this enhanced product line. BI was planning to supply ancillary automotive components directly to the Indian automobile OEMs such as Tata Motors, TVS and Mahindra & Mahindra as a vendor.

Leveraging the *Lit-lite* Brand for Promoting GPK

Recently, BI had got its other trademark named 'GPK' registered. As far as the brand awareness of two trademarks was concerned, *Lit-lite* was more popular at both local and international level. Initially, GPK was promoted to counter some of the local issues in a few countries. For example, there was more than one importer interested in the similar product line but desired it under a different brand name. At times, there were exclusivity class with the customer and hence, GPK was introduced to accommodate it. Recently, the board of directors had decided to promote GPK as a trademark which would include high-end best quality products with a high premium on it.

Forward Integration

BI was in dilemma whether to directly market its products in the international market or not. This would remove the intermediary leading to high profit margins. BI would be in direct touch with the customers which would give the organization the opportunity for cross-selling customized products to the customers. It would also build a strong relationship with the customers. However, the cost of setting up marketing offices, including the manpower cost, was holding up the BI management to take this decision. It could have antagonized the existing BI dealer too. It was a risky initiative but would have given BI the desired profits.

Duplicity

The duplicity of the *Lit-lite* brand name was rampant in some of the countries where BI had a good market standing. In these markets, the demand for *Lit-lite* products was more than the supply. This shortfall was capitalized by local counterfeit manufacturers. BI officials and owners had witnessed and verified this duplicity during their regular visits to these countries. BI could have sued these counterfeit manufacturers for trademark violation; however, the financial implications and time involved in pursuing such cases in that particular country of violation was inhibiting the management to go for it. According to Mr Kahlon, to tackle this problem BI planned to quickly enhance its production capacity.

Domestic Market Share

As per Mr Kahlon, BI presently had a ratio of approximately 80:20 for its international and domestic operations. However, due to rising instability in the Middle East market and other markets, the organization envisioned to change this portfolio to 50:50 by 2014. One of the reasons behind this strategic reorientation was the repeated dollar fluctuation. It had given the Chinese manufacturers a further edge in the international market vis-à-vis pricing. BI had incurred huge losses due to this trend. The domestic manufacturers of the respective countries got subsidies from their local governments, which gave them added advantage, thus enabling them to price their product at a much lower price. Being a company of

Indian origin, BI found it more comfortable in competing with domestic competitors. In case of changes in the government policies and fluctuation in steel prices, all manufacturers would be equally affected and it would make competition more consistent.

Mr G.S. Kahlon wanted the company to emerge as a major domestic player in the spare parts market. The export market was throwing a lot of challenges. He knew that a balance had to be struck by taking a calculated risk so that BI became the most successful company in the Indian automotive heavy vehicle spare parts industry. He was looking for answers regarding strategy to be followed in the coming years so as to achieve the desired goals.

DISCUSSION QUESTIONS

1. Suggest a suitable segmentation, targeting and positioning strategy for increasing the domestic targeted sales basket to 30 per cent for BI?
2. What challenges do you think BI will face in pushing its product in the domestic market?
3. Enumerate the difference in marketing strategy for BI in the domestic market as compared to the international market.
4. Discuss the measures to be undertaken by the product management team to tackle the duplicity issue in the international market.
5. Suggest low-cost promotional strategy for BI to enhance the visibility and sales of the *Lit-lite* brand in the Indian market.

ENDNOTES

1. BI is better known as Bharat International amongst its customers, vendors and in the industry.
2. www.ficci-b2b.com/sector-overview-pdf/sector-automotive.pdf, accessed on 11 July 2011.
3. www.travelmadeeasy.in, accessed on 25 July 2011.
4. http://www.cci.in/pdf/surveys_reports/automotive-auto-ancilliaries-industry.pdf, accessed on 11 July 2011.
5. A 'small scale enterprise' has an investment in plant and machinery of lower than ₹5 crores (50 million) whereas a 'medium enterprise' has an investment in plant and machinery of more than ₹5 crores (50 million) but less than ₹10 crores (100 million).

REFERENCES

www.bankofindia.com/smepol.aspx, accessed on 15 July 2011.

www.rbi.org.in/scripts/NotificationUser.aspx?Id=2502&Mode=0, accessed on 25 July 2011.

6

ALLUMEZ INFOTECH: SOCIAL MARKETING APPROACH TO BUSINESS

THE BEGINNING

During December 2005, when Mr Parwinder Singh, CEO, Allumez InfoTech (Exhibit 6.1) was on vacation from United States after completing his industrial automation project, and was enjoying his early morning tea in his village, he saw a little boy fixing his tractor. The little boy's technical skills impressed him. Parwinder was a visionary and had been introspecting for a long time on how to ameliorate the lifestyle and economic status of the rural community of his home state, Punjab (Exhibit 6.2). Hailing from a rural background himself, Parwinder knew that rural economy based on agriculture would shrink more in the coming years. He wanted to motivate rural boys and girls who in all probability would choose agriculture as a means to earn their livelihood to some online hi-tech world which could provide them a better platform to become successful entrepreneurs of the world. A little boy's ability to restore a tractor without any mechanical engineering diploma or degree further strengthened his belief in the rural talent and acted as a trigger to start his dream project. IT (Information Technology) seemed one of the obvious industries as he had prior experience in the field and importantly all the villages of Punjab had easy access to basic infrastructure required, namely, the 'internet'. Importantly starting business in this industry did not require any huge initial investments unlike other manufacturing businesses. The low investment factor in IT-based business helped Allumez motivate many of his 'associates' to start their own ventures. The CEO Mr Parwinder Singh believed that good 'exposure to IT' and 'specialized training' were two major obstacles which were thwarting young rural boys and girls to become successful entrepreneurs.

To start with actualizing his vision, Mr Parwinder formed an NGO named 'DEC' in 2005 with the aim to find talented and enthusiastic boys and girls from rural community within Punjab (Exhibit 6.2),

Exhibit 6.1 | *CEO Mr Parwinder's Profile*

Mr Parwinder, an industrial automation programmer by profession had a lot of attachment not only to his village but the entire community and the state. An engineering graduate with masters in business administration (MBA), he had worked with leading multinational corporations. His last stint was with DG Drives as manager (projects). He was also a visiting faculty in various business schools. Apart from IT business, Mr Parwinder had planned to build a state-of-the-art old age home with modern facilities. An extrovert by nature, he is fond of travelling. He had travelled all the continents and many countries around the world. Besides heading Allumez InfoTech, he was also founder-President of a NGO called 'DEC'.

Source: As per interview with Mr Parwinder dated 2 December2011

Exhibit 6.2 | *The State of Punjab (India)*

Source: mapsofindia.com

who had strong inclination to become successful entrepreneurs. This was how Mr Parwinder's dream to provide path to deserving candidates started and his vision—*'to nurture entrepreneurs from rural community of Punjab'* saw the light of the day. In an endeavour to provide training and exposure to these juvenile minds, he formed a company named Allumez InfoTech in 2006. Allumez means 'to illuminate'. He had a vision to create one entrepreneur from each village of Punjab. In the coming year, he was all set to launch his dream project, namely, www.101dollarearningtips.com. However, he perceived numerous marketing problems in its rollout and in achieving the desired result.

THE BUSINESS MODEL

Allumez InfoTech[1] had a business model which was quite common in the Indian IT industry. However, its implementation was unique. The company had four divisions, namely, web hosting, web marketing, web designing and bioinformatics. The CEO and his team of more than 30 senior programmers and analysts were continuously involved in research and development for finding new ideas to earn more and more revenue through their online business model.

Allumez InfoTech had its in-house training centre which exposed new ideas to trainees apart from providing requisite training to the new employees. According to the present company employees, Allumez's training modules on online marketing are an eye-opener and a great learning resource on that topic. The USP (Unique Selling Proposition) of Allumez InfoTech business model was that it promoted business partnership model among its colleagues who initially join Allumez as trainees. As part of this model, they were completely empowered and made business partners, which ultimately satisfied trainee's entrepreneurial instincts besides generating a sense of loyalty for the overall system. This partnership model also made the entire business of Allumez more transparent and sustainable. Allumez had official tie ups with Google AdSense for promoting advertisements and thereby generating revenue for Allumez.

These business partners were called 'associates. The 'associates' were entrepreneurial owner of their Web site-based business. The associate/entrepreneurial owner shared a percentage of revenue with Allumez. The 'associate' would further form more associates on similar lines; where Allumez would also have some revenue share. Allumez provided the entire technical know-how, training and backend support including servers for its associate Web site-based businesses and further also to the associate's associate.

WEB HOSTING

Allumez's web hosting division allows users to host their Web sites on dedicated Allumez servers located in India and the United States. Along with customized web space, Allumez's dedicated call centre provided 24 × 7 support and monitoring, thus, ensuring continuous network connectivity, server health and URL (Uniform Resource Locator) response. The company had network of around 70 associates across the globe, who have outsourced their backend operational business to Allumez. Although these associates were Allumez's creation but they were running their businesses independently. This was akin to 'business within a business' model.

In addition to that, Allumez has more than 300 industry-related domains registered in its own kitty on varied topics such as www.plctutorials.com, www.searchguruz.com, www.machibazar.com, www.bluemirchi.com, etc. (Exhibit 6.3). On each well conceived, designed and developed Web sites, Allumez earns revenue through Google AdSense advertisements. During the course of Allumez's business operations, count of domains registered with Allumez keeps on varying depending upon footfall or

Exhibit 6.3 | *Web Sites of Allumez (Indicative List)*

www.22gee.biz
www.allarticledirectories.com
www.anandkarj.com
www.bestplacementagency.com
www.bluemirchi.com
www.freeplctutorials.com
www.freewallpapersport.com
www.freewebhostingplan.com
www.hostingfunda.com
www.jattbros.com
www.machibazar.com
www.myteacheronweb.com
www.postyourcomplaints.com
www.searchguruz.com
www.searchpg.com
www.spidernetworld.com
www.starplushosting.com
www.veerg.com
www.webdomainspace.com
www.website-welcome.com

Source: Company Records

traffic the particular Web site captures. The footfalls and the revenue through Google AdSense was the major input for the decision to upgrade or close a site. Allumez keeps consistently adding new domain names and Web site content after rigorous analysis of content demand in respective industry sectors. The decision on subject topics and related Web site content on specific domains was solely taken by the top management after intensive inputs by the R&D team. For instance, the website www.plctutorials.com provided information to electronics graduates on the subject of microcontrollers and was attracting large number of students, practitioners, faculties and amateur footfalls.

Allumez invested large amount each year in getting these domains and associated web space renewed. The sites lacking potential and with inadequate traffic were removed from Allumez's portfolio. Allumez's website hosting division provided eight services, viz., e-mail accounts with related domain name; web-based e-mail interface; online web stats; web site backup utility; product image and logo; custom error pages; FTP (File Transfer Protocol) access and other customized features.

WEB DESIGNING

Web designing is one of main divisions for any IT software services organization and so was it for Allumez InfoTech. Allumez's dedicated team of senior programmers were continuously involved in designing web sites for its associates and also for internal requirements of Allumez. All design variants such as custom web design, professional web design, corporate web design and web site template design were developed by Allumez's team. Apart from that, Allumez possessed huge expertise in designing product image and logo besides graphical/flash banner design. According to business requirements, Allumez has many e-commerce specialists to facilitate its customers with customized business solutions.

WEB MARKETING

Web marketing was one of the starting training modules in Allumez's curriculum for budding entrepreneurs. Various modules in web marketing included search engine optimization (SEO); affiliate marketing; PPC (Pay Per Click) marketing; banner ads; e-mail campaigns and blogs and forums.

- **Search Engine optimization:** It was one of the primary web marketing tools used by every IT company. SEO is the way to improve raking or visibility of the web site or web page. In general, higher the rank of web site on the search results, higher is the probability of attracting traffic on to the web site. Optimizing a web site was more of the tedious hard work rather than any strategic planning type of a job; as it involved amending the web site content (HTML and associated coding) to both enhance the relevance of specific keywords and to eliminate barriers to the indexing activities of search engines. Allumez had entire pool of talent from rural community who were novice to various IT courses. However, with little training in the SEO module; they were able to do the SEO quite comfortably. In fact the SEO training module was the easiest for them than the other Allumez IT training modules.
- **Affiliate Marketing:** Affiliate marketing was a marketing technique in which the web site rewarded its affiliates for increasing traffic on to the web site due to affiliates[2] own initiated marketing efforts.
- **Pay per Click:** PPC was a widely used online advertising model in which advertisers paid its promoters whenever their advertisement was clicked by an individual. It was at times referred to as cost per click.
- **Banner Ads:** Allumez had a portfolio of about 300 own web sites. Allumez embeds advertisements in the form of banner ads on various web pages of web sites. The charges for displaying banner ads varied across different web pages along with the location on the web page.
- **Email Campaigning:** Bulk e-mails to intended recipients were another major marketing tool used by Allumez InfoTech while marketing its own and customer's products.

Allumez had good reputation in Punjab and surrounding states. It often got new projects and contracts from various industries. Allumez had initiated 'subject matter expert' mechanism owing to growing business operation complexities each day. Under this subject matter expert scheme, Allumez had segregated its list of associates depending upon their interest and expertise. Allumez outsourced its assignments to subject matter expert associate, thus enhancing their business operations effectiveness for the all the stakeholders, viz., Allumez, associate and the client.

BIOINFORMATICS

Bioinformatics is interdisciplinary research area involving knowledge of biology and information technology. Bioinformatics was the latest addition to Allumez's portfolio and it was exploring various IT-related revenue generating models in this area. Bioinformatics was a growing industry and it had huge revenue potential. Allumez was capitalizing on its IT services capability and strength to monetize the revenue opportunity in the bioinformatics.

INFORMATION TECHNOLOGY INDUSTRY OUTLOOK

The Indian IT industry had given India a special recognition in the world. IT had played major role in altering India's image from a low quality, high cost product producing country to a preferred destination for competitively priced, high quality products and services. Some of the major Indian IT giants which have been globally successful included Infosys, TCS, HCL, Wipro and Mahindra Satyam. Few highlights of Indian IT industry were[2].

- According to NASSCOM (National Association of Software and Service Companies), in FY2011, Indian IT exports revenues rose to approx $59 billion, thus, contributing 26 per cent as its shares in total exports.
- As per NASSCOM, domestic IT-BPO revenues, excluding hardware, rose to almost 16 percent, thus, reaching $ 17.35 billion in FY 2011.
- Data centre service market in the country was anticipated to grow at CAGR of 22.7 per cent and expected to touch $2.2 billion by end of 2011.
- As forecasted by TRAI (Telecom Regulatory Authority of India) broadband subscribers to touch 100 million by 2014.
- IT firms to grow between 23–27 per cent in FY2012.
- According to NASSCOM, IT export component to reach $175 billion in revenue by 2020.
- Domestic IT revenues are likely to touch $50 billion by 2020.

Initiatives taken by the government to enhance growth of the IT sector:

- Constitution of technical advisory group for unique projects (TAGUP).
- Plans to formulate information technology investment regions (ITIRs).
- Enactment of Information Technology Act, 2000.

GLOBAL IT INDUSTRY

Information technology has witnessed many big investments since last decade. The advent of social media channels like Facebook, Twitter, LinkedIn, MySpace and Google+ has revolutionized the lifestyle of consumers and integrated business communication model of the organizations not only in the developed countries but also in the developing countries. Total investment of approximately $1.5 trillion was recorded in information technology sector in 2011, in contrast to approximately $1.2 trillion in 2007. As of now, the United States bags the highest market share of about 38 per cent in the entire world for investments in IT industry. Other nations where heavy investment in IT industry had been made include BRICS (Brazil, Russia, India, China and South Africa). Investments in BRICS countries rose by approx 12 per cent per year in last 4 years from $108 billion in 2007 to $172 billion in 2011. IT industry includes varied product lines such as hardware, software, prepackaged software, etc.. Globally total investments in IT services that excluded hardware and pre-packaged software had seen increase of approximately 5.9 per cent per year from $489 billion in 2007 to $616 billion in 2011.However within BRICS countries, this figure was expected to jump from $27 billion in 2007 to $51 billion in 2011[3]. India held the top position in terms of revenue among BRICS countries in IT outsourcing business (Exhibit 6.4).

THE INITIAL HURDLES

Like all business start-up ventures, Allumez InfoTech had its own set of problems during its initial years of operations. Motivating and training the rural youths, who were completely unaware of IT and online world, was itself a big hurdle. The enthusiasm and intense desire to become a successful entrepreneur helped a lot in imparting the desired training in a short span of time to these young youths. Even many near and dear ones of Parwinder were never quite convinced with his dream to successfully revolutionize the state rural community with his IT-oriented business model. The family wanted the young next generation to carry forward the stable family run agricultural business instead of moving in to any kind of risky hi-tech IT business. The other hiccup that Allumez faced was its inability to recruit

Exhibit 6.4 | *Global IT Industry*

World Total IT Spending

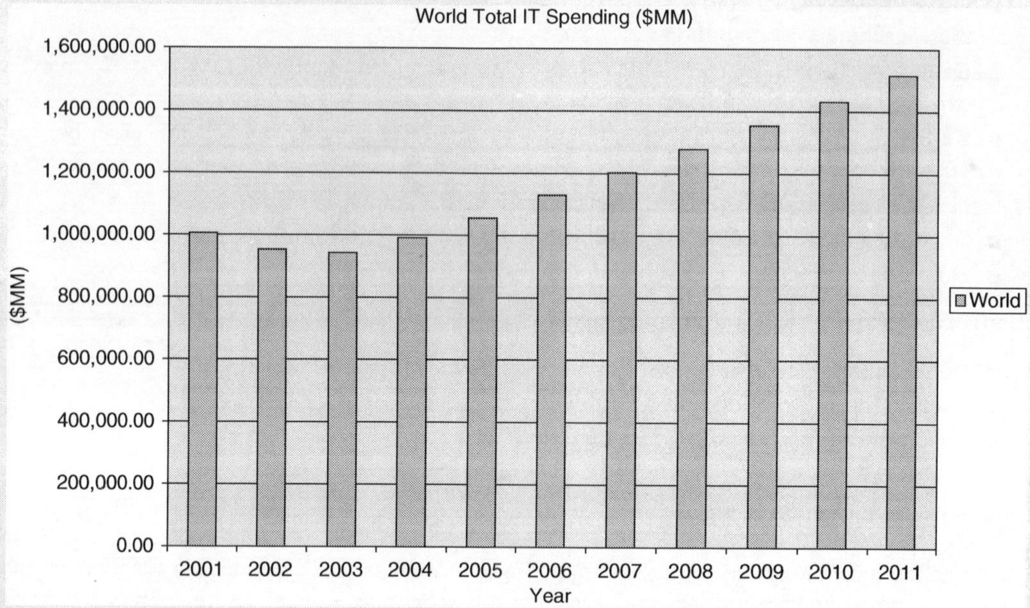

BRICS Total IT Spending

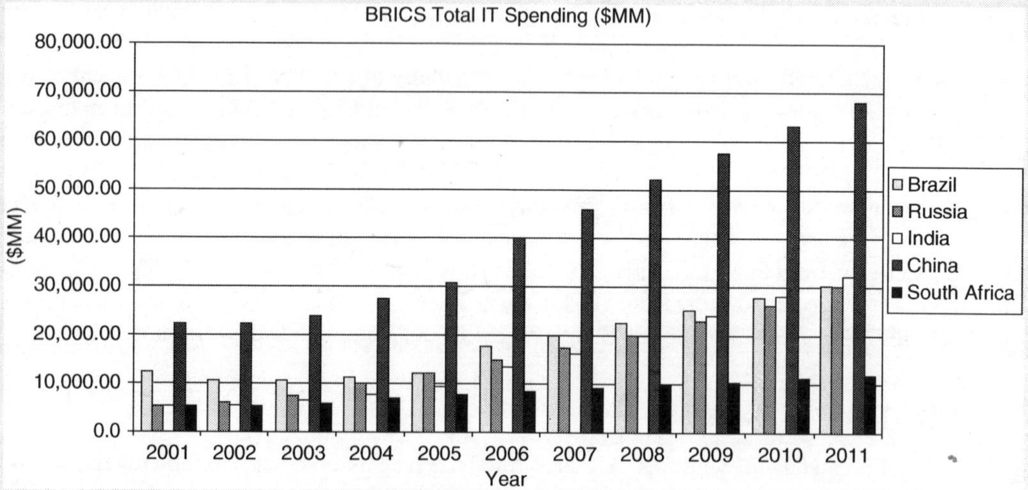

Source: http://www.ibef.org/artdispview.aspx?in=38&art_id=28792&cat_id=121&page=2

quality trainers because of the financial constraints. Other than financial aspects, Mr Singh stated that although web developers were easily available but there was scarcity of quality trainers on online business module who had expertise on Linux-based operating systems and servers in the Punjab region.

This shortage of quality IT trainer was one of the major hindrances in the smooth functioning of Allumez's operations in the initial years.

When Allumez started, it was just a family of immature and talented young rural boys and girls who were not quite familiar with information technology. It took Mr Parwinder three years to train and develop an inhouse team of web developers and online marketers who could help Mr Singh in Allumez assignments. During those three years Mr Parwinder was himself engaged 'day and night' in imparting knowledge to these young minds that were all new to this technological world. It also took Allumez three years to reach breakeven in the business.

According to CEO Mr Parwinder, the problem to find quality trainers for Allumez was associated with the level of education being imparted by technical schools of Punjab. He believed state engineering course was more theoretical with little practical exposure. He opined that since overall curriculum of majority of technical schools lacked hands-on experience, it ultimately frustrated individual's effort to sustain and grab better jobs in today competitive world. He was of the view that it was not essential although preferred to have some technical degrees to initiate entrepreneurial career. According to him strong determination, hands-on experience and ability to take calculated risk were more important than just bookish knowledge or impressive credentials for becoming a successful entrepreneur.

SUCCESS STORIES AT ALLUMEZ

Parwinder, a proud entrepreneur, had a vast collection of successful stories in his memory which really motivated him and gave a sense of satisfaction for his entrepreneurial choice. He proudly shared some of his interesting experiences in identifying the best talents and grooming them to be the best entrepreneurs of the country.

A 17-year-old boy, who grew up in a small rural family of Kharrar (located close to headquarters of Allumez), was roaming joblessly a few years back. The eldest son of a cab driver, he intended to join his father's profession. He happened to meet Mr Parwinder and had a discussion about his future plans. On hearing the intentions of the 17-year-old boy, Mr Parwinder counselled him to join Allumez training institute, although he was not an engineering graduate and the boy did agree. The young boy's hard work, aggression to achieve his goals, positive attitude and sharp learning curve stunned Mr Parwinder who personally imparted training to him. Presently, the young boy is heading a small company by name AS Web Info in his village. Interestingly, the little boy recorded profits in its first month of operations. The proud father had sold out his cab to help his son in setting up the infrastructure of his company. Mr Parwinder was confident enough to acclaim that the young boy would be among one of the leading business tycoons of the nation in the coming years.

In 2007, Mr Parwinder, by chance, met a young boy outside his office. He was rushing with a stockpile of documents and accidently some of those fell down. The scattered documents had beautifully designed landscapes, which motivated Mr Singh to enquire about them. The young boy confidently acclaimed that those were his drawings. In course of his discussion, the boy revealed to Mr Parwinder about his job. This 20-year-old boy, whose father had passed away, was working in one of the bulb manufacturing firms for a monthly salary of ₹1800. The boy also told about his passion for drawings. After the entire discussion and looking all his drawings, Mr Parwinder offered him to join Allumez for a monthly salary of ₹3,000 along with the commitment to offer him further training on drawing-related subjects. Mr Parwinder trained him into computers and on various modules of web designing for a year. The young boy was quite talented and creative and picked up web designing lessons very fast. Though Mr Parwinder had desire to convert him to partnership model, that is, as 'associate' in coming years, but unfortunately the boy left Allumez and joined some other company. But Mr Parwinder was proud to acclaim that boy was earning more than ₹35,000 per month and Allumez had a major contribution in shaping the life of that 20-year-old young boy.

There were many such interesting success stories that Mr Parwinder had to share. It gave him a lot of contentment and energy to move further towards his mission of changing the rural economic face of Punjab. Thus, Allumez InfoTech was also shaping up as an entrepreneurial school of young rural boys and girls in the region.

MARKETING STRATEGY

Allumez did not have any large dedicated budget for its existing product lines. However, for its upcoming project www.101dollarearningtips.com, Mr Parwinder had decided to hire marketing executives who could effectively position the unique idea among prospects. He had asked the GM (Finance) to keep separate marketing budget provision in next year's annual operating plan (AOP). For the existing product lines, instead of focussing on any kind of mass media promotion, the company with the help of its NGO 'DEC' was intensively promoting and counselling rural candidates among various villages of the state. 'DEC' had been targeting students who were yet to start their college life but had completed their school education.

Allumez's marketing strategy included the following four simple steps:

- Inspire young Indian rural talent to be engaged in the prospering IT industry.
- Educate and attract interested individuals on various IT modules as per their interest.
- Make the interested candidates as 'associates', that is, business partners after adequate training and help them start their own web-based organization with their own trademark and brand name.
- Extend full support to the 'associate' so that they may further expand the same model in their respective companies, that is, each associate will further make one or more associates.

According to Mr Parwinder's findings, the positive word of mouth spread by these young rural minds was far more effective than any other medium of marketing. Every expansion by each 'associate' automatically acted as a revenue source for Allumez's operations. It was a win-win situation for both Allumez and its related associate partners.

This marketing strategy for attracting prospective 'associate' seemed to work well as it had been successful in converting many prospects to actual customer/entrepreneurs (associate). However, it was never an easy task in entire Allumez's journey of 6 years as Allumez targeted niche population of rural youth community. Therefore, generating leads and converting them finally as 'associate' (business partner) besides imparting product and industry awareness and training to such a focussed target market was nothing less than a challenge for Allumez. Undoubtedly, it was a time-consuming activity for the entire team of Allumez but importantly it was conforming to the ethics of the organization and was satisfying the organization's goal to produce young entrepreneurs from the rural pockets of Punjab.

Above all, Allumez was in a way extending its corporate social responsibility (CSR) by educating and bringing up the talents of rural youths of India. Certainly such activities were undertaken by big corporate houses, however, for any Indian software organization operating as a small medium enterprise (SME), it was quite unique. Allumez had undertaken a noble mission which had a potential to change the economic status of millions of rural youths in the state. Mr Parwinder believed that irrespective of qualification, it was our social responsibility to engage young talent in some activity that was productive to them; else they may go astray.

REVENUE GENERATION

In 2006, Allumez started its operations with one associate and gradually it was able to augment to 70 business partners at the end of 2011. The target for each 'associate' was to generate revenue of $500 before that associate was exposed to next idea in 101dollarearningtips.com. By successfully meeting these targets, Allumez earned ₹1.7 million through its associates with the rise of over 48 percent in comparison to 2010. Allumez had planned to enhance 'Earning through Associates' by ten fold by 2015–16 (Exhibit 6.5). Similarly, Allumez was consistent in registering relevant domains. With one domain in 2006, company touched an impressive figure of 300 in 2011. Depending upon the subject, content and relevance, some Web sites had been able to garner quite high traffic and fewer mere rarely visited by internet users. On an average, each domain was earning $60 per year.

Allumez InfoTech has multiple sources of revenue to sustain itself. The alliance with Google AdSense for placing advertisements on its 300 owned Web sites acted as one of the major revenue generation sources for the company. As industry interaction was an integral part of curriculum in most of the engineering colleges in Punjab, Allumez got many student training and industry visit assignments from these engineering colleges. The organization was doing exceptionally well on its web hosting business. In its web hosting business, each expansion by Allumez 'associates' automatically scaled up the business operations of Allumez. It was quite akin to multi-level marketing business strategy. However, Allumez allowed each associate to promote its own brand name, with negligible trademark marketing of Allumez. Allumez only handled backend web support system for all its associates and charged a fee based on revenue-sharing model.

Some of Allumez associates had insufficient infrastructure and expertise to perform high end web designing/development. In those cases, Allumez team located at its headquarters did the contract job for its associates to meet its requirements of their associate's further clients and charged extra on per assignment basis. Allumez InfoTech had high hopes in terms of revenue generation from its forthcoming project www.101dollarearningtips.com. Though, it had not been marketed to the outside world as of now, but as per the company officials, the organization was making profits even during it R&D phase.

THE NEXT BIG LEAP

Mr Parwinder and his top management team were all set to launch the biggest and dream project of Allumez till date. It took three years for Allumez's top management to plan various features of this project. The project had been named as www.101dollarearningtips.com. Mr Parwinder had been introspecting and drawing outlines on various challenges, ranging from pricing issues, promotional issues, security issues to other market competition related issues that the project might encounter. The top management was doing intensive background preparation so as to ensure successful accomplishment and effective execution of the project 'www.101dollarearningtips.com'.

7PS OF WWW.101DOLLAREARNINGTIPS.COM

Product

Www.101dollarearningtips.com business module would provide young minds an access and training on 101 fresh ideas to earn online. All the ideas mentioned would be best as per R&D done by the in-house experts of Allumez, including the top management. This project would be unique in comparison to other business ventures which generally involved substantial initial capital investment. With complete

Exhibit 6.5 | *Allumez Infotech Performance (2006–2011) (In Indian Rupees)*

	2006–07	2007–08	2008–09	2009–10	2010–11
Number of associates	1	13	19	37	70
Earnings through associate/s	25,000	3,25,000	4,75,000	9,25,000	17,50,000
Number of domains registered	1	70	120	210	300
Earnings through Advts. (Google Ad Sense, etc.)	3,000	2,10,000	3,60,000	6,30,000	9,00,000
Total revenue	28,000	5,35,000	8,35,000	15,55,000	26,50,000

Revenue Projections *(In Indian Rupees)*

	2011–12	2012–13	2013–14	2014–15	2015–16
Number of associates	137	268	399	525	700
Earnings through associate/s	34,25,000	67,00,000	99,75,000	1,31,25,000	1,75,00,000
Number of domains registered	375	469	633	918	1,376
Earnings through Advts. (Google Ad Sense, etc.)	11,25,000	14,06,250	18,98,438	27,52,734	41,29,102
Total revenue	45,50,000	81,06,250	1,18,73,438	1,58,77,734	2,16,29,102

Cost and Profit Projections *(In Indian Rupees)*

Cost Projections	2011–12	2012–13	2013–14	2014–15	2015–16
New domain and webspace registration	7,50,000	9,37,500	12,65,625	18,35,156	27,52,734
Website designing	15,00,000	18,75,000	25,31,250	36,70,313	55,05,469
Old registered domains renewal fees	5,38,000	7,72,375	10,88,781	15,47,570	22,35,754
Salaries and wages	3,00,000	330000	363000	399300	439230
Office rentals	35,000	38,500	42,350	46,585	51,244
Security deposit	1,00,000	–	–	–	–
Marketing budget	50,000	55,000	60,500	66,550	73,205
Total cost	32,73,000	40,08,375	53,51,506	75,65,474	1,10,57,636
Total revenue	45,50,000	81,06,250	1,18,73,438	1,58,77,734	2,16,29,102
Income	12,77,000	40,97,875	65,21,932	83,12,260	1,05,71,466

Source: Company Records

flexibility on financial investment, the only requirement to be a part of this ambitious business model was to join hands as an 'associate' with Allumez operations. After registering as an 'associate' with Allumez, each individual would be given an access to 101 ideas to earn online under certain terms and conditions. Consistent sincerity for aspiring entrepreneur/'associate' was one of the key conditions put forth by the company's CEO. He wanted few but determined 'associates' to be the part of this mega-project. According to the CEO Mr Parwinder, the ideas in www.101dollarearningtips.com business module would be divided into different slabs. Each 'associate' will have to perform upto certain threshold performance before s/he gets access to the next hierarchical stage of www.101dollarearningtips.com business module. The training, R&D support for next idea along with key strategies on how to earn more through that particular idea would be provided by Allumez. The CEO further stated that it was required by each 'associate' to generate a revenue of $500 (₹25,000) transaction before they would be exposed to the next idea under www.101dollarearningtips.com business module. Also in order to motivate the 'associate', after completion of the first stage, Allumez would gift an individual with new a domain, hosting and website of a second idea. Likewise, Allumez would give incentive at each stage, besides giving access to further ideas from www.101dollarearningtips.com.

Allumez would also provide complete consultancy report to its 'associate' which would not only include details regarding idea proposal but will also share training sessions and infrastructure that need to be deployed for achieving the desired goal. Allumez would give flexibility with the scheme, depending upon individual's interest and capacity to invest in the venture. Allumez's in-house team would provide complete operational and marketing training to its 'associate' on all ideas. If required, Allumez would help in recruiting manpower for its associates venture. The operational training for idea implementation would not be a time bound activity as it might vary from associate to associate. For instance, a heavy investor associate who desires to have its own dedicated servers or even call centres might require more training sessions in comparison to other associate who wants to commence venture with little initial capital.

For all the extended support required to make its associates venture successful, Allumez will not charge anything. Allumez would go for revenue-sharing model, once the business starts getting revenue. According to Mr Parwinder, www.101dollarearningtips.com business module had an enormous potential, and each idea out of 101 would have very wide scope and any associate can sustain his entire life by just sticking to one idea, however, that would not be recommended by Allumez. The organization would always foster its associates to continuously grow through increased revenue generation and get shifted to next slabs, thus getting exposed to further more ideas. Allumez's top management had designed its training curriculum of all ideas in very streamlined manner and all the parameters such as earning potential of particular idea, difficulty in grasping, security and others related issues had been fully taken care of.

Price

An exceptional product would certainly have a unique pricing strategy. There would be no price for joining www.101dollarearningtips.com business module. It involved no fixed initial capital investment. It would be a customized investment project as per capacity of each aspiring entrepreneur/associate. Once an individual will get registered as associate with Allumez, CEO and his team of analyst and programmers would formulate a project report for the concerned individual which would include all information regarding strategies and infrastructure that could be developed using the same amount. For instance, an individual who can afford high initial capital cost, the CEO and his team may recommend him to have his own dedicated servers or may guide him to have in-house data centre. Allumez had even plans for the individual who has nil initial investment capacity. The CEO Mr Parwinder believed that on imposing threshold in investment criteria, some of the interested candidates might feel reluctant in adopting the entrepreneurial path.

Promotion

Mr Parwinder knew that the www.101dollarearningtips.com required innovative marketing techniques, besides right positioning among the target population. Allumez planned to promote his dream project both online and offline. In the offline promotion, the target population would be any young candidate who was passionate enough to start his own business venture. However, during initial phase of offline promotion, the company desired to target young minds pursuing engineering courses. The senior management of Allumez believed that it would be easy to convince tech-savvy students of the present times as compared to other youths. Also the engineering students as part of their present curriculum were already exposed to theoretical and practical IT related knowledge. Due to social networking sites like Facebook, Orkut, LinkedIn and Twitter, these students were better exposed to online world. Hence, it was comparatively easy for Allumez to persuade them to start their own business and make them their future associates.

On the other hand, the company was not ready to compromise on its goal in promoting rural youth, as CEO Mr Parwinder had already decided to delegate the entire backend operational business of 101dollarearningtips.com to the students of Allumez's training institute. All the students of Allumez's training institute were from the rural community. Allumez would try to encourage its future associates to train and include rural community in their support team of their respective ventures. The top management had decided to target population that was below 26 years of age as they believed that success of any new business venture required high energy levels, higher risk-taking ability besides hard work and enthusiasm. These traits could be easily found among young college students.

Few students of various technical colleges had enrolled themselves for regular six months industrial training (mandatory in all engineering courses). They had been given assignments to promote www.101dollarearningtips.com during their training with a monthly stipend. They were being trained by professional trainers on various skills such as high impact presentations, effective communications and advanced IT skills. The training would also enable them to effectively deliver structured technical presentations while promoting www.101dollarearningtips.com. Interestingly, after getting inspired by Mr Parwinder's talks, some of the trainees have formed a partnership company named 'Youth2Business' to attract youth towards entrepreneurship. The CEO himself had planned to address some of the reputed technical schools as a part of the company's marketing campaign for www.101dollarearningtips.com.

In the online promotion, Allumez planned to use one of its domains, namely, www.dollarearningtips.com as a linkage source for its new project. It would be an open house platform for all creative individuals with unique ideas but are incapable of investing and promoting it further. The ideas would be kept confidential. In such cases, Allumez will either invest or will arrange investors, provided the idea was approved by a panellist comprising of experts from the IT industry. Undoubtedly, www.dollarearningtips.com being a meaningful user interactive domain name, may garner heavy traffic. Allumez planned to link it with their dream project www.101dollarearningtips.com so as to improve its visibility.

Allumez has associates who migrated abroad like United States, Europe and Australia and are operating and expanding their business from there. Allumez had planned to promote www.101dollarearningtips.com on international level through its associates. Recently, Allumez signed a contract with Indian Air Force (IAF), Ludhiana, to provide training on web development and web designing to select IAF personnel. Mr Parwinder has also planned to hold marketing campaigns regarding upcoming projects among household members of IAF residential colony.

Place

Though www.101dollarearningtips.com would be an online venture by Allumez, its entire support system would be controlled from Allumez's headquarters located in SAS Nagar or Mohali of Punjab. The majority of the Indian population still do not have confidence in e-business. People are apprehensive about their background and location. In order to address such concerns, Allumez had ensured its physical presence since its inception. Allumez's training institute is also located at its corporate office in Mohali, Punjab.

People

Allumez in its organizational structure had employees mainly from rural community. It was expecting high-tech IT specialists to be part of Allumez family as their future associates for its upcoming project, www.101dollarearningtips.com. Locating, inspiring and converting young rural prospects to start their own businesses has remained an ongoing activity in Allumez operations. In an effort to motivate Indian talent from rural community to join the organization, Allumez InfoTech was being actively assisted by its NGO 'DEC'. Presently, majority of youngsters from rural community of Punjab were crazy about foreign jobs because either their families are already settled there or the huge currency convertibility difference which impresses them. Hence, making them believe to start their own venture in India against the option to migrate to other countries was a quite tough task, which was being performed by NGO 'DEC'.

Process

The company had been doing its web hosting business and would operate its latest project on Linux-based operating servers and operating systems such as Fedora and Ubuntu instead of windows. The reason behind the usage of such technology was that it was less prone to virus attacks and was available for free of cost. As far as the database was concerned, Allumez had been always using MYSQL. PHP and JAVA were the two server side technologies being used in all assignments of Allumez.

Physical Evidence

Allumez had sufficient infrastructure to sustain any large project like www.101dollarearningtips.com. Starting from manpower to technological resources, the latest physical state-of-the-art resources at Allumez would certainly give the 'associates' a nice experience and boost their confidence for being associated with Allumez.

NEXT 5 YEARS

After three years of involvement in the planning phase, Allumez plans to expand and market its unique idea of www.101dollarearningtips.com for the next five years. Allumez had plans to convert at least 700 prospects as 'associates' in coming five years along with expansion of its infrastructure. It had already started grooming its support staff at its in-house training school on various subjects, such as web development, web designing, search engine optimization and other IT tools for its new project, www.101dollarearningtips.com. The support staff would be mentored by subject matter experts.

FINANCIAL POTENTIAL

As per the company officials, www.101dollarearningtips.com had immense earning potential. Also India is rated as one of the best destinations to start any IT-related business because of low cost skilled and semi-skilled manpower, large English-speaking population, IT environment friendly government policy as compared to other developed and developing countries. Allumez started personal web hosting business as it was a very lucrative product line and had enormous untapped business potential. Presently across the world there were approx 1.2 million registered domains; with 70 million booked only in the United States. India was quite lagging as it had only close to 0.6 million domains registered thus capturing only 0.5 per cent of total market share[4]. The logic behind revenue generation in web hosting business was quite simple and acted as source of income for an entire life time. For instance, one of the leading web hosting companies in the United States had more than 40 million domains registered. Each domain was sold out for subscription fees of approximately $12 yearly; however, it cost $9 to the hosting company. Thus, the company had been making a recurring profit of approximately 120 million each year (40 million*$3).

Mr Parwinder had many interesting statistics to highlight high revenue potential in web hosting business. He shared his experience of his friend's visit who was working as business development executive (BDE) in one of the New Delhi (Capital of India) based multi-level software marketing organizations. His friend's organization had similar web hosting business model and was selling domain, web space and doing CMS (Content Management System). His friend readily shared his first performance appraisal results with Mr Parwinder. He had successfully completed the target of 80 sales during his first quarter of the year and received an incentive of ₹25,000 by the company. Then, Mr Parwinder showed the monetary difference to his friend which he would have received if he had been running the same web hosting business on his own. His friend's company was selling its complete web site package for ₹7500 by selling 80 packages; the company increased its revenue by ₹6 lakhs (0.6 million). However, the actual costing of the product to the web hosting company was under ₹1 lakhs (0.1 million). Thus, the company made a profit of nearly ₹5 lakhs (0.5 million) in just one quarter through one BDE; out of which only 5 per cent was shared with the employees. These interesting figures by Mr Parwinder surprised his friend and the friend had decided to become a future associate with Allumez and run his own business.

Thus, web hosting profession was a very profitable business. Interestingly, web hosting would be one of the ideas in entire www.101dollarearningtips.com gamut as disclosed by the CEO. Besides, there are hundred more ideas to earn online. Therefore, www.101dollarearningtips.com had the potential to be a lucrative platform to initiate entrepreneurial career.

WHY INDIA?

In comparison to the United States and other developed countries, Indian IT industry had very less operational overheads. Presently, Indian SME in IT business has employed workforce, whose average salary ranged from 10,000 to 15,000 per month; however, in the United States workforce was paid about $200 per day. Hence, it was quite appropriate to choose India as the destination to start any kind of operations.

Secondly, as per latest reports titled 'Internet's New bn', by the Boston Consulting Group (BCG), India would see its number of Internet users triple to 237 million by 2015, from 81 million registered in September 2010. Further Internet penetration rate in India was expected to reach 19 per cent by 2015, up from the current 7 per cent[5]. Because of the huge demand expected by experts in IT industry, it may a good decision for young minds to initiate any kind of IT-related business in India.

LOOKING FOR 'PLAN B'

Though Mr Parwinder had already developed Plan A to execute his dream project, he anticipated numerous challenges as he was discussing expansion road map with his team for www.101dollarearningtips.com. Being confident on product attributes, the CEO was still further brainstorming on ways to strengthen various parameters of marketing, such as pricing, promotion, revenue model and STP (segmentation, targeting and positioning), which will play pivot role in the acceptance of the project. Though he had planned to launch it in separate phases but was looking for more innovative ways through which he could effectively promote his unique product. The stakes for Allumez were high as it took a lot of time to develop complete product, that is, www.101dollarearningtips.com. Market awareness on various ways of earning through online was quite low in India. Also due to large number of counterfeit web sites, people may feel reluctant to show their involvement in any online business model. Mr Parwinder was discussing with his management team so as to come up with Plan B for its marketing strategy; in case the present marketing strategy for www.101dollarearningtips.com fails to get the desired response from the target population.

DISCUSSION QUESTIONS

1. What do you mean by 'social marketing'? Do you agree that Allumez InfoTech is following social marketing approach for attracting the rural youth for IT-based training modules? Suggest innovative social marketing tools for Allumez InfoTech so as to attract more number of talented rural youths from the state.
2. What are the current revenue sources of Allumez InfoTech? Suggest new product lines and innovative profit sharing models so as enhance the revenue sources of Allumez InfoTech.
3. Discuss the similarities and differences between Allumez InfoTech business model and a multilevel marketing (MLM) business model.
4. What is the future of bioinformatics with regard to web-based service delivery? How can Allumez InfoTech leverage its core competence of IT-enabled services to generate more revenue through its engagement in bioinformatics domain?
5. Should CEO Mr Parwinder consider a detailed marketing research programme before deciding on his marketing strategy for www.101dollarearningtips.com? If so, what are the marketing areas he should research on? Should he hire a marketing research agency?
6. What should be the future marketing strategy of Allumez InfoTech, given its wide product portfolio and IT industry scenario?
7. Suggest Plan B for marketing strategy of www.101dollarearningtips.com, in case the Plan A did not give the desired result.

ENDNOTES

1. Allumez InfoTech would be referred to as Allumez.
2. http://www.ibef.org/artdispview.aspx?in=38&art_id=28792&cat_id=121&page=2, accessed 2 December 2011.
3. http://www3.qeh.ox.ac.uk/slptmd/Newman-Ross.pdf, accessed 2 December 2011.
4. http://www.hostingfunda.com, accessed on 1 December 2011.
5. http://www.ibef.org/artdispview.aspx?in=38&art_id=28792&cat_id=121&page=2, accessed 2 December 2011.

REFERENCE

http://www.mapsofindia.com, accessed December 5, 2011.

7

Moniba Pumps: The Sales Enigma

It was a Thursday afternoon of March 2010 and Mr Rakesh B. Engineer, Managing Director, Moniba Anand Electricals Private Limited (MAEPL), was mulling over the reasons for the decreasing sales growth rate of Moniba industrial pumps. He was confident that in terms of technology and quality, Moniba Pumps was superior to their competitors. His presumption was that if marketing and sales were effectively managed, the Moniba brand could become the market leader in a specific class of industrial pumps. It was an enigma for Mr Rakesh that in spite of being superior in technology, quality and reliability, the company was not presently performing well in sales.

MONIBA PUMPS

Moniba is the brand name of products from MAEPL, Mumbai. This organization started as a sister concern of Waterman Industries Limited, which was established in 1972 (Exhibit 7.1). MAEPL started manufacturing water purifiers to provide bacteria-free and virus-free water for the domestic and industrial market. However, later on, Mr Rakesh B. Engineer, a mechanical engineer turned entrepreneur (Exhibit 7.2), decided to add the industrial pumps to its product portfolio. Innovation and new product development was his passion. As a result, year after year, high quality innovative pumps (Exhibit 7.3) were consistently introduced by involving company engineers, vendors and customer feedback.

MAEPL (henceforth, MAEPL is referred to as Moniba Pumps[1]) is an ISO 9001:2000 certified manufacturing and trading organization in Mumbai and an exporter of superlative Moniba AODD pumps, double diaphragm pumps, portable submersible sewage pumps, sealless magnetic driven pumps, polypropylene pumps, electronic metering pumps and other allied products. Besides manufacturing a comprehensive range of industrial pumps, Moniba Pumps also imported AODD pumps from Belgium and marketed them in India. It was also the only distributor of Verde Air Double Diaphragm pumps in India which was originally produced by Verder Air, Belgium. All these products were trusted by leading industries and Moniba had clients like Reliance, IOCL, L&T, HAL and various other major industrial organizations (Exhibit 7.4). Moniba Pumps was also exporting some of its products to the United Kingdom.

Exhibit 7.1 | *Evolution of Moniba Pumps*

Mr Rakesh B. Engineer joined Waterman Industries Limited in 1984 to assist his elder brother. During that time, Waterman Industries Limited had the largest market share in the industrial chemical pumps category. In 1993–1994, Mr Rakesh B. Engineer's elder brother added water purifiers into their product line by the brand name of Moniba Pumps and sold the product for two years. However, Moniba Pumps was not able to garner a good market share. Hence, in 1996 they had a collaboration with a family friend's company named Batliboi Limited, and as per the collaboration agreement they sold their water purifiers jointly by the brand name Moniba Batliboi Limited till 1998. However, in 1998 Videocon came into picture and Waterman Industries started selling their entire water purifier inventory to Videocon, with the condition that Moniba Batliboi Limited would not sell its water purifier products in the market. However, this agreement could not last longer than a year because of the mounting payment disputes between Videocon and Waterman Industries. Ultimately, the plant of water purifiers was shut down by Mr Rakesh B. Engineer's elder brother. Till this time, Mr Rakesh B. Engineer was looking after industrial pumps. He took another challenge of reviving water purifiers from where his brother had left in late 1999 under the brand name Moniba Pumps. Mr Rakesh focused on his core competence of new product development (NPD) and marketing. He hired 20 new marketing executives along with a general manager who was then working with Bajaj. By 2002, though Moniba Pumps' turnover reached 6 crores, the company was still in loss of nearly 1 crore after 3 years of operations. This happened due to disproportionate advertising budget and huge loan from the bank. Ultimately, the water purifier unit was shut down in 2002. Since then, Moniba Pumps has been totally focusing only on industrial chemical pumps.

Source: www.monibapumps.net and interview with Rakesh B. Engineer, dated 22 May 2010

Exhibit 7.2 | *Profile of Mr Rakesh B. Engineer, MD*

Mr Rakesh B. Engineer, Managing Director of MAEPL (Moniba Pumps), graduated as a mechanical engineer in 1984. Soon after the graduation in 1984, he joined Waterman Industries—the family-run business of manufacturing and trading pumps. He increased the volume of the business from the manufacturing of just 30 pumps per month to 1,000 pumps per month within a few years of his joining at Waterman Industries. Innovation and new product development has always remained a passion and the focus area for Mr Rakesh B. Engineer. Since 1999, he has led MAEPL into the manufacturing of all kinds of industrial chemical pumps. A Bangalore University graduate, he is a very dynamic, versatile and challenge-loving person. He has taken a lot of responsibilities of Moniba Pumps on his shoulders. Mr Rakesh B. Engineer is eagerly waiting for his son to join him who is about to complete his post-graduation in engineering from California University. A combination of traits such as sincerity, perseverance, commitment and innovative bent of mind is what makes Mr Rakesh B. Engineer a successful entrepreneur. He started off his carrier jointly with his elder brother, remained together for 15 years and ultimately started of his own entrepreneurial career in 1999.

Source: Interview with Rakesh B. Engineer, dated 23 May 2010

Moniba Pumps represents millions of SMEs (Small and Medium Enterprises[2]) dotting across India, that contribute to 40 per cent of the country's GDP and 50 per cent of exports. The SMEs in India provide employment to approximately 40 million people.[3] Many organizations start as an SME and

Exhibit 7.3 | *Product Launch by Moniba Pumps*

Year	Products Introduced by Moniba Pumps
1991	Handy vacuum cleaner*
1992	Instant cooler cum water purifier*
1993	Trading of blag don AODD pump to UK*
1996	Magnetic seal-less pump*
1999	Polypropylene pump
2001	First fabricated SS (stainless steel) pump (CEMRON)
2002	5 mm SS sheet die press pump in technical collaboration with Mencarelli Italy
2003	Portable submersible pump
2004	SS investment casting self-priming and rubber impeller pump
2006	Peristaltic hose pump with technical collaboration from Ragazinni, Italy
2006	Manufacturing of AODD pump
2007	Verder imported AODD pump
2008	SS investment casting pump

** with Waterman Industries*
Source: www.monibapumps.net

later scale up into bigger corporations. The SME organizations in India like MAEPL run on a unique business and revenue model. The SMEs, in spite of contributing immensely to the industrial growth of the country, suffer from a low capital base, lack of professionalism and infusion of modern management practices. The delegation of power is lacking and the concentration of management is in few hands.

The Government of India is supporting SMEs through easy bank credit facilities, infrastructural support, skill development and technology upgradation. Moniba Pumps is SME with a strength of 32 dedicated employees with an annual turnover of about 2 crores (20 million rupees). It includes 1.5 crores (15 million rupees) from its own manufacturing pumps and 50 lakhs (5 million rupees) from its trading products which it bought from other manufacturing companies. In the trading business of Moniba Pumps, some of the pump categories are sold under the Moniba brand, while some pump categories are sold with the original brand name with Moniba Pumps acting as an exclusive distributor.

MARKETING DEPARTMENT

Moniba Pumps' marketing department is headed by its managing director. Next in the hierarchy is Mr Shenoy who has been given the responsibility of follow-up with customers to whom quotations had already been sent from the organization. Mr Shenoy is in his sixties and recently retired from an MNC as production manager in a manufacturing organization. He also assisted the MD, Mr Rakesh, in monitoring day-to-day sales activities of the organization.

The company had only one sales engineer, Mr Kapil Patil, who was responsible for giving quotations and handled all enquiries posted by clients through phone, postal mail and email from all across India as per the requirement. The average number of enquiries that Mr Kapil Patil received each day ranged from 10 to 15. Only 65 per cent of the enquiries were being answered within a specific lead time, that is, 3 days (72 hours) and the rest of the enquiries exceeded the stipulated lead time. The company did not have any other sales engineer, but for Mr Kapil Patil, to take the follow-up of the quotations sent to

Exhibit 7.4 | *Key Clients and Competitors*

Key Clients

1.	Apcotex Lattices Ltd, Secunderabad
2.	Apex Corp, Indore
3.	Asian Paints Ltd, New Delhi
4.	Bharatiya Communications, Calcutta
5.	Hotel Samrat, Delhi
6.	HAL
7.	IOCL
8.	Larsen & Toubro
9.	Radisson Hotel, Delhi
10.	Reliance
11.	Hotel Kemps, Ooty
12.	Centaur Hotel, Mumbai
13.	Nanavati Hospital, Mumbai
14.	Air India, Mumbai
15.	Southern Railway, Mysore

Key Competitors

1.	Kirloskar Pumps
2.	KSB Pumps
3.	Antico Pumps
4.	Raje-Dia Pumps
5.	Kweng Alloys
6.	Macbow Pumps

Source: Company records

clients. Due to his excessive workload, Mr Kapil was unable to devote adequate attention to the follow-up activities. Recently, the appointment of Mr Shenoy was done to fill this gap.

The conversion rate from prospects (who asked for quotations) to actual customers (who placed the order) was approximately 10 per cent. Mr Rakesh had given Mr Kapil and Mr Shenoy a conversion target of 15 per cent for the next year, that is, 2010–2011. The process of lead generation was carried out only through secondary sources such as directories, yellow pages and CDs obtained from industrial associations. Four marketing executives reported to Mr Kapil and MD, Mr Rakesh. Out of these four marketing executives, two were recently appointed. Mr Hemant looked after Gujarat, Rajasthan and Madhya Pradesh; Mr Rahul was in charge for Maharashtra; Mr Vijay looked after Mumbai; Mr Ajit looked after northern India; and Mr Sarkar was responsible for the eastern region (Exhibit 7.5). All these executives had been given the responsibility to increase the customer base, besides expanding and setting up new distribution channels. The marketing executive's roles included generating leads, getting queries filled by the customer and passing the same to sales engineer Mr Kapil Patil, who was stationed at the head office in Mumbai. However, all marketing executives had been informed to get familiar with all technical specifications within a month so that they would be capable enough to generate quotations on their own instead of being dependent on Mr Kapil Patil.

Exhibit 7.5 | *Marketing Department*

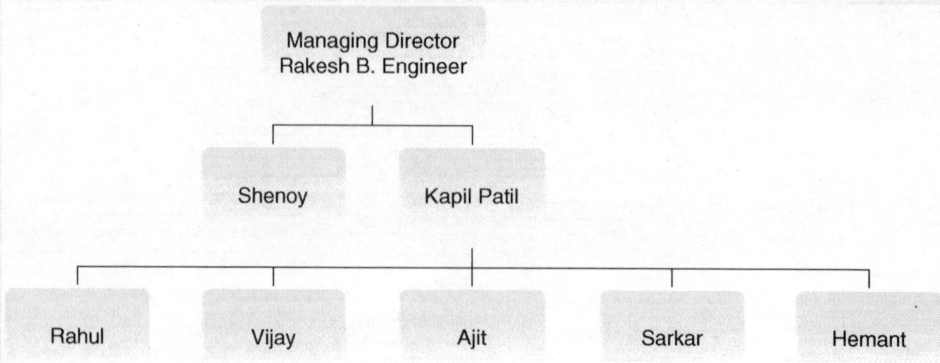

Source: Interview with Rakesh B. Engineer, dated 27 May 2010

MARKETING MIX OF MONIBA PUMPS

Moniba Pumps had a wide range of product line which comprised its own manufactured products as well as trading products which it bought from other manufacturing organizations and sold as a distributor and some under its own brand name. There was a total of 13 products out of which 8 were manufactured and the remaining 5 were traded products. Despite being equipped with the latest technology and superior quality, decreasing sales of these products was a major concern for Moniba Pumps.

Manufactured Products

Polypropylene Pumps (PP)/PVDF/PFA

Moniba Pumps started manufacturing Polypropylene Pumps (PP)/PVDF/PFA in 1999 (Exhibit 7.3). It is widely used in the paper industry, fertilizer plants, and thermal and atomic power plants. The sale of this pump was a concern for the company despite being excellent in quality. Its competitors such as Antico Pumps, Raje-Dia Pumps and Swaraj Pumps had a complete hold over the market. According to company officials, low sale of PP pumps was due to Moniba being a late entrant in this pump category. Usually, customers are satisfied with the competitor's products. Moreover, these customers have already maintained an inventory of spare parts such as impeller, casing, inlet, etc., of the competitor's products. This inventory issue was a major roadblock for Moniba in acquiring new customers. Keeping multi-brand inventory spares was not desirable by a customer. So, acquiring new customers and motivating existing customers to switch to Polypropylene pumps was an area of concern for Moniba.

Portable Submersible Sewage Pumps

A portable submersible sewage pump was specially designed for applications such as the drainage of sewage water and septic tanks, of dirty water or drainage in small purifying installations. Such sewage pumps were most economical and reliable to handle water with suspended solid. Moniba Pumps was a market leader in this category of pumps. The sales of this pump, since its manufacturing in 2003 (Exhibit 7.3), was high as compared to its competitors such as Darling Pumps and Modi Pumps.

Peristaltic Hose Pumps

The peristaltic hose pump had a wide range of applications as it could be used to transfer all types of liquids, paste, viscous liquids, and abrasive and corrosive liquids in almost all types of industries. The manufacturing of this pump started in 2006 (Exhibit 7.3) with technical collaboration with Ragazinni, Italy. Moniba Pumps was a market leader in this category as there was hardly any competitor in India. However, it was only used for laboratory applications in India. The sales of peristaltic hose pumps for industry applications were negligible due to lack of awareness about the product and its usage.

Self-priming SS (Stainless Steel) Pumps (CEMRON)

Moniba Pumps started the manufacturing of self-priming SS (stainless steel) pumps (CEMRON) in 2001 (Exhibit 7.3). Despite being an early entrant than its competitors such as Investa Pumps, KSB Pumps, etc, sales were not up to the mark.

In-line Self-priming SS (Stainless Steel) Pumps

Moniba recently started manufacturing in-line self priming SS (stainless steel) pumps keeping in mind specific applications such as salt water pumping, water treatment, in-line booster for chemical pipe line, chemical pumping like caustic transfer, acid unloading, and monomer and polymer transfer. The sales of competitors such as Investa Pumps were far ahead than Moniba Pumps, as Moniba was a late entrant in this pump category. Also, the huge stock of spare parts inventory for the existing products was a negative inertia for switching to the Moniba brand.

SS 316 (CF&M) Centrifugal Pumps (Investment Casting)

A similar problem existed in the case with SS 316 (CF&M) centrifugal pump (investment casting), that Moniba started manufacturing in 2004 (Exhibit 7.3). The product was best in quality and technology. It had extensive applications in chemical solutions, industrial liquids, petrochemicals, electroplating solutions, food products and pharmaceuticals. However, the market demand of Moniba Pumps in this category was quite low as compared to its competitors such as Sulzer Pumps, KSB Pumps and Johnson Pumps, as Moniba was a late entrant in the market and the spare part inventory acted as inertia for new buyers.

AODD (Air Operated Double Diaphragm)

Innovation and new product development had always remained the passion of MD Mr Rakesh. As a result, again in 2006 (Exhibit 7.3), high quality AODD (air operated double diaphragm) pumps were introduced for handling abrasive, adhesive, cement ceramics, drilling, inks and dyes. It was also widely used in food oils, pharmaceuticals and the plating industry. The sales of AODD pumps manufactured by Moniba Pumps had always been in high demand as compared to its competitors. The product was free from problems such as leakage, had variable flow, ability to run dry, lighter weight, self priming with no foot valve required, and most importantly it stopped automatically on closing the discharge valve. Moniba was closely monitoring the high sales of its own manufactured AODD pumps vis-à-vis Verder Air double diaphragm pumps, produced by Verder Air, Belgium.

AP-50 Pumps

Moniba also manufactured AP-50 pumps and exported it to Blackdon Pumps, United Kingdom. This product was a cash cow for Moniba.

Quality and technology for Moniba Pumps had never remained an issue as per the company officials. Production and service of all the manufactured pumps in Moniba Pumps was carried out by the manufacturing personnel. As such, there is no separate service or maintenance department in the company. During complaint calls, depending upon the availability of the workforce and the raw material, the customer's problem was handled.

Trading Products

The sales of trading products were also an area of concern, according to MD Mr Rakesh B. Engineer.

Barrel Pumps

Barrel pumps were suitable for handling any type of chemicals or viscous liquids. It was one of the trading products of Moniba Pumps. The company received tough competition in this particular pump from Mandar Pumps. According to company officials, the vendor provided the product with excellent quality but there were a lot of problems and inconveniences in logistics, ease of availability and after-sales service. The service engineer, in spite of being trained by the vendor, was not very comfortable with the trading products.

Seal-less Magnetic Driven Pumps

Moniba Pumps was doing quite well in terms of sales in another trading product known as a seal-less magnetic driven pump, leaving its competitors such as Kweng Alloys and Macbow Pumps far behind. This product category had its extensive application especially where thin liquids were involved, namely, chemical, pharmaceutical, textile processing, dye baths, electroplating industries, metal finishing machines, filtration units, general laboratories and ultrasonic cleaners.

Metering and Dosing Pumps

The metering and dosing pump was another bought-out pump being traded by Moniba in the industrial market. It was widely used in the pharmaceutical, food and chemical industry. The sales of this product had always remained an issue with the company because of the high price from the vendor. Excellent quality and appropriate logistics was one of the key factors in metering and dosing pumps. After-sales service from the vendor was a serious issue and a majority of Moniba Pumps service engineers had inadequate product knowledge for this category of pumps. This had increased customer dissatisfaction with metering and dosing pumps from Moniba.

Muddy Water Self-priming Pumps

This was widely used for sewage, dewatering basements, trenches, swimming pools, construction sites, for desk wash and engine cooling, or any application where priming had to be avoided. This was another product which Moniba Pumps traded and was facing tough competition from Kirloskar Pumps, KSB Pumps and Suzlar Pumps. Despite a high demand in the market, receding sales of this product because of inappropriate in-bound logistics had become a key concern for the organization.

Centrifugal Back Pullout-type Pumps

These were widely used for pumping clear or turbid water up to 3,000 PPM. It was ideally suited to circulating systems in industries, irrigations, sprinkler systems, booster service, fire fighting, air-conditioning and pumping liquids having a temperature in the range of 10 to 100 degrees. The sales had always remained an issue because of a high price by the vendor for this product. Moniba Pumps also suffered from poor in-bound logistics and after-sales problems from the vendor side.

Nearly all the trading products faced logistics issues. The vendor's inability to provide after-sales service or repair due to some reasons, along with the lack of product knowledge of trading products with Moniba Pumps service engineers, had compounded customer dissatisfaction level for most of the trading products.

Distribution and Logistics

Recently, Moniba has appointed four marketing executives for different states, such as Gujarat, Rajasthan, Madhya Pradesh, Maharashtra, northern India, and eastern India. Mumbai was appointed separately due to its high potential. The new marketing executives' mandate was to increase the customer base and set up new distribution channels in the above states (Exhibit 7.6). There was no specific market analysis by Moniba Pumps while entering into these markets.

The brand and product awareness of Moniba Pumps was relatively low in these regions as per the opinion of MD Mr Rakesh. Apart from that, the company also had four technical dealers (who deal specifically with chemical pumps) in regions like Andhra Pradesh, Baddi, Bangalore and Chennai, apart from 30 inactive non-technical (who do not specifically deal in chemical pumps) dealers. These 30 non-technical dealers worked purely on a commission basis. They were spread over various parts of India. On receiving the order, it took nearly 7–12 days for a product to be dispatched. The company used private shared transportation for sending its products to the different states and cities of India.

Promotion

Moniba Pumps experimented with various modes of advertisement in the past few years. In 2001–2002, Moniba Pumps used yellow pages of all districts as a mode of advertisement. However, from 2003–2004, Moniba Pumps focused more on exhibitions where they used to display their products. The company displayed its product line in approximately 6–7 exhibitions each year. In 2005–2006, the company advertised its products in about 20 magazines.

Exhibit 7.6 | *Distribution Channel*

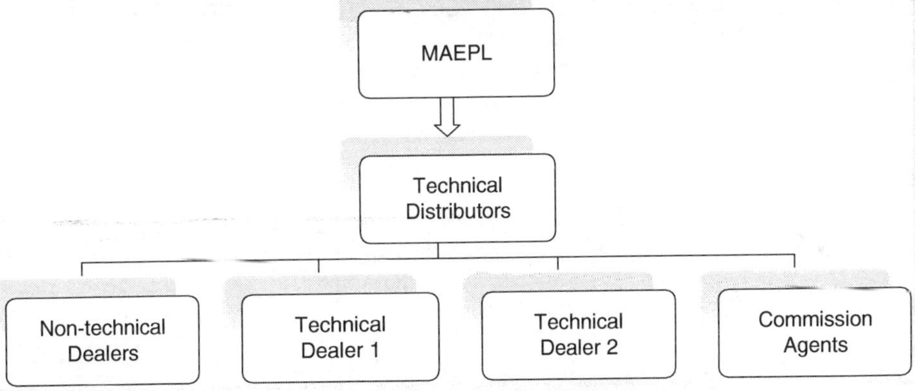

Source: Interview with Mr Hemant (Marketing Executive), dated 28 May 2010

In 2007–2008, 'yellow pages' besides magazines were used as a medium. However, in 2008–2010, an innovative way of promotion comprising glossy handouts/pamphlets of each product with clear specifications, along with the pros and cons of the product, were colour-printed and sent in the form of mailers to the target market by taking data from industrial directories. In 2010–2011, in addition to handouts, the system of bulk email was started with a reminder every 15 days. This proved to be very efficient as it had increased the company's sales by 24 per cent in comparison to the previous year's sales. Since its inception, Moniba Pumps regularly used to give advertisements in local newspapers.

ORGANIZATIONAL CULTURE

There was no fixed hierarchy in the organization. The production capacity of Moniba Pumps was 120 pumps per month. However, as of now, only 30 pumps were being produced each month. Moniba Pumps had some of its orders pending. The entire workforce was on a fixed salary in contrast to other manufacturing units located nearby where the total salary consisted of a fixed salary and a variable salary depending upon the performance.

As per company officials, a lot of changes had been observed in the shop floor employee behaviour. For instance, as per company policy, every worker on the shop floor was supposed to fill up a leave form and get it duly signed from the head supervisor before taking a leave. However, since a few months, workers on the shop floor did not find it important to abide by the company's rules as quoted by Mr Patil (Head Supervisor, Shop Floor). In the past, the culture inside the organization was quite good. It involved standing meetings between the managing director and all employees so as to understand the employees' problems and feedback were recorded for further action. However, such meetings have not taken place since the last one year.

PROCESS FLOW

Moniba Pumps' operations involved five main steps (Exhibit 7.7). Raw material from the inventory department was brought to the shop floor and raw materials such as castings were inspected manually in order to check their basic dimensions. After a basic inspection, machining was done, which involved working on jobs with the help of lathes, drilling machines, etc. This was followed by the manual inspection of specific minute dimensions of jobs by the company's quality control personnel. As soon as it was approved by the quality control personnel, the raw materials were sent for painting, if required. The approved raw materials were painted green. After inspection and painting of sub-parts, they were moved on to the assembly floor where all the sub-parts were joined to form a complete product. The development of a complete product was followed by a rigorous testing process, followed by packaging and dispatching. As far as the layout of machines was concerned, they had been placed depending upon the space available.

Exhibit 7.7 | *Manufacturing Process at Moniba Pumps*

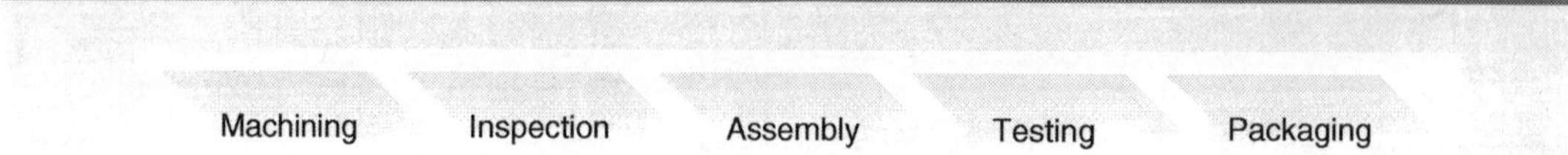

Source: Interview with head supervisor (shop floor), dated 28 May 2010

INVENTORY MANAGEMENT OF MANUFACTURED PUMPS

Moniba Pumps followed a simple logic while maintaining the stock of its manufactured pumps. According to Mr Rakesh B. Engineer, the company followed a simple rule which involved the total production of all the pumps in the year. The production of a specific type of pump for the entire year was taken into account and dividing that number by 12 gave the number of specific pumps that had to be kept in stock per month as per company's policy. For example, according to the production data sheet (Exhibit 7.8), the company manufactured a total of 637 pumps in 2007–2008. Hence, 637/12 = 53 pumps is the total

Exhibit 7.8 | *Production Record as Maintained by MAEPL*

Production for 2007–2008

Product	April	May	June	July	Aug	Sept	Oct	Nov	Dec	Jan	Feb	Mar
PP/PVDF	10	6	31	39	38	19	21	14	3	11	17	19
AP-50	1	0	0	0	0	40	1	0	2	0		5
Sewage	8	23	6	21	12	3	0	4	4	2	17	7
Hose Pump	0	0	0	0	2	1	0	1	1	0	1	1
SS Pump	5	10	3	2	1	2	4	12	1	7	3	5
Magnetic Pump	2	3	6	1	1	3	2	1	10	1	0	6
AODD Pump	1	7	4	15	4	4	4	4	5	11	13	10
Metering Pump	5	0	6	1	0	0	2	0	0	0	2	0
Cemron Pump	1	0	3	4	2	2	2	0	6	4	1	2
Coller	6	2	0	3	1	0	0	0	0	0	0	0
Barrel Pump	1	0	0	2	1	3	0	0	0	1	0	0
Slurry Pump	0	1	0	0	1	2	2	0	0	0	4	0
TOTAL	40	52	59	88	63	79	38	36	32	37	58	55

Production for 2008–2009

Product	April	May	June	July	Aug	Sept	Oct	Nov	Dec	Jan	Feb	Mar
PP/PVDF	8	15	13	27	14	30	6	16	34	23	17	27
AP-50	0	0	1	0	0	28	20	1	0	0	0	0
Sewage	2	15	13	6	7	3	10	13	2	6	1	7
Hose Pump	0	1	0	0	0	0	1	3	1	1	1	0
SS Pump	2	1	6	10	6	4	1	8	14	6	7	3
Magnetic Pump	2	18	6	2	0	5	0	0	6	0	2	2
AODD Pump	7	7	10	8	3	7	11	7	7	9	9	8
Metering Pump	2	0	0	1	2	2	0	0	0	0	0	0
Cemron Pump	0	6	2	3	1	2	1	3	0	1	3	2
Coller	0	1	17	0	0	0	0	3	0	0	0	0
Barrel Pump	0	0	4	0	0	1	1	3	0	0	3	1
Slurry Pump	0	5	0	1	0	2	1	0	0	0	3	2
TOTAL	23	69	72	58	33	84	52	57	64	46	46	52

Source: Company records

number of pumps Moniba would try to maintain in stock per month for the next year. Further, the company manufactured 228 PP/PVDF pumps in 2007–2008. Thus, 228/12 = 19 pumps is the total number of PP/PVDF pumps that Moniba endeavoured to maintain in stock per month for the following year.

INVENTORY MANAGEMENT OF RAW MATERIAL

Moniba Pumps had manual inventory management system. According to company officials, raw materials were generally available in stock but sometimes a particular sub-part of some pumps had shortage because of the prevalent manual management system. Keeping record of very small components through the manual management system sometimes became difficult and was also easily susceptible to human errors. This shortage resulted in delays in delivery of the final products. Also, sometimes the number of sub-parts was larger in inventory than actually required, due to which the company incurred various types of inventory costs.

E-INTERFACE

Moniba Pumps had maintained an e-interface (Web portal) for its customers by the name of www.moniba.net. The portal gave information about industrial chemical pumps manufactured and marketed by Moniba Pumps. Lately, customization had been implemented inside the Web portal through which customers could generate a query regarding their requirement by filling important parameters such as the liquid to be handled, capacity, viscosity, specific gravity, suction head, discharge head, solid size and temperature. However, the queries generated through the e-interface were being handled without any specific standard response time.

EMERGING ISSUES

Decreasing Sales

Managing Director, Mr Rakesh B. Engineer, was worried about the decreasing sales of Moniba Pumps. He was wondering if he should decrease the cost so as to increase the sales revenue of the company. However, decreasing the cost would have given a negative signal to the clients that the product quality was inferior. Mr Rakesh and the management team working with him were passionate and enthusiastic about devising methods for enhancing the sales of Moniba Pumps; however, the shop floor workers were passive towards this effort. Though the shop floor workers were not directly involved in the marketing of products, many a time there were orders pending due to absenteeism and employee turnover. Mr Rakesh also thought of recruiting more sales persons so as to increase the sales in spite of the fact that it would further add to the cost in the short run. He was not sure why the sales of pumps were going down month by month. He regularly exhorted his sales team for exerting more effort towards increasing the sales revenue of MAEPL.

Locating Technical Dealers and Distributors

Moniba Pumps dealt with technical industrial products. Technical implies chemical industrial pumps which required a full awareness of all kinds of liquids, acids, concepts like viscosity and specific gravity. Identifying such distributors and dealers capable of handling a technical query and submitting quotations was a matter of concern for the company. The flow of quotation handling was such that dealers, whether active, inactive (who worked purely on commission basis), non-technical (who did not deal in industrial chemical pumps), and Moniba marketing executives sent queries from customers to a single point, that is, to the sales engineer Mr Kapil Patil available at the corporate office in Mumbai.

In reply, Mr Kapil Patil provided dealers with the best available recommended product and quotation. The dealer/marketing executive further recommended it to the customer.

Increasing Attrition Rate

The company was also facing attrition issues. The availability of an adequate number of shop floor workers for smooth production was increasingly becoming a matter of concern. In the recent past, one of the sales persons resigned and joined another company. According to Mr Rakesh, once employees gain a certain amount of experience, they switch to another company at a higher salary though the salary structure at Moniba Pumps was as per the industry norms.

OPTIONS AVAILABLE

MD Mr Rakesh was mulling over various options that would lead to increase in sales. These included the following options.

Recruiting More Sales Engineers

Recruiting at least another sales engineer or more was one of the options available for Mr Rakesh. This would not only balance the workload of Mr Kapil Patil but would also improve his efficiency by reducing his work-related stress. Further, it could also help in increasing customer satisfaction and help customers in getting better services in the form of timely response to quotations and other marketing-related issues. If the company appointed another sales engineer, an aggressive approach may be followed. The present reactive approach would be replaced by a proactive planning. This could lead to higher customer conversion rates and increased sales revenue.

Implementing Customer Relationship Management Effectively

Another option could be the implementation of formal customer relationship management (CRM) at Moniba Pumps. Maintaining customer relationships would give a feeling of recognition among customers, which would ultimately increase customer loyalty. A formal customer relationship management would spread a positive word of mouth for Moniba Pumps amongst prospective clients. CRM is considered to be one of the best and most effective tools of marketing, and given the prevailing conditions at Moniba Pumps there is no reason to believe why the sales would not increase with the implementation of a formal CRM.

Aggressive Lead Generation Process

A drastic change in the lead generation process was another option available with Mr Rakesh. Instead of being entirely dependent on secondary sources such as yellow pages, directories and CDs from industry associations, an aggressive initiative needs to be taken by marketing executives to locate the new industries coming up in their respective areas. Also, managing relationships with contractors and builders was imperative since they may recommend Moniba in their various infrastructural projects. The dealers may also be given a target to provide at least 10 leads every month to Moniba Pumps. This approach had the potential of enhancing sales to a great extent. The conversion rate of the provided leads for prospective clients would be quite high due to high quality products from Moniba Pumps.

Wait for His Son

Instead of bringing in any changes in the present system at Moniba Pumps, another option was that Mr Rakesh should wait for his son to return to India. His son was completing his post-graduation in engineering from California University and would be joining the business the following month.

Mr Rakesh was keen that his son should take over as the managing director of the company. He wanted to be relieved from day-to-day involvement in the company and wanted to play the role of a mentor. As his son was going to take over the reins of the company in the coming years, all major initiatives required his consent and involvement. Mr Rakesh had an ambitious plan of scaling the operations to next higher level in order to become a bigger player. He planned to discuss it with his son upon his return to India as it involved huge bank loan liabilities.

Selling-off

Mr Rakesh was also mulling over the option of selling-off the entire business. He recalled the various lucrative offers that he had received in the past for the sales of Moniba Pumps' business. Every time he refused these offer as he believed that with superior quality products, consistent innovation and high brand equity, Moniba Pumps would one day be amongst the top Indian pumps company. Also, at times Mr Rakesh became doubtful whether his son would really take over and sustain his interest in Moniba Pumps, which was an SME and comparatively smaller than MNCs, where his son had already worked for and was exposed to over the years. Mr Rakesh recently celebrated his 50th birthday and felt that he had become more risk-averse than he was 20 years ago.

DISCUSSION QUESTIONS

1. 'Moniba Pumps' present marketing and sales problem is a common issue in most of the SMEs in India.' Do you agree with the statement? Give examples in support of your answer.
2. Among the five options before MD Mr Rakesh for enhancing the sales and a better future of Moniba Pumps, which option is the best? Enumerate facts from the case to justify your answer.
3. Discuss the factors that are inhibiting the revenue and market share growth of Moniba Pumps.
4. Comment on the integrated marketing communication strategy being followed by Moniba Pumps to enhance the sales of its industrial pumps.
5. What should be the future marketing strategy of Moniba Pumps, given the prevailing organization and industry scenario?
6. Should Mr Rakesh consider a detailed marketing research programme before deciding on his sales and marketing strategies? If so, what are the marketing areas he should research? Should he hire a marketing research agency?

ENDNOTES

1. MAEPL is better known as Moniba Pumps amongst its customers, vendors and the industry.
2. A 'small scale enterprise' has an investment in plant and machinery of lower than ₹5 crores (50 million) whereas a 'medium enterprise' has an investment in plant and machinery of more than ₹5 crores (50 million) but less than ₹10 crores (100 million).
3. www.bankofindia.com/smepol.aspx, accessed on 23 September 2010.

REFERENCES

www.monibapumps.net, accessed on 21 September 2010.
www.rbi.org.in/scripts/NotificationUser.aspx?Id=2502&Mode=0, accessed on 23 September 2010.

8

JAWANDSONS: THE DOMESTIC MARKET ENTRY

Managing Director, Mr G. B. Singh, was discussing with his son Mr Gian Singh (Exhibit 8.1) about the challenges that they would have to overcome if they started a new product line of Indian ladies suits and saris with their own trademark in the Indian market. As Jawandsons was already a successful vendor to one of the world's leading home furnishing retail chains, they were confident about their own product's quality. Also, currently Jawandsons was dependent on only a few international buyers, for example, approximately 90 per cent of the revenue came from a single international buyer. The owners realized that it may negatively affect Jawandson's stability and growth in the near future. On 15 July 2011, the board of directors at Jawandsons, in a major decision, decided to foray in the domestic market for ladies suits and saris and also extend their relationship to newer international buyers.

INCEPTION

Jawandsons made a humble beginning in 2001 under the leadership of Mr G. B. Singh who had always set high targets for himself and those around him. The vision to provide the customers with unmatched quality and affordability led to high revenue. By 2011, Jawandsons crossed a revenue turnover of over ₹100 crore (1 billion). G. B. Singh attended an international fair in Germany, where he met delegates from various home furnishing retail chains. Fortunately at that time one of the home furnishing giants was looking for some suppliers who had prior experience in textile business and also had the capability to provide quality products at par with international standards. G. B. Singh's samples impressed various buyers, thus contacts were exchanged and travel plan to India was scheduled by the buyers. This was how relationship between Jawandsons and a leading buyer from Sweden started. Since then Jawandsons had never looked back, and today it was one of the most reputed vendors for home furnishings, supplying its manufactured products in all major countries of the globe. Training, motivating and developing human resources had been at the forefront of Jawandsons' growth.

Exhibit 8.1 | *Top Management Profile*

Mr G.B. Singh

A first generation entrepreneur initiated his entrepreneurial career by opening a small industrial textile unit. Combination of traits such as sincerity, calmness, enthusiasm and astute visionary is what made him a revered personality in the textile industry. His hard work and passion had enabled him to set up an export unit at Ludhiana which is growing at an exponential rate.

Mr Gian Singh

Mr Gian joined Jawandsons few years back after he completed his post graduation from the University of Nottingham (U.K). He completed his Bachelors in Commerce from University of Delhi. Fostering his existing business, on one hand, he was also actively involved in diversifying his current business by starting up a new product line.

Source: As per an interview with the MD Mr G. B. Singh, dated 29 August 2011

PRODUCT PORTFOLIO

Jawandsons was primarily manufacturer and exporter of home furnishings products such as blankets, baby blankets, quilts, throws, bed covers, etc. Being a vendor company, all the products manufactured were entirely dependent on the demand of the organizational buyer. The manufacturing steps from raw yarns to finished products were carried out in-house (Exhibit 8.2).

Exhibit 8.2 | *Production Process*

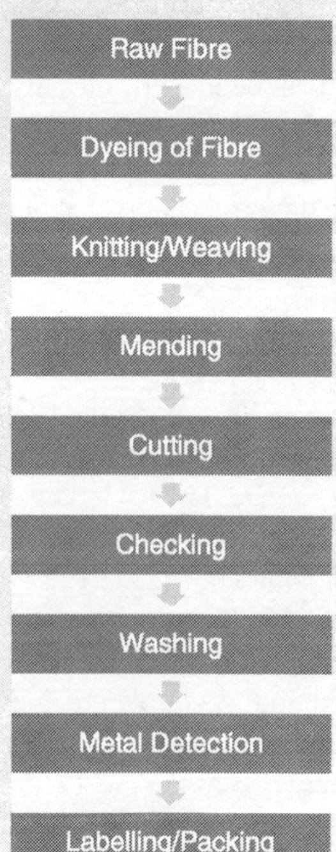

Source: As per an interview with the MD Mr G.B. Singh, dated 29 August 2011

NEW PRODUCT DEVELOPMENT (NPD)

Jawandsons followed all stage of new product development process, while conceptualizing and introducing new products (Exhibit 8.3). The majority of the lead generation occurred as organizational buyers themselves approached Jawandsons. The demand for new products always existed as the retail giants had hired market research agencies to understand the ever-changing consumer behaviour. These market research agencies used to advise about new product requirements to their client about the changing consumer demands. The marketing/sourcing department of Jawandsons always remained in close touch with the various executives of the buyers in order to upgrade themselves with the new design requirements.

As soon as a request for any new kind of product was received, the proposal was shared with the top management, quality and production department. The top management in consultation with the production, marketing/sourcing and quality departments would finalize the timelines for sample submission. Simultaneously, the top management will also start working on the cost-benefit analysis, risk factors and capacity issues related to the new order. In case of any issues, Jawandsons negotiated with the buyer. As soon as the samples got approved from the buyer, the responsibility of fulfilling the complete order went to the production and quality department.

THE FOUR PILLARS

The strong foundation of Jawandsons was based on the following four pillars:

Competitive Price

Competitive price was one of the most critical parameters for which Jawandsons had been rated high by the buyers. They were able to provide best competitive prices amongst their competitors. This was

Exhibit 8.3 | *New Product Development*

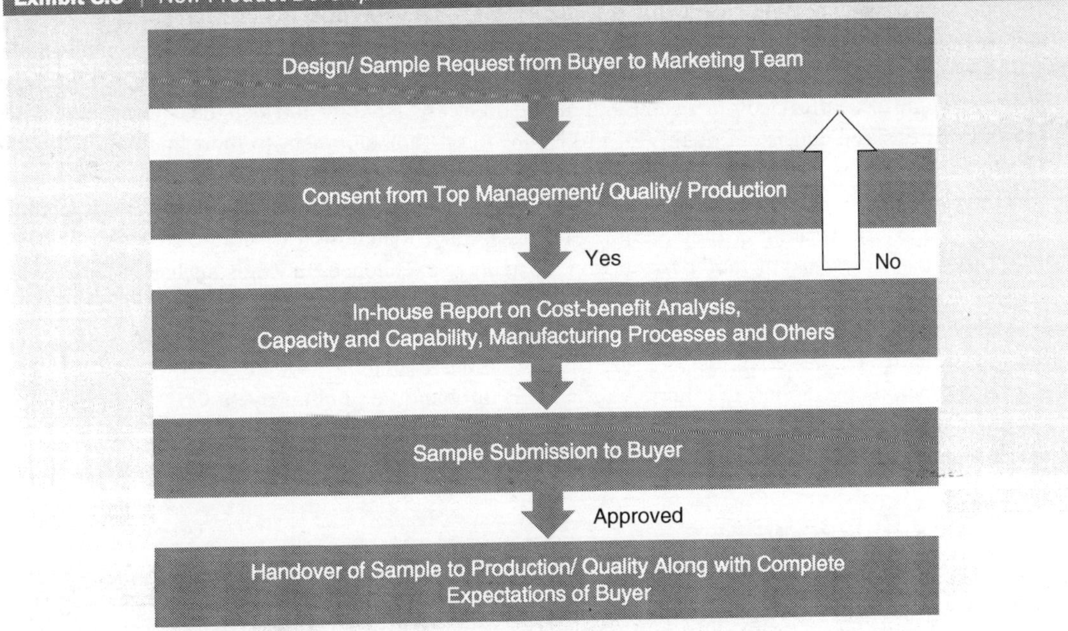

Source: As per an interview with the MD Mr G. B. Singh, dated 29 August 2011

Exhibit 8.4 | *Ludhiana*

Ludhiana is called the industrial capital of Punjab. It is one of the principal producers of woollen and acrylic knitwear. Ludhiana is also known for cotton and blended fibre which is used to produce hosiery, knitwear and various ready-made garments. Ludhiana contributes to nearly 28 per cent industrial output of Punjab. Textile industry in Ludhiana mainly fulfils the requirements of the domestic market, although since last one decade it has also exported its products. Majority of the textile industries in Ludhiana are small scale. The Ludhiana textile industry has about 10,000 industrial units.

Source: www. travelmadeeasy.in accessed on 18 August 2011

possible because of varied factors like procuring bulk raw materials such as acrylic and cotton directly from large suppliers, and optimum utilization of resources such as raw materials, manpower and energy. Being located in Ludhiana, Punjab (Exhibit 8.4), which was the hub of textile industry in northern India, also helped it reduce overheads to a great extent.

Jawandsons possessed a highly motivated technical team who were able to conceptualize and design large machine tool infrastructure using their innovative skills. It saved Jawandson's large CAPEX budget. A well-equipped infrastructure also helped in reducing production cost in the long run. The marketing/sourcing department was supported by an equally efficient quality and production department in providing the most competitive price to the buyer besides ensuring on-time delivery. All departments worked closely on different manufacturing process alternatives that could be used in meeting the quality and production benchmarks.

Best Quality

Jawandsons was committed towards quality. Quality policy was given due importance and the top management was passionate about achieving the quality goals. Each product underwent numerous rounds of quality tests before it was packed for the customers (Exhibit 8.5). The quality products of Jawandsons were well received in the international market. Having gained experience in the fabric business, Jawandsons knew the value of comfort, colour-fastness, functionality, care, labeling and also the external appearance. Jawandsons ensured consistent quality of products and on-time shipment to their international clients. The focus was on fast, accurate and friendly service apart from providing quality products.

The organization had numerous in-house testing facilities such as PH value test, blend test, composition, shrinkage test, washing fastness, rubbing fastness, shade matching, yarn count, construction density and appearance after washing and twist testing. To achieve excellence, Jawandsons had obtained testing certifications from leading testing laboratories like TUV, Germany; Intertek, Hong Kong; ITS, Istanbul; FIRA, United Kingdom; Euro Fins, Denmark; Texanlab, India and Govmark, New York. They also had the latest quality testing equipments in-house like colour matching cabinet-greatmecbath, conditioning rock, crock metre digital, LG fabric washer, IFB tumble dryer, hot air oven, GSM cutter, hot plate, leandro metre-automatic, microscope, twist tester-prasto, count checking warp real digital, magna scope, viscosity metre, metal detectors, UV light boxes, calibrated weighting scales, pick glass, etc.

Complete Compliance

The compliances followed by Jawandsons may be classified into social, legal and environmental. All the compliances were given extreme importance in daily operations of the company because of mandatory requirement by its largest MNC client. However, the other competitors were not quite particular about

Exhibit 8.5 | *Quality*

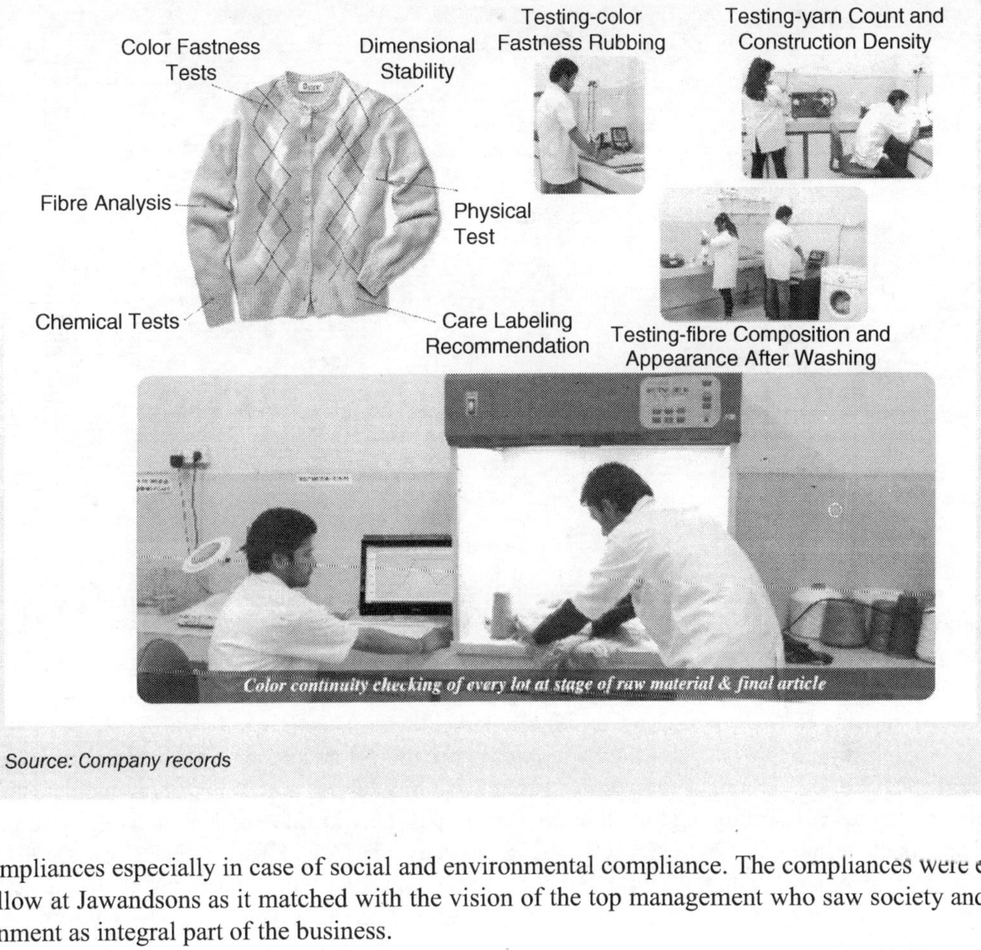

Source: Company records

compliances especially in case of social and environmental compliance. The compliances were easy to follow at Jawandsons as it matched with the vision of the top management who saw society and environment as integral part of the business.

On-time Delivery

Jawandsons had a good on-time delivery record in the international market. The buyer–seller relationship was streamlined leveraging IT in the organization. The demand–supply equilibrium, along with reorder data and order size data, was efficiently exchanged between Jawandsons and the foreign client. Thus, Jawandsons was honoured with the prestigious award of 'Supplier of the Year' by one of the major retail clients.

PROMOTION

The top management never gave much importance to promotion as they were already flooded with orders. One of major Sweden-based retail chain buyers was already buying bulk of their production. So the entire finished products, due to its top quality and competitive prices, was normally over-booked. However, off-late Jawandsons decided to diversify the existing business by starting a product line of Indian suits and

Exhibit 8.6 | *Exhibition Fairs*

Source: Company records

saris for the domestic market. Jawandsons saw this as critical requirement for the future growth of the organization. They wanted to promote their own brand name to the end consumer. Until now they were anonymous to the retail consumer as they were only catering to large retail chains. Jawandsons wanted to initiate its market presence in the domestic market, apart from existing B2B (Business to Business) market, by entering B2C (Business to Consumer) market under its own brand name.

The organization had never allocated any budget for special advertisements or promotions earlier. However, the company officials rarely missed an opportunity to visit and project their competent deliverables at various textile fairs and exhibitions throughout the world (Exhibit 8.6). They were regular participants at Heimtextil (Germany), CITME (Shanghai), ITMA and Textile Fair (New Delhi) since last one decade. According to the MD G. B. Singh, these fairs educated the company on the latest developments of yarns, fibres, machinery, production process and products. Moreover, these fairs acted as a single platform where a lot of renowned buyers were available at one place.

INFRASTRUCTURE

Jawandsons moved from city to the outskirts of Ludhiana for more space and growth.The manufacturing unit was well-equipped with latest circular knitting machines, flat knitting machines, linking machines, washing and warping machines manufactured by the world's best manufacturers such as Universal, Stool and Aries. The company also had an in-built boiler unit which produced steam for washing, pressing and softening. The company also had the latest power loom and handloom machinery in the shop floor (Exhibit 8.7).

The entire infrastructure design had been installed and maintained at par with international standards. The manufacturing unit also possessed various in-house labs, metal-free zones and R&D department which acted as innovative engine for the organization. To ensure safety of the workers, fire alarms, emergency exits, pure drinking water and other amenities had been provided at all floors in the manufacturing unit.

Exhibit 8.7 | *Infrastructure*

MANUFACTURING FACILITIES

Circular Knitting Machines

Power Loom Machine

Warp Knitting Machine

Fabric Dyeing Machine

Fabric Printing Machine

Source: Company records

LOGISTICS

The inbound logistics included procurement of yarn directly from vendors such as Reliance, Pashupati and Indian Acrylic; and raw material such as cotton, polyester, acrylic, etc., directly from the suppliers. The frequency of the order varied depending upon the intensity of the demand. Wool was imported from countries such as Kenya and South Africa.

Out-bound logistics included local road transport to deliver the goods upto the sea port and further ship containers were used to deliver the goods to the destination. Depending upon the distance between countries, the lead time varied. Majority of the international supplies were through sea route.

PRODUCTION

Production involved various phases. Depending upon the product requirement, yarn has to be knitted or weaved. Sometimes international buyers specifically mention the manufacturing process that needs to be followed. Generally, the manufacturing process is chosen with the concurrence of marketing/sourcing, quality and production team after discussing the client's requirements. Knitting and weaving are the main operations. While knitting, machine rider moved in a horizontal direction and horizontal movement could further take place either in circular rotation or straight direction. In weaving a cloth, two machine plates run simultaneously and in parallel direction. For example, sweaters are knitted and shirts are weaved. After warping, raw clothes are sent either to handloom machines or power-loom machines depending upon the thickness of the yarn. High density yarns are weaved on handloom machines. Further the cloth undergoes drafting. This is done to print designs on the cloth. After drafting reeding is done to adjust the required weight. Further clipping (mending) and knotting are done to give finishing. However, in case of power looms all the above steps are automated. After a long sheet of cloth was manufactured, the cloth is cut as per the size specifications. As soon as it is cut, tarpai, washing, pressing and quality checking are done. This is followed by packing and dispatch. The entire lead time including in-bound logistics and production takes nearly 5–7 weeks.

CORPORATE SOCIAL RESPONSIBILITY

Jawandsons had been actively involved in taking social and environmental initiatives and fully abiding by their corporate social responsibility towards their clients and society (Exhibit 8.8).

Saving Water

Jawandsons had installed modern washing machines at all the units with automatic dosing of water and chemicals to control the wastage of water and preventing any harm to underground water aquifer. Also rain water harvesting was being practised to recharge the water aquifers in and around the factory premises.

Water Treatment and Recycling

Company was undertaking environmental improvements with installation of modern ETP (Effluent Treatment Plant) with automatic chemical dosing, aeration and use of environmental friendly chemicals.

Encouraging Plantation

Jawandsons had been encouraging green belt area on top priority. They have acquired 5 acres of land and planted more than 3,000 trees to ensure healthy future for younger generations.

Exhibit 8.8 | *Corporate Social Responsibility*

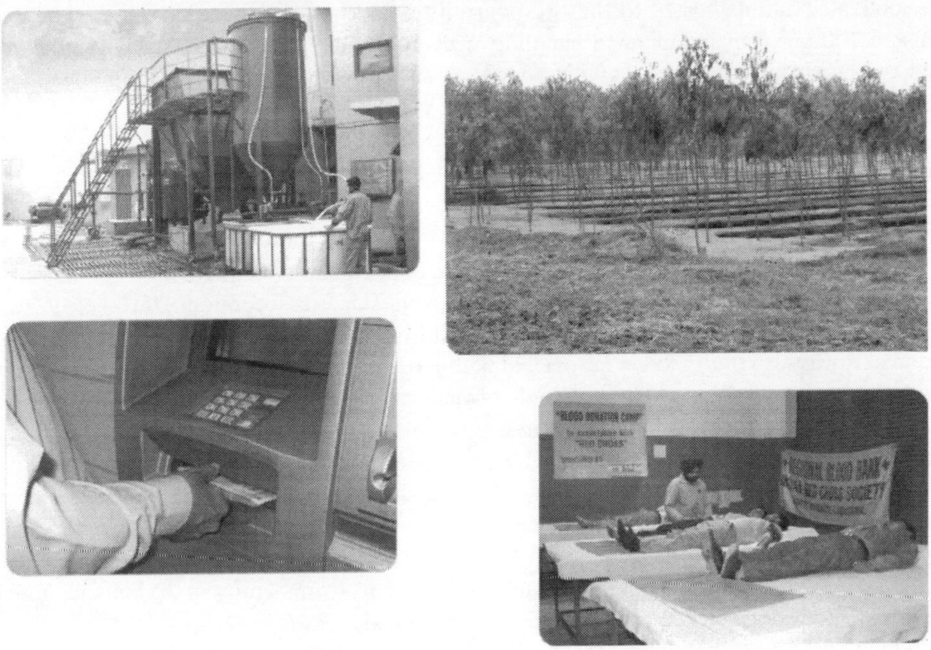

Source: Company records

Employee Welfare

Company had installed fire safety systems like fire extinguishers, manual call points, smoke sensors, fire alarms and hydrant systems. Fire engine vehicles were placed by the organization at each manufacturing unit to handle any potential disaster. Safety trainings were conducted periodically to encourage safe and secure working conditions. The company had also provided suitable personal protective equipments and trainings to avoid any accident. All the workers were insured by the organization against any major accident.

Social Activities

E-salary to workers was started to facilitate transparency. Blood donation camps were organized periodically by the organization to promote social welfare. First aid training in collaboration with Red Cross was conducted twice a year. The top management had shown keen initiative in providing free books and notebooks to the children of the Government High School, Ludhiana. Jawandsons also sponsored three orphan children every year for free education up to matriculation level. It also provided financial support to the cultural body 'Sur Sabad Manch' for promotion of regional language and music. It also provided monetary support for medical treatments and marriages of its poor workers.

Organization Culture

Organization culture at Jawandsons was employee friendly and professional. Majority of employees were motivated and dedicated to their responsibility. Special grievance department had been created to ensure 100 per cent compliance handling with in allotted time frame. As per company officials, Managing Director often interacts with workers at the shop floor, thus giving them the due recognition and motivating them.

THE ROAD AHEAD

Despite exponential growth Jawandsons had achieved since its inception, still a lot needs to be achieved felt Mr Gian Singh. Being a dedicated export unit, the company had maintained strong business relations with one of the biggest home furnishings buyers since its inception. However, to further stabilize its operations, the top management envisioned to enter other product line in the domestic market. Jawandsons was also trying to get associated with more international buyers so as to neutralize the risk factor of being mainly dependent on a single buyer. According to Mr Gian Singh, Ludhiana was getting stronger in weaving and nearby producing centres such as Amritsar has gone low on production. So, Indian suits and saris were one of the favourite options available as far as new product line was concerned. Although Ludhiana (Owner's native place) and hub of Indian suits and saris (Ladies dress material) had a lot of competition, but as per the M. D. Mr G. B. Singh, ladies dress material was a product which sold throughout the year, and there were very less chances that the sales would become stagnant. Besides hedging risk, Jawandsons also wanted to initiate its own identity in the consumer market, starting with the domestic market, by launching its own brand.

Undoubtedly, the existing association with the world's leading retail chain would facilitate Jawandsons desire to get associated with more number of buyers. However, there would be other challenges like:

Market Choice

Ensuring smooth operations during the expansion phase would be one of the main hurdles. Jawandsons had to maintain the balance. On one side, existing business partners were continuously demanding larger order size with higher frequency. On the other side, new business partners of the proposed new product line would have their own demands. There was also dilemma whether to join hands with new domestic partners or new international partners. Mr G. B. Singh was pondering over two options, viz.,

(a) Case-1 (Existing business partners + New domestic partners): To include new domestic business partners into the existing international business model did not seem feasible to Mr Gian Singh, as domestic buyer's stressed mostly on lesser cost of production with little concern over compliance handling, which is a key requirement with the international buyers. To include domestic buyers into the existing system was not at all possible as the present system was internationally validated with fixed norms such as no overtime, holidays on weekends, no child labour and corporate social responsibility compulsions. Because of intense competition in the domestic market, achieving highly competitive price with existing standards was not possible. Thus, the top management perceived major hurdles on including new domestic partners. If this model has to be executed, the company may have to handle its operations in an entirely different manner.

(b) Case-2 (Existing business partners + New international partners): Including new international partners into the existing system was the other option available while achieving the mission of making it a long-term sustainable business. Jawandsons wanted to expand its customer base as currently it was lopsided with a basket of few buyers. However, the company's present production capacity was only good enough to handle the demands of the existing buyers and few domestic buyers. Therefore, increasing business relations with new international partners may affect the stability of Jawandsons business model. It might reduce the satisfaction level of the existing customers besides impacting the delivery schedules.

Operational Challenges

Operating in new product line for entirely new market, that is, domestic market, involved different processes and strategies in terms of designing, manufacturing, marketing/sourcing and distribution. According to the company officials, Jawandsons cannot afford to start the manufacturing of ladies dress material in their existing export manufacturing unit. The management will have to look for entirely new manufacturing plant with new infrastructure in terms of machines and work environment. Moreover, the company had no existing domestic distribution network. However, since all the ladies dress material manufacturers were shifting from Amritsar to Ludhiana, setting up of a new industrial plant seemed a lucrative opportunity.

If top management initiates this new business opportunity, the entire focus will be diverted to a new manufacturing unit. Since the company was already progressing exponentially in their export business, would it be right to compromise on the attention on exports at this juncture?

DISCUSSION QUESTIONS

1. Suggest a market entry strategy for Jawandsons in the domestic market.
2. As per the constraints given in the case, what is your opinion in case Jawandsons decides in favour of Case 1, i.e., it chooses a domestic business partner? Would it be a good decision for Jawandsons' future business prospects?
3. 'Corporate social responsibility (CSR) and business profitability may go hand-in-hand'. Do you agree with the statement? Justify your answer with examples from the case study of Jawandsons.
4. 'Jawandsons was able to serve its business customers better due to smaller customer basket'. Do you agree with the statement? What are the business implications of having smaller customer basket?
5. What is your advice on Jawandsons plan to launch a new product line for ladies suits and saris in the domestic market? Will it impact their current business model? Do you think Jawandsons would get the same level of success it achieved in the export market?
6. Should Jawandsons engage outside communication agency to build brand equity before launching new products for domestic markets? Can high priced products meeting international norms be sold in India? Would branding help Jawandsons in achieving substantial market share in the domestic market?

9

Prodigy Recruitment Consultants: Managing Brand Extensions

It was a cold evening of 31 December 2011, when the CEO of Prodigy Recruitment Consultants, Yuvaraju, (Exhibit 9.1) was introspecting his entrepreneurial journey, which he started about two years back. He felt satisfied the way the organization had grown since its inception. He also thought of the challenges in the next phase of the company's growth. The corporate client response towards Prodigy services had been encouraging. The organization had achieved its breakeven in less than two years. Prodigy had been passionately providing customized talent acquisition services to enterprises based in and around Chennai, the automotive and IT hub of India. Prodigy had been successful in understanding the clients' unique business requirements and their organizational culture and, hence, was able to match their HR (human resource) talent requisition expectations. Prodigy endeavoured to win credibility and trust from all its clients. The core competence of Prodigy was providing recruitment services for automotive, logistics and IT (information technology) industry. Yuvaraju knew that the world was a small place and valued 'word of mouth' promotion from its clients than any other form of marketing. Prodigy had planned not only to scale up its operations but also enter into new service product lines through brand extension. Yuvaraju articulated that Prodigy Recruitment Consultants as an organization was at a critical stage now, where these strategic decisions would have a long-term bearing on the organization's sustenance and future growth trajectory.

PRODIGY RECRUITMENT CONSULTANCY

The word 'prodigy' means 'genius'. In May 2010, Mr Yuvaraju started Prodigy Recruitment Consultancy as a recruitment consultancy organization with the aim to bridge the gap in talent acquisition through in-depth knowledge of the industry and the expertise in understanding of talent pool, thereby, adding

Exhibit 9.1 | *Profile of Founder CEO Yuvaraju*

Yuvaraju, an outgoing person, had a pleasing and charismatic personality. Yuvaraju did his MA (Master of Arts) and MPhil (Masters in Philosophy) in History, prior to joining his recruitment consultancy job. Due to his personal traits of gelling well with people, he wanted to enter an industry which had direct interaction with customers. Tourism and human resources emerged as his preferred choices. Yuvaraju joined a reputed manpower consultancy company in Chennai as his first job. He worked there for more than 4 years before quitting as key account manager (KAM) for Cognizant Technologies Solutions in SAP module. Being an entrepreneur was a long cherished dream of Yuvaraju and he had already started to accomplish milestones as Prodigy founder-CEO in less than 2 years of his operations.

Source: As per interview with Mr Yuvaraju, dated 28 December 2011

value to company and the client. Prodigy provided services to both industrial (B2B) and individual clients (B2C). Yuvaraju, during his stint with a reputed recruitment agency, had realized that there was a large gap between talent requirement by the organization and timely availability of suitable candidates for the job. His recruitment market research showed that there were a lot of openings in the job market but candidates were not aware of the same and thus industrial clients were unable to locate right candidates at right time. This was more so in some specific industry verticals.

He planned to create a structured database and fulfil this talent acquisition gap leading to a win-win situation for the job seeker and the employer. Since Yuvaraju wanted to design and implement this in his own way and envisioned it as a great business opportunity, he decided to open recruitment consultancy as his first business venture. He wanted his venture to have the best professional standards and highest ethical values. The Indian software company 'Infosys' was a benchmark for Prodigy to emulate its professionalism, organizational culture and ethics.

Yuvaraju's recruitment industry exposure and expertise over the business processes gave him a strong foothold for the initial start. Prodigy was an interface between clientele and various companies. To the individual clients (B2C), Prodigy gave an opportunity to express their credentials and provided them the best matching job opportunities available in the industry. Each individual was treated with respect and provided all help and facilitation to secure suitable job matching his/her credentials. The motto of Prodigy for its client services was *People are at the heart of everything we do, nothing is more important to us than the relationships we have built.*

Due to excellent industry response, Yuvaraju also received lucrative business offers for franchisee model; however, he politely declined those proposals. His vision was to grow the organization according to his operational, ethical and professional standards for the next five years before going for any further expansion in other cities. He was greatly inspired by Tata Group with regard to their organizational culture and employee policies. Yuvaraju's dream was to make his company the most trusted and valued global brand in the recruitment industry.

GLOBAL RECRUITMENT INDUSTRY

The global economic downturn had significantly impacted the recruitment market since 2009 but recruitment agencies were hopeful for its revival. Most of the recruitment organizations were diversifying into new businesses besides cost cutting initiatives. The global recruitment companies were expanding in emerging markets such as Eastern Europe, Latin America and Asia. The spotlight on these markets was becoming an essential part of their long-term growth strategy. The current highlights of global recruitment industry were[1]:

- The total global recruitment market was valued at over $420 billion and had grown at an average of 12 per cent per annum during the last decade.
- The generalist sector accounted for 70 per cent of the continental European market, while in the United Kingdom and the United States, the proportion was around 54–56 per cent.
- In terms of specialist recruitment, the total worldwide market was likely to be worth $29.6 billion on a net fee/gross profit basis.
- The US recruitment industry received around 81 per cent of its revenues from placing temporary/contract employees.

INDIAN RECRUITMENT INDUSTRY

The Indian recruitment industry had shown an upward trend since 2009. According to a study conducted by leading international HR (human resource) service provider MaFoi Randstad, the Indian organized sector would create more than 1 million jobs in the year 2011 alone and the top recruiting industries would be real estate, health care, hospitality and IT and ITES (information technology enabled services)[2]. The main factors contributing to growth in job market included easy availability of skilled resources with good communication skills, favourable socio-political environment and a stable government.

ERA (Executive Recruiters Association), an association of Indian recruitment industry, had broadly classified the recruitment industry into three domains, viz., search, selection and staffing. The size of the recruitment industry was estimated at ₹20,200 crores (202 billion) with each of the domains predicted to have an increasing growth in the coming years[3].

FUTURE PROSPECTS

The future of Indian recruitment industry looked bright. The global markets were slowly and steadily recovering from the economic downturn, customer spends were comparatively higher and a general optimistic mood had been witnessed across industry in the financial year 2010–11. The optimistic business growth will lead to newer projects, foreign direct investments, expansions and new business initiatives leading to increased demand of manpower. This was good news for recruitment consultants like Prodigy.

MARKETING MIX AT PRODIGY

The CEO Mr Yuvaraju had planned the marketing mix of Prodigy so as to uniquely position it in terms of talent acquisition for the client and the job seeking candidates. Yuvaraju had used his own research, prior industry experience and training insights in finalizing the marketing mix. The underlying idea was to achieve customer satisfaction through customized quality service delivery thereby adding value to the organization and the client.

Product

The company's product focussed on 'client', 'candidate' and 'company'. According to Yuvaraju, Prodigy's success lied in connecting both the client and the candidate to their mutual satisfaction and importantly within the defined time frame. This was possible with rich HR database along with specialized databases in different industry verticals. Prodigy specialized in recruitment services for automotives, logistics and IT (Information Technology).

For Prodigy, 'client' was an independent entity who was a business provider to the organization. The client was expected to share complete information regarding the manpower requirements in the company along with the key desirables. On the basis of the information collected from the client, Prodigy provided customized recruitment solution within the given timeframe. For individual candidates, Prodigy facilitated 'appropriate job' as per his qualifications and expectations. Both with the clients (B2B) and candidates (B2C), Prodigy endeavoured to build a strong relationship based on professional ethics and quality service delivery.

Price

Prodigy charged industrial clients as per the number of 'candidates' referred to for requisite positions. It did not charge any fee to the candidates/job-seekers. The recruitment industry norm for referral commission from the client organization is 8.33 per cent of total CTC (cost to company). Prodigy apart from charging this fee also provided customized recruitment solution as per the agreement fee. However, the payment realization after the completion of the requisite service delivery took time because of the client processing bill time. Normally it took 45–60 days for each invoice to get billed and processed after completion of the services.

Prodigy like other recruitment consultancy organizations was directly affected by the economic downturn. The client organizations generally freeze recruitment as a first reaction to such crisis. Such move directly impacted the revenue inflow of recruitment consultancy companies. Prodigy was mulling over option of extending its domain to a being a full fledged HR consultancy company; to hedge its risk again such uncertainties.

Place

Prodigy Recruitment Consultants had their corporate office in Chennai, India. It had planned to extend its network in metro cities of Mumbai, Calcutta and New Delhi in the near future. Prodigy had received multiple requests for franchise options due to positive 'word of mouth' promotion in the recruitment industry. However, Yuvaraju was not in a hurry and wanted to build a strong foundation before opening its own company branches across the country. Yuvaraju was against the franchise model in the recruitment industry. He opined that since people and process are the key deliverables in this industry it cannot be easily replicated in franchise model unlike other product and service franchise model. Presently, CEO Yuvaraju was completely focussed on building strong relationships with clients and candidates through quality service delivery, developing trust and professional integrity.

Promotion

Prodigy was involved in both push and pull marketing for its promotion to its customers. It followed push marketing when holding meetings/presentations with its potential industrial clients. During the initial entrepreneurial journey, CEO Yuvaraju himself was involved in making presentations and meeting with the clients. The general query of the industrial client was regarding the quality of manpower database, scrutiny process of profiles, working capital, employee strength and their competence, infrastructure and previous client list. Being a start-up enterprise, many a times initially there was not much to elaborate on these issues. In such circumstances, based on his prior experience in the industry, comprehensive knowledge of processes and clarity of client's expectations had enabled its prospects to generate initial sense of trust and confidence in the company. In less than two years, Prodigy had successfully registered itself as a permanent manpower provider for two large MNCs (multinational corporations) and many other Indian organizations in automotive, logistics and information technology industry (Exhibit 9.2).

For individual candidates, Prodigy followed pull marketing approach. It was job seekers who approached Prodigy to provide a better job opportunity or employment for them. Prodigy had responded sensitively to the needs and expectations of candidates thereby building a network of professionals at all levels and in all functional areas.

Prodigy had been using social networking sites such as Facebook, LinkedIn, Twitter and Orkut to enhance the visibility of its brand name (Exhibit 9.3). Due to financial constraints Prodigy had avoided any form of mass media advertisements. Mr Yuvaraju was himself involved in interaction sessions at colleges and professional institutions in and around Chennai. He discussed about the job opportunities and industry expectations and how Prodigy may help realize their potential. Referrals along with such interaction sessions provided Prodigy enough leads. Prodigy's specialized recruitment solutions, strong adherence to timeframes and competitive liasoning with its potential clients had ensured it sufficient number of industrial clients and individual job seekers.

People

Since Prodigy was purely a services provider, 'people' was the most critical resource for Prodigy. Yuvaraju had very competent team taking care of the business development and its operations. As Prodigy had limited capital, Yuvaraju had employed many part time employees from his social networking circle to work for Prodigy. This was working quite well for Prodigy. Yuvaraju had also planned to recruit some more full time staff in the near future as he was expecting some more MNC clients to

Exhibit 9.2 | *Clienteles of Prodigy (Indicative List)*

Hema Engineering

India Nippon Electricals Limited

Tenneco Automotives India Pvt. Ltd

Chep India Pvt. Ltd

Nihon Technology

Sundaram BNP Paribas Fund Services Limited

Spensers Travels

Source: Company Records

Exhibit 9.3 | *Marketing Campaigns*

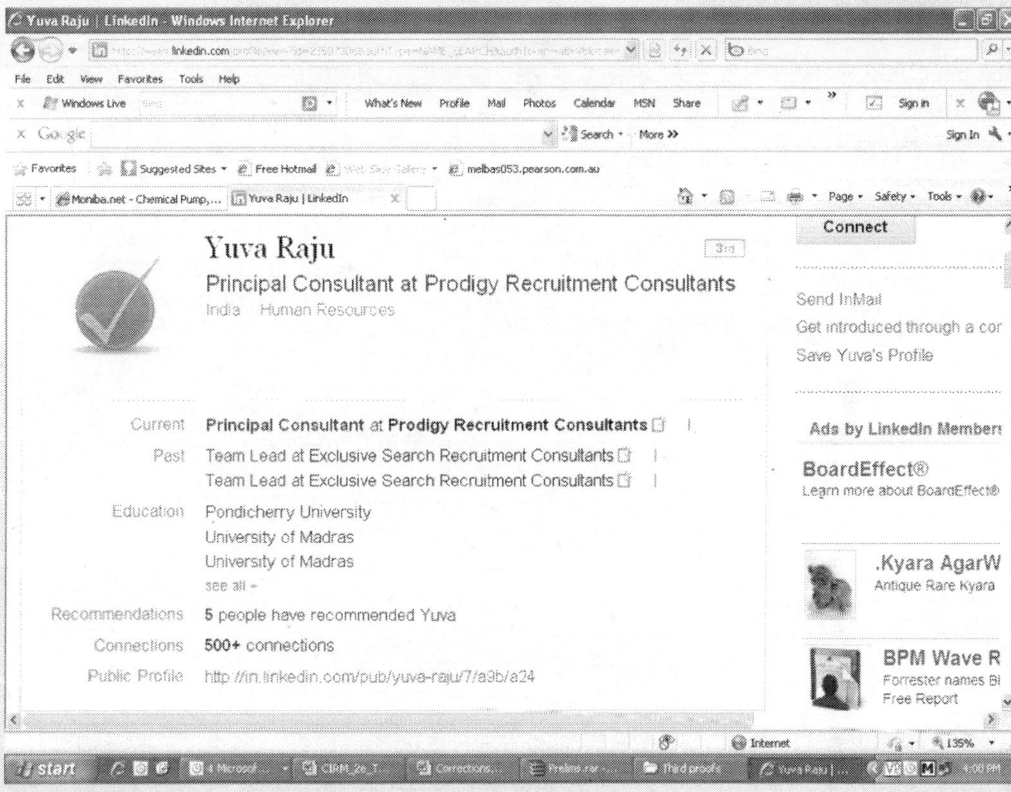

Source: Company Records

register it as manpower provider. In its organizational structure, Prodigy had designated senior members from its business development team as KAM (Key Account Managers) who had expertise in specific industry verticals.

Recruitment Process

Prodigy employed a comprehensive and structured process so as to understand each client's needs, backgrounds and specific position requirements. Search stages were customized for individual candidates as well as for industrial clients. Each talent exploration and acquisition was personalized, addressing the specific needs of the assignment and thus incorporating the best search practices. The entire search mechanism was methodical and well-organized (Exhibit 9.4). Prodigy was closely involved till the end process to ensure that the interests of all stakeholders were adequately met.

Exhibit 9.4 | *Recruitment Process*

Process for Industrial Clients

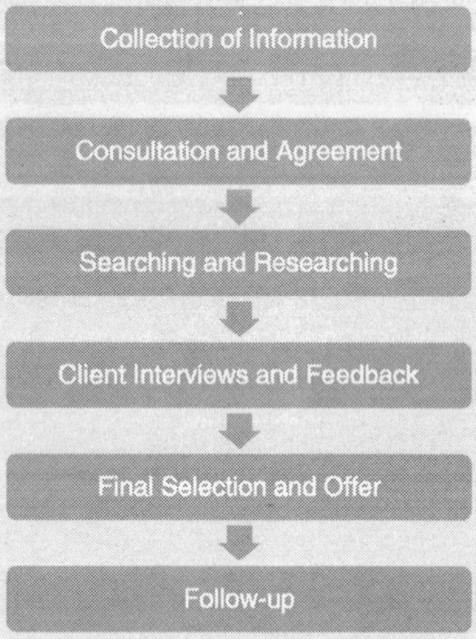

Process for Candidates

Source: Company Records

TALENT ACQUISITION: INDUSTRIAL CLIENTS AND INDIVIDUAL CANDIDATES

The recruitment process at Prodigy Recruitment Consultants was process oriented with professional delivery standards. In case of talent acquisition services for industrial client, Prodigy followed the following process:

Stage 1: Collection of Information

The first step after receiving the lead or request of recruitment services by the client involved collection of complete background information about the client. It included details about organizational culture, business model, vision and mission, HR practices, KRAs (key result areas) and strategic initiatives by the organization. The information about requisite technical qualifications, interview process and time-frame was also collected by Prodigy executives.

Stage 2: Consultation and Agreement

The second step involved direct discussion between Prodigy and the client. The client gave presentations regarding position, responsibilities, compensation and interview process. Based on the industry knowledge and recruitment expertise, Prodigy gave their inputs to the client. The timeframe for the requisite search was discussed and finalized. After the mutual consent an agreement was signed by both Prodigy and the client.

Stage 3: Searching and Researching

The third step of search process was performed by Prodigy's in-house team to locate requisite talent as per client requirement. It involved designing blueprint elaborating the database research and search strategy, allocation of organizational resources and delegating responsibilities to Prodigy executives for implementing this search strategy. It also included leveraging website applications for adding more information to profiles obtained through research and headhunting. Thereafter, Prodigy conducted screening interviews to filter out candidates from large HR pool for next level of interview/interaction with the client.

Stage 4: Client Interviews and Feedback

From the large HR pool, selected candidate resumes were forwarded to clients by Prodigy along with reasons for recommendations. Coordination with the client and lining up initial and subsequent (if required) interviews of candidates were the next step in this critical stage of recruitment process service delivery. Client shared its feedback regarding the candidate interview with Prodigy.

Stage 5: Final Selection and Offer

This step involved Prodigy sharing details about candidate's potential, compensation expectations and other relevant details to assist the client in making their final decision. Prodigy held an important responsibility of ensuring acceptance of offer by the candidate and their subsequent joining on the agreed date. Prodigy also had to maintain sufficient backup to handle any last minute fall outs.

Stage 6: Follow-up

Ensuring customer satisfaction and to gain customer loyalty was one of the important goals of Prodigy. Prodigy maintained regular contact during the initial period with the company as well as with the candidate. This practice provided differentiation to Prodigy's recruitment services. Though some recruitment agencies stay connected with industrial clients for future business but taking feedback from joining candidates was rarely done in the recruitment industry. In case some dissonance was there either from the client or from the candidate, immediate corrective actions were taken by Prodigy to resolve it in the best possible manner.

The recruitment service philosophy and professional integrity adopted by Prodigy Recruitment Consultant had earned it 'word of mouth' promotion and client appreciation besides many referral leads. The motivation and passion among the Prodigy employees to consistently deliver quality service came from their CEO Yuvaraju who believed in 'walk-the-talk' philosophy and followed 'management-by-heart' leadership.

CANDIDATES

Prodigy believed that full potential of individuals could only be achieved if they were provided right platform as per their capability and expertise. According to Yuvaraju, understanding candidate's aptitude and matching it with related industrial profile was mutually beneficial proposition for Prodigy and the candidate. Prodigy as an organization was fully aware of the moral responsibility of providing right direction to candidate's career and ensured that great care was exercised while assessing candidate's experiences, proficiencies and career objectives and matching it suitably with the required role.

Prodigy followed the following steps in fulfilling its commitment to the candidates:

Stage 1: Interview and Assessment

The first step was an ongoing activity where any candidate, either fresher or experienced, may approach Prodigy for a job. In fact, it was one of the most important steps in the entire recruitment process. It involved understanding and evaluating short-term and long-term career goals, interest areas, and monetary expectations of the applicant/candidate. It also included thorough understanding of their skill set, profiles handled by the candidate in the past (for experienced candidates), expectations from the next job or any kind of constraints with regard to location and industry. After thoroughly understanding about the candidate background and competence, it is checked whether the candidate's profile and expectations match with any of Prodigy client's current open position. In case a potential match was found between the two, the candidate qualified for the second step of consultation and advice by Prodigy recruitment consultant. In case there was no match, the candidate was put in category of 'continuous communication and career counselling'. Such candidate's resume database was retained by Prodigy for future match. The candidate was informed about the same and asked to wait for the next communication from Prodigy. Also such candidates were given career counselling on how to upgrade their skill sets and informed about those skills sets which had got high employability and better salary packages.

Stage 2: Consultation and Advice

The candidates whose profiles were matching with Prodigy client's current open positions were elaborated about different job options. They were also counselled on how they could achieve their short-term and long term-goals by choosing among those options. The idea was to facilitate candidate to ask queries freely so that they may take an informed decision. Prodigy experienced consultants helped candidate make their choice objectively by helping them match it against their priorities, viz., location, industry, salary, responsibility, etc. This step ensured that candidate made better job choice which reduced the chances of post-job joining dissonance to the minimal level.

Stage 3: Matching with Current Open Positions

After comparing clients open positions with available candidates' profile, candidates' consent for forwarding their profiles to the client company was obtained. Prodigy forwarded the resume after the candidates' consent to the client company. Once the client company approved the profile an interview date was decided and the candidate through Prodigy was informed of the same. In case of disapproval of the profile, feedback was shared with the candidate through Prodigy.

Stage 4: Client Interviews

Prodigy assisted candidates in the interview preparation by making them thoroughly aware about company's background, business operations, vision of the company and client expectations. Prodigy shared the feedback received from client with the candidate and also gave feedback to the client received from candidate.

Stage 5: Offer and Follow-up

Prodigy helped candidate in evaluating potential job offers besides providing insights regarding negotiations for competitive compensation packages. It also coordinated logistics and communication for the candidate during their resignation and joining processes. Prodigy helped the candidate in settling in the new job and resolving the expectation gap, if any, both from the client side and candidate side.

The track record of providing excellent recruitment services to the candidates had helped Prodigy earn credibility amongst the student community in the Chennai region. Prodigy was quite popular in some colleges. Moreover, Prodigy was providing recruitment services without any charge. Prodigy Recruitment Consultancy was the leading choice among the candidates seeking jobs in the automotive, logistics and IT sector.

THE ROAD AHEAD

Mr Yuvaraju was mulling over various options like scaling up the business, foraying into other product lines and undertaking brand extensions. The opportunities and challenges that accompanied each option had put Yuvaraju in dilemma as he was planning proactively for next financial year:

- **Scaling up:** Scaling up was one of the obvious future goals of Yuvaraju. No doubt, the core competence of Prodigy was in automotives, logistics and IT industry; however, expansion was required to sustain the present business growth rate and also to transform into a bigger enterprise. Large capital infusion by venture capitalist was one of the viable options before Prodigy. However, Yuvaraju was not much keen for this. He opined that he may think of this option after at least 5 years once Prodigy becomes a leading recruitment consultant at the national level. He further added that it would give him a level playing negotiating space with venture capitalists, who may demand a sizable equity at this stage.
- **Prioritizing other Industry verticals:** Yuvaraju saw a direct correlation between growth rate of an industry and growth of manpower requirement in that industry. He was discussing with his core team about focussing on other industries too apart from automotive, logistics and IT, which Prodigy may also target for its recruitment services in the coming years. The discussion based on the limited statistics data with them concluded that telecom and communication; banking, financial services,

insurance (BFSI); FMCG and consumer durable and healthcare and lifesciences were most promising industry verticals for growth in the coming years.

- **Diversifaction:** Yuvaraju was thinking of adding contract staffing and executive search to its product line. In contract staffing, Prodigy would act as manpower vendor to its industrial clients. The employees (contract staff) would be on the payroll of Prodigy, however, they would work at client's location. This business model had high profit potential, with margins accumulating each month and lasted till the employee worked with the client. However, it involved administrative staff to seamlessly coordinate with the client besides providing social benefits like PF (Provident Fund) and medical reimbursements. The executive search focuses on recruitment of senior executive positions. It is highly profitable business but requires large pool of expertise, offices in metro cities and strong corporate network.

However, one of the ideas that caught much active attention of Yuvaraju was that of brand extension. He had read about Dettol, Amul, ITC, Caterpillar, Pierre Cardin, Johnsons & Johnsons, Virgin, Apple, Dove and Google brand extension articles and was impressed how new brand derived brand equity from successful existing brands.

PRODIGY BRAND EXTENSION

Yuvaraju did a BCG analysis (Exhibit 9.5) of its product portfolio. Its recruitment services had 'star' status in automotive, logistics and IT sector as a regional player. He had plans of providing brand extension through introduction of new product lines. Prodigy commanded good brand equity in the recruitment market in Chennai region especially in the automotive, logistics and IT sector. Brand extension would help Prodigy hedge risks of instability in recruitment market in specific sectors. The spin off

Exhibit 9.5 | *Boston Consulting Group (BCG) Matrix*

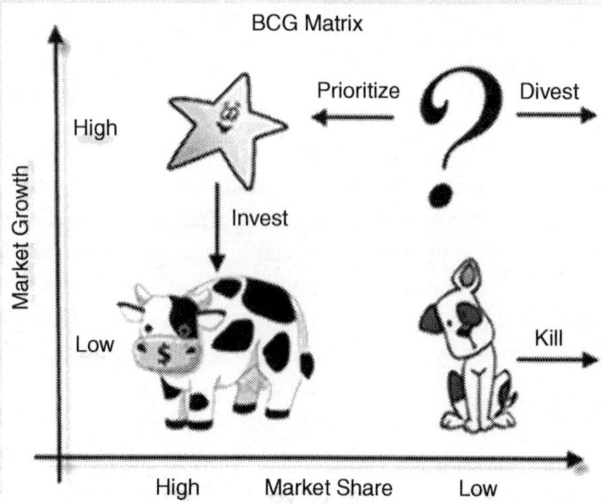

Source: http://www.maxi-pedia.com/BCG+matrix+model, accessed on 29 December 2011

products of Prodigy as part of brand extension would include Prodigy training and development services (PTDS); Prodigy organizational development services (PODS) for change management services; Prodigy compensation and benefits services (PCBS) and Prodigy career consultancy services (PCCS). Yuvaraju opined that to start with Prodigy would find many takers for these new services in automotive, logistics and IT sector due to its strong brand image in these verticals (Exhibit 9.6).

However, Yuvaraju was concerned about challenges that brand extension exercise would put forth to Prodigy. He was well aware that brand extension was a double edged strategy. If it worked and was able to transfer the brand equity of the existing Prodigy product lines to the new product lines; it had potential of bringing high profitability and many new clients to the Prodigy. It would also ensure that Prodigy offers a portfolio of products under the same umbrella name thus transferring the brand value that it had built in last 2 years to the new brands. This may also enhance the acceptability of newer Prodigy product lines. However, if the new product lines did not do well in the recruitment market, and if Prodigy had to withdraw any of those services, it might negatively affect the current successful product lines. Also the clients associated with new product lines; perceived new product services with the same old quality benchmarks, no matter how improved and best services an organization provides.

Yuvaraju was in a dilemma and thought he will discuss the proposed Prodigy brand extension plan with his core team within the organization. He also planned to call his mentor, who had more than 30 years of recruitment industry experience and had recently retired as Chairman of a leading recruitment agency of the country to take his opinion in this regard. He wondered whether Prodigy brand extension could help in making Prodigy Recruitment Consultants climb the next big growth trajectory.

Exhibit 9.6 | *Financial Projections*

Cost Projections	**2011-12**	**2012-13**	**2013-14**	**2014-15**	**2015-16**
Website Cost, AMC, SEO, etc.	35,000	38,500	42,350	46,585	51,244
Salaries and Wages	3,50,000	4,02,500	4,62,875	5,78,594	7,23,242
Stationery	75,000	82,500	90,750	99,825	1,09,808
Postal Expenses	50,000	55,000	60,500	66,550	73,205
Office Rentals	40,000	46,000	52,900	60,835	69,960
Hardware & Softwares	80,000	1,00,000	1,00,000	1,00,000	1,00,000
Marketing Budget	1,00,000	1,15,000	1,32,250	1,52,088	1,74,901
Logistics	40,000	44,000	48,400	53,240	58,564
Miscellaneous	60,000	66,000	72,600	79,860	87,846
Total Cost	8,30,000	9,49,500	10,62,625	12,37,576	14,48,769

Revenue Projections	**2012**	**2013**	**2014**	**2015**	**2016**
Fees from clients					
Automobiles	4,00,000	4,60,000	5,29,000	6,34,800	7,93,500
IT	3,00,000	3,45,000	3,96,750	4,76,100	5,95,125
Logistics	2,50,000	2,87,500	3,30,625	3,96,750	4,95,938
Telecom & Communication	1,00,000	1,15,000	1,32,250	1,58,700	1,98,375

(Continued)

Exhibit 9.6 | *Financial Projections (Continued)*

Revenue Projections	**2012**	**2013**	**2014**	**2015**	**2016**
Banking and Financial Services	1,30,000	1,49,500	1,71,925	2,06,310	2,57,888
FMCG	-	2,00,000	2,30,000	2,76,000	3,45,000
Consumer and Health care	-	50,000	57,500	69,000	86,250
Life Sciences	-		75,000	90,000	1,12,500
Fees from HR services					
Prodigy Training and Development Services (PTDS);	-	1,00,000	1,15,000	1,38,000	1,72,500
Prodigy Organizational Development Services (PODS)	-	1,00,000	1,15,000	1,38,000	1,72,500
Prodigy Compensation and Benefits Services (PCBS)	-		9,00,000	10,80,000	13,50,000
Prodigy Career Consultancy Services (PCCS).	-	50,000	57,500	69,000	86,250
Total Revenue	11,80,000	18,57,000	31,10,550	37,32,660	46,65,825
Total Cost	8,30,000	9,49,500	10,62,625	12,37,576	14,48,769
Income	3,50,000	9,07,500	20,47,925	24,95,084	32,17,056

Source: Company Records

DISCUSSION QUESTIONS

1. What do you mean by brand extension? Taking Prodigy as an example, discuss the role of perceptual mapping in brand extension.
2. Do you suggest Yuvaraju to go for brand extension while introducing new product lines of training and development services; organizational development services; compensation and benefits services and career consultancy services? Support your answers from the facts given in the case study.
3. Do a SWOT analysis of Prodigy Recruitment Consultants. Suggest future marketing strategy for Prodigy keeping in mind the given resource constraints.
4. What do you mean by core competence? What was Prodigy's core competence? Enumerate facts from the case study to support you answer.
5. Comment on marketing mix of Prodigy Recruitment Consultants. Suggest refinements in the marketing mix to enhance competitive advantage for Prodigy in the recruitment industry.
6. Should Yuvaraju engage marketing consultants before introducing new product lines through brand extension or he may rely on his mentor for the crucial decision on brand extension? If Yuvaraju opts to go for marketing consultants, what are the marketing areas that should be researched by the marketing consultants?

ENDNOTES

1. http://www.linkedin.com/answers/hiring-human-resources/staffing-recruiting/HRH_SFF/496369-46631227, accessed on 31 December 2011.
2. http://www.maintec.com/blog/indian-recruitment-industry, accessed on 31 December 2011.
3. http://www.era.org.in/ERAStats.aspx, accessed on 31 December 2011.

REFERENCE

http://www.maxi-pedia.com/BCG+matrix+model, accessed on 29 December 2011.

10

GILLTECH PHYTOWORLD: THE MARKETING STRATEGY

M.S. Gill, Director and founder of Gilltech Phytoworld, was intensively thinking about innovative marketing strategy through which Gilltech's ayurvedic products (Exhibit 10.1) could be better positioned and marketed to the allopathic and homeopathic doctors. The Gilltech ayurvedic (herbal) products were already well received amongst the ayurvedic doctors in northern India. But there was general reluctance among allopathic and homeopathic doctors regarding its acceptance. Ayurvedic products were being perceived as slow acting medicines. Mr Gill wanted to change this perception through his innovative ayurvedic medicines. He saw many challenges towards achieving this goal. However, with the kind of initial response he had received from doctors and patients, he was certain of bringing such transformation soon.

THE FOUNDATION

Mr Gill founded Gilltech Phytoworld in 2008 after breaking out of his old partnership business. Prior to this partnership business, he had served at a middle level management in an MNC. But his entrepreneurial passion and love for phyto (plants) world made him start partnership business. Mr Gill looked after the marketing and customer relationship and his partner, an ayurvedic doctor by profession, took up the responsibility of production. However, due to differences in approach towards the business, Mr Gill walked out of the decade-old partnership.

At Gilltech Phytoworld, Mr Gill had conceptualized and developed all product formulations on his own. Mr Gill, an MBA, had set an ambitious goal for the company. The mission of Gilltech Phytoworld was to practice ayurveda through scientific and technical procedures by doing an appropriate research work to balance tridosha, that is, maintaining equilibrium between air, water and fire. The ayurveda industry was doing well as the government was investing heavily in it through AYUSH (Department of Ayurveda, Yoga and Naturopathy, Unani, Siddha and Homoeopathy) (Exhibit 10.2).

Exhibit 10.1 | *Ayurveda*

Ayurveda is the oldest form of medication in India. It had been derived from two Sanskrit terms namely 'ayus' meaning life and 'veda' meaning knowledge. Therefore, it is called knowledge of life. Ayurveda aims to maintain equilibrium between body and mind. It uses characteristics of environment to achieve harmony between nature and man. It also enables human to promote firmness of mind. The ayurvedic medicines tend to eliminate the disease rather provide a temporary relief. Ayurvedic medicines also increased immunity of various body systems.

Air, water, fire, earth and ether are the five key elements in ayurveda. In human body, these elements are represented as energy and termed as 'Doshas'. 'Air' and 'ether' are collectively called as 'Vata Dosha' controlled the theory of movement thus pedalling nerve impulses, circulation, respiration and elimination. Similarly, 'Fire' and 'water' are jointly called as 'Pitta Dosha' directing process of metabolism. Communality of 'Water' and 'Earth' known as 'Kappa dosha' was responsible for the growth and protection of the body. Proportionate balance among all these five determinants facilitates perfect equilibrium.

Source: http://www.ayurved.com/article_details Accessed on 13 September 2011

Exhibit 10.2 | *Indian Ayurveda Industry*

- Number of registered medical practitioners: 366,812
- Number of dispensaries: 22,100
- Number of hospitals: 2,189
- Number of hospital beds: 33,145
- Number of teaching institutions (undergraduate): 187
- Number of upgraded postgraduate departments: 51
- Number of specialties in postgraduate medical training: 16
- Number of pharmacies manufacturing Ayurvedic medicines: 8,400

Source: www.itmonline.org/arts/ayurind.htm Accessed on 13 September 2011

THE MARKETING MIX

Gilltech Phytoworld had a unique marketing mix which augured well for the organization's future. These were reinforced by the founder M.S. Gill's passion for innovative herbal products and his technical expertise in the area. He was well supported by a motivated technical team and other staff in the organization.

Product

Gilltech Phytoworld manufactured about 30 herbal products (Exhibit 10.3) used for curing different allergic problems, brain tribulations, sex problems, liver troubles, hair problems, cough, detoxifiers, etc. Broadly ayurvedic treatment had been classified into two categories, namely, classical and patented (modernized). Classical medicines involved single ingredients and modernized medicines included multiple ingredients. Presently the products manufactured by Gilltech Phytoworld were only modernized products.

Exhibit 10.3 | *Product Mix*

- ALER-H Capsules (Antiallergic)
- ALER-H Gel (Antiallergic)
- ALER-H Syrup (Antiallergic)
- ASPAS Capsules (Antispasmodic)
- ASPAS Syrup (Digestive tonic)
- CALCITUFF Capsules (Calcium Supplement)
- COUGHEND Syrup (Cough Syrup)
- CUROTOX Capsules (General Tonic & Detoxifier)
- CUROTOX Syrup (General Tonic & Detoxifier)
- EATALL Capsules (Appetizer)
- FERTORYL-F (Female hormonal balancer)
- FERTORYL-M (Male Sex Tonic)
- GLOWRITE Gel (Fairness cream)
- GRAYTONE Capsules (Brain tonic)
- GRAYTONE Syrup (Brain tonic)
- LOMECARE Capsules (Hair care)
- NEEMOSEP Capsules (Antiseptic)
- NEEMOSEP Gel (Antiseptic)
- NEEMOSEP Syrup (Antiseptic)
- REGEN-L Capsules (Liver tonic)
- REGEN-L Syrup (Liver tonic)
- SCURNILL Lotion (Antiallergic)
- SEPTITUF Capsules (URTI, Immunomodulator)
- SEPTITUF Syrup (URTI, Immunomodulator)
- UROCID Capsules (For Uric Acid)
- UTROTONE Capsules (Uterine Tonic)
- UTROTONE Syrup (Uterine Tonic)
- VITALOME Hair Oil (Hair Vitalizer)
- WALKFIT Capsules (Anti-arthritic)
- WALKFIT Gel (Anti-inflammatory, Analgesic)

Source: Company records

Classical medicines required completely different manufacturing process and Gilltech Phytoworld had no plans to enter into this market segment. All the products being manufactured were in line with the company's vision of balancing tridosha. The USP (unique selling proposition) of Gilltech Phytoworld's products was that unlike other herbal medicines, its impact was comparatively faster. Gilltech Phytoworld never compromised on the processing time while manufacturing the medicines. The brand names of all the products (Exhibit 10.3) were kept with a view to correlating it with the name of the disease so that its customers had an easy recall.

Gilltech had received appreciative feedback from its customers during initial product promotion. For example, some of the products such as Walkfit capsules had high demand. The production manager Mr Ashish Jagdev said:

> I am waiting for that day when my reply to our customers for Walkfit products will be 'no shortage now, we have enough goods in our stock'.

Gilltech Phytoworld products like Fertoryl-M (male sensual tonic) and Fertoryl-F (female hormone balancer) were widely accepted amongst all doctors including allopathic doctors in the north-western India. The Fertoryl-M was being used for overcoming sexual weakness, erectile dysfunction, and to maintain motility and mobility. According to the company officials there was no single allopathic and ayurvedic medicine which could cure all the three problems simultaneously with a single medicine. Gilltech had also developed herbal anti-allergic gel named Aler-H. Many allopathic gels comprising of steroids were available but came with side effects unlike the Gilltech herbal gel. Gilltech was the proud producer of the same to fulfil this latent requirement.

Each product being manufactured underwent in-house clinical side effect tests and stability tests besides statutory testing from the government agencies. Majority of the Gilltech's products were well accepted by the doctors. Dr. Manjit Vashisht, a homeopathic physician said:

> Almost my every prescription to the patients carries out at least one product of Gilltech Phytoworld and the patients are cured faster.

Another Patiala-based ayurvedic physician Dr. Mandeep Singh opined that antibiotics were used on every second or third patient which ultimately lowered the immune power of the body. He opined that the doctors should ensure that patients are not frequently given hard antibiotics. Gilltech's endeavour was to replace use of antibiotics with useful herbal products. Mr Singh said:

> Gilltech Phytoworld's 'Neemosep' is an herbal antibiotic which gave a perfect alternative to these synthetic chemical antibiotics. Neemosep is a drug of choice for me to treat infections. I have found it to be excellent for its efficient immune-modulatery and anti-inflammatory effects.

Depending upon the usage and dosage, all the products were being designed and packed in different product formats such as syrups, capsules and tablets. In the recent past, ayurveda was given least priority in comparison to allopathic medicines. However, realizing its immense medication potential with minimal or no side effects, the Government of India had started creating resources to attract talent and create more opportunities in the ayurveda area. Being located in Patiala, gave Gilltech added advantage of easy access to one of the largest botanical garden situated in the historic city of Punjab. However, the quality and quantity of raw materials required for manufacturing tridosha-balanced herbal medicines were not available in abundance in the Patiala region. It was an area of concern for Gilltech and it was exploring neighbouring regions of Himachal Pradesh, Jammu & Kashmir, Haryana and the national capital region of Delhi for procurement of herbal raw material.

Gilltech had 25 products in the testing phase and planned to launch them soon. Strong passion towards phyto sciences motivated Mr Gill to consistently experiment many new mixtures of ingredients whose combination had potential for a new herbal drug. Mr Gill stated enthusiastically:

> Exploring and researching ayurveda is my worship, whereas marketing is my passion. I have always intended to do something different. Changing the concept of slow acting herbals to fast acting herbals was a challenge for me. I gave around seven years to this concept and succeeded in doing so by a method called BALANCING TRIDOSHA. Processing is another part where I have used technical and scientific aspects to eliminate the side effects. In all, I want to assert that nature is the best healing therapy, believe it or not.

Pricing

Gilltech's products were priced higher in comparison to other local ayurvedic medicine manufacturers. Gilltech used quality raw materials sourced from the best climatic regions of India. The quality of the raw material was highly dependent on various parameters such as climatic conditions like soil, rainfall, temperature, humidity, etc. Though the raw material used for manufacturing such herbal medicines were available from local sources and also at lower prices, Gilltech Phytoworld preferred best quality raw materials in order to have desired medication effects of the finished products. For example, one of the ingredients named *atis* used in the medicine for curing digestive disorders was available from local sources at ₹800 per kg; however, Gilltech sourced *atis* at ₹5,000 per kg from other states as it was up to the desired quality parameters of the company.

The usage of such high quality raw materials was also the driving force behind Gilltech's USP—*Fast acting herbal medicines*. Though the products were priced high, still it had been well accepted in the market especially among the ayurvedic doctors. One of alternatives for reducing price was through economies of scale. But Gilltech Phytoworld being an SME had a lot of constraints such as finance, production capacity and limited workforce which was hampering its fast scaling up.

Promotion

Gilltech Phytoworld had broadly followed two promotional strategies, namely, prescription and dispensing. Gilltech medical representatives made presentations to doctors and convinced about the efficacy of herbal drugs and requested for prescriptions to their respective patients. The medical representatives also regularly interacted, educated and convinced chemists about the fast-acting effectiveness of particular Gilltech herbal drugs. Thus, the targets for 'prescription' promotional strategy were allopathic, ayurvedic, homeopathic doctors and chemists. This conventional marketing strategy was working quite well for Gilltech Phytoworld. 'Dispensing' involved hospitals and nursing homes stocking medicines in their in-house stores and, thus, removing the intermediary chemist. Gilltech, being an SME and a start up venture, had limited promotional budget. However, it gave discounts on bulk deals and launched incentive schemes depending upon the market conditions.

Gilltech did not prefer OTC (over the counter) push strategy, rather they focused their promotions to doctors and patients. The company had developed product literature which mentioned the details of ingredients of the drug and its medicinal value. The medical representatives of Gilltech gave this literature to doctors and chemists during their field interactions/visits. Mr Gill was also planning to come up with a magazine called *Phytoworld*. Gilltech would distribute it to hospitals, nursing homes, doctors and chemists free-of-cost. The organization was also using e-mail and social media like Facebook, Linkedin and Twitter to enhance its product and visibility. Mr Gill was also planning to update the Gilltech Web site features and provide interactive services like forums and live chat rooms.

Distribution

Gilltech Phytoworld followed simple distribution strategy (Exhibit 10.4). Presently the company has its operations in seven states of the country, namely, Punjab, Haryana, Himachal Pradesh, Rajasthan, Uttar Pradesh, Jammu & Kashmir and Union Territory of Chandigarh. Gilltech had appointed one C & F (Carrying & Forwarding) agent in each state. The C & F agent would supply products in bulk to the various stockists located throughout the state. The stockist would supply to chemists, hospitals and nursing homes in each city as per their allocated area. The patients received these herbal drugs through chemists or hospitals/nursing homes.

Exhibit 10.4 | *Distribution Channel*

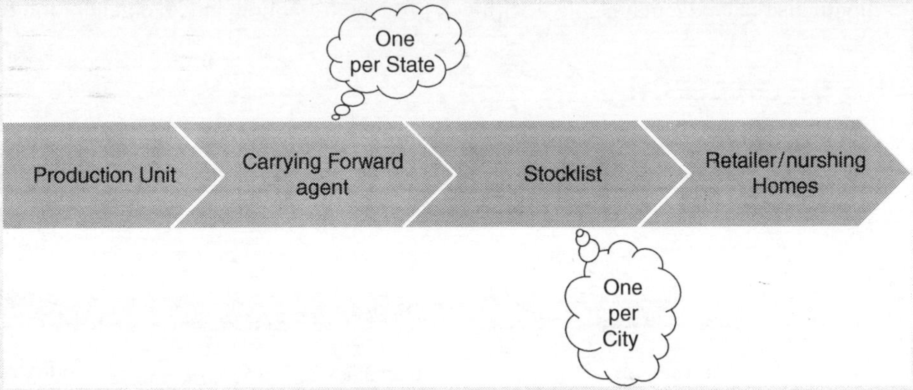

Source: As per interview with company officials dated 27 September 2011

Marketing Strategy

Gilltech Phytoworld had a well-thought out marketing strategy. The company had been actively targeting all categories of doctors. Although a herbal manufacturer, Gilltech's medical representatives met and gave presentations to all doctors. It largely followed similar strategy being used by allopathic companies, that is, representatives had been trained to project the technical analysis. The medical representatives explained how each herbal ingredient of the drug was directly correlated with the disease and how it will create impact on a specific part of the body.

All the products were positioned as fast acting and safe medicines unlike other ayurvedic medicines which were slow acting. According to the marketing executives, initially doctors were requested to test the medicines on small sample of patients; especially in cases where they showed any reluctance to endorse Gilltech's products. Mr Gill was confident about quality and effectiveness of Gilltech's herbal drugs on the patients. The strategy was that the trail on small patients would certainly lead to repeat prescriptions by majority of the doctors due to its effective impact within the desired time period. The patients may also adopt the Gilltech products realizing its cure effectiveness to the particular disease.

This promotion strategy worked for Gilltech and doctors started repeatedly prescribing Gilltech drugs in their respective category. For example, one of the Gilltech's drug Utrotone is highly successful in cases of uterus problem and iron deficiencies. One of doctors based in Sirhind, Punjab; Mr Shelly opined:

> Anemic females often come to me with imbalanced hormone and uterus problems leading to infertility. Gilltech's Utrotone helped me in curing many such cases. Also natural hormones in Utrotone do not have any adverse effects on the patients.

LEAD GENERATION

Lead generation process at Gilltech Phytoworld was carried through medical representatives (MR) posted across seven states. Each MR planned before start of the month his/her scheduled visits to doctors in nursing homes and hospitals in the allocated area for the entire month. The MR gave a structured presentation to the doctor during the interaction process and answered queries of doctor, if any. The MR also regularly interacted with chemists to inform about new drugs and their fast-relief effectiveness. Word of mouth also played a major role in Gilltech product promotion and lead generation process.

FUTURE OF GILLTECH

Mr Gill was reading *John Mullins* 'New Business Road Test' model (Exhibit 10.5) and introspected whether these applied to Gilltech Phytoworld. He was fascinated by the model and its approach. He tried to see this model in the Gilltech's framework perspective.

Exhibit 10.5 | *New Business Road Test Model*

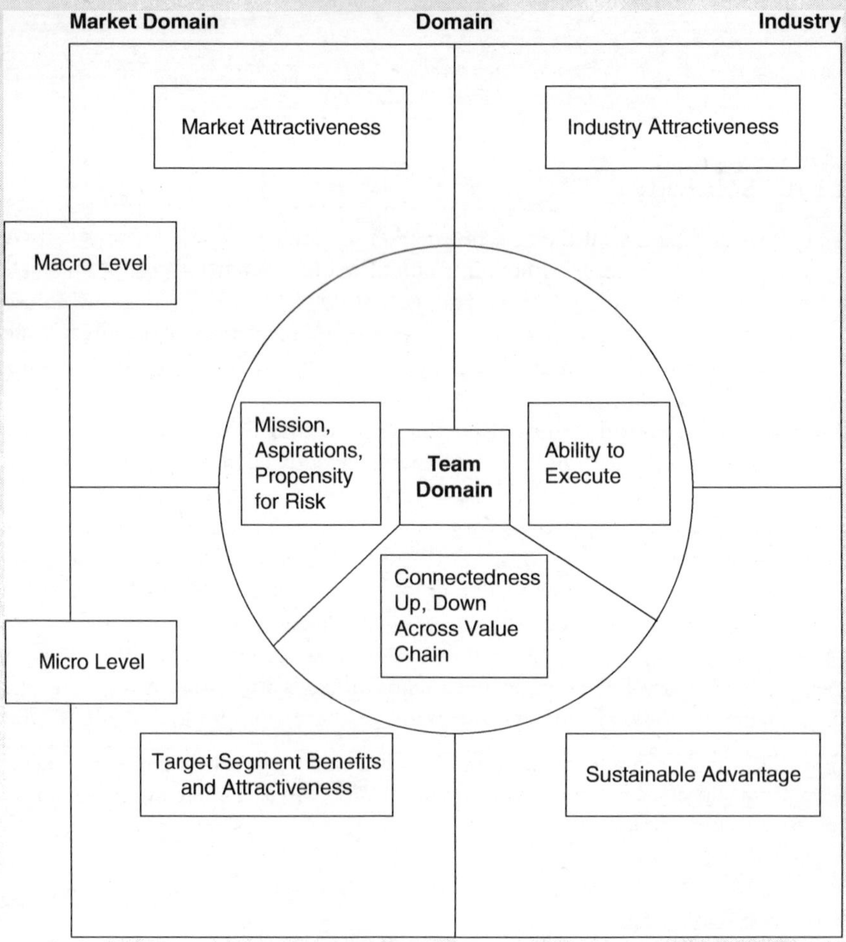

Source: http://www.kubernetes.co.uk/2009/01/19/new-business-road-test-and-mindmanager-8/Accessed on 30 September 2011

Industry Attractiveness—Macro Level

1. Industry had high growth rate with increasing number of ayurvedic hospitals and government funding.
2. High potential for modern ayurveda which included fast acting and safe herbal drugs, that is, without any side effects.
3. Competition was comparatively lower in ayurveda than allopathic and homeopathic domain.
4. The product quality of local manufacturers was inferior due to poor quality of raw materials in the region.

Sustainable Advantage—Micro Level

1. Fast-acting herbal medicines.
2. Safe and pure herbal medicines (no synthetic ingredients).
3. Had unique positioning strategy backed by scientific analysis.
4. Balancing tridosha principle in each herbal drug.

Target Segment Benefits

At micro level, the target segments for Gilltech Phytoworld were people who were suffering from acute and chronic diseases. Gilltech was also planning to enter into the cosmetic and veterinary section. This segment's attractiveness in terms of benefit was high due to the following reasons:

1. Demand of product is high, especially herbal products without any side effects.
2. Some of the products such as Fertoryl-M & Fertoryl-F are uniquely customized.
3. Huge customer potential in cosmetic/veterinary division.

MARKETING ISSUES

Market Awareness

One of the main issues faced by Gilltech Phytoworld was low market awareness about modern ayurveda amongst allopathic and homeopathic doctors and the patients. Ayurveda, as a branch of medicine, was not quite popular in the country. The government sponsored grants and employment opportunities were comparatively much lower than other branches like allopathic and homeopathic medicines. However, of late, the government has started investing money into Ayurveda through various sponsored schemes and programmes and things have started improving. In November 2003, the Government of India renamed the Department of Indian Systems of Medicine and Homoeopathy, established in 1995, to the Department of Ayurveda, Yoga and Naturopathy, Unani, Siddha and Homoeopathy (AYUSH) so as to enhance the promotion of Ayurveda and other older Indian medicinal methods.

The acceptance of herbal drugs was not easy. There were fewer ayurvedic doctors in the country. Gilltech planned to penetrate the market of allopathic and homeopathic doctors besides ayurvedic doctors. The main reason for this was that there were large number of allopathic doctors and most of them had quite higher number of patients' visiting them. The endorsement of these herbal drugs by allopathic doctors would have a larger revenue impact for Gilltech. Besides, promotion of these herbal drugs would become quite easy to homeopathic and ayurvedic doctors and the patients, once they get accepted by allopathic doctors in the country.

Initial Reluctance in Acceptance

Allopathic doctors showed high initial reluctance in acceptance of the ayurvedic medicines. This was because of old perception carried by allopathic doctors regarding ayurvedic medicines as slow-acting herbal drugs. Gilltech had been successful in converting most of such reluctance into acceptance with the 'trial' marketing strategy. The doctors and patients were educated about balanced tridosha. The MRs tried to convince allopathic doctors giving technical details and citing clinical trial results.

Availability of High Quality Ingredients

Easy availability of high quality raw materials was an area of concern for Gilltech. Presently, the organization was highly dependent on limited number of vendors who supplied quality raw materials as per company specifications. Gilltech Phytoworld was planning to set up its own botanical garden where quality raw material herbs and plants as per requisite soil, temperature and humidity conditions would be grown. This would mean a long-term investment by the company for ensuring uninterrupted supply of high quality raw materials (Exhibit 10.6).

Exhibit 10.6 | *Financial Statement*

FY 01-04-2010 to 31-03-2011

To Opening Stock	8,10,377	By Sale	35,00,000
To Purchase	13,70,000	By Closing Stock	12,08,387
To Freight/Cartage	8,010		
To Gross Profit	25,20,000		
	47,08,387		47,08,387

Profit and Loss account

To Printing and Stationery	50,000	By Gross Profit	25,20,000
To Rent	1,57,500		
To Salary	18,00,000		
To Bank Charges	25,000		
To Telephone	15,000		
To Interest Canara Bank	90,000		
To Interest Term Loan	30,000		
To Net Profit	3,52,500		
	2,520,000		2,520,000

Balance Sheet (2010-2011)

Liabilities	Amount	Assets	Amount
Manjit Singh Gill (Prop.)	9,98,972	Closing Stock	12,08,387
Canara Bank OD	8,00,000	Machinery	4,56,000
Canara Bank Term Loan	2,50,000	Plot	1,70,000
Sundry Creditors	2,00,000	Sundry Debtors	4,00,000
VAT Payable	2,000	Cash in Hand	16,585
	22,50,972		22,50,972

Exhibit 10.7 | *Production Chart*

Sl. no.	Name of products	No. of batches	Monthly production
1	Neemosep cap	1 (20 kg)	40,000 capsules
2	Aler-h cap	1 (20 kg)	40,000 capsules
3	Fertoryl- F cap	1 (20 kg)	40,000 capsules
4	Fertoryl- M cap	1 (20 kg)	40,000 capsules
5	Walkfit capsules	1 (20 kg)	40,000 capsules 1800x200 ml (bts*) 300x200 ml
6	Utrotone syrup	3(360 litres)	600x100 ml (bts)
7	Gray tone Syrup	1 (120 litres)	300x200 ml 3600x100 ml (bts)
8	Aspas syrup	4 (480 litres)	1200x200 ml (bts)
9	Curotox syrup	2 (240 litres)	4800x100 ml (bts)
10	Cough end syrup	4 (480 litres)	4800x100 ml (bts)

NOTE: These are production figures for some of the fast-moving products
**bts represents bottles.*
Source: Company records

FUTURE PLANS

Gilltech Phytoworld envisaged rapid spreading out to the other states of India by setting up new production facilities (Exhibit 10.7) and marketing departments. Mr Gill also planned to add a new product line, namely, veterinary division in their portfolio. Mr Gill was of the view that there were many veterinary problems for which there was not any effective cure. He saw a huge herbal medicine market opportunity for animal care. Mr Gill was also toying the idea of coming up with herbal cosmetic products. However, his prime concern presently was to develop the marketing strategy so that Gilltech herbal drugs are accepted by allopathic doctors of Punjab and other states in the country.

DISCUSSION QUESTIONS

1. Suggest a marketing strategy for Gilltech Phytoworld for gaining acceptance of Gilltech's herbal products by allopathic and homeopathic doctors.
2. Discuss the relevance of *John Mullins* 'New Business Road Test' model to Gilltech Phytoworld herbal products business.
3. 'Gilltech's products were priced higher in comparison to other local ayurveda medicine manufacturers'. What is this kind of pricing strategy called in marketing literature? Comment on the present pricing strategy being followed by Gilltech Phytoworld?
4. What is lead generation process at Gilltech Phytoworld? Suggest few more cost-effective innovative method of lead generation for Gilltech Phytoworld.
5. Do you think that it is the right time for Gilltech's to make a foray into veterinary herbal medicinal products and cosmetic herbal products?

6. Comment on the present NPD (new product development) process of Gilltech Phytoworld. Give your suggestions on improving the NPD process so that Gilltech achieves strategic competitive advantage in future.

REFERENCES

www.ayurved.com/article_details, accessed on 13 September 2011.

www.itmonline.org/arts/ayurind.htm, accessed on 13 September 2011.

www.kubernetes.co.uk/2009/01/19/new-business-road-test-and-mindmanager-8/, accessed on 30 September 2011.

INDEX